Protection and civilization

Frank Hermans

Protection and civilization

How shocking events left their mark on human history

Uitgeverij Aspekt

Protection and civilization
Frank Hermans
© 2017 Aspekt Publishers
Aspekt Publishers | Amersfoortsestraat 27
3769 AD Soesterberg | The Netherlands
info@uitgeverijaspekt.nl | www.uitgeverijaspekt.nl

ISBN: 978-94-6338-114-7
NUR: 775

Coverdesign: Mark Heuveling
Lay-out: Paul Timmerman

All rights reserved. No part of this book may be reproduced or translated in any form, by print, photoprint, microfilm, microfiche or any other means without written permission from the publisher.

Content

Introduction		9
The perspective		10
Civilization and empathy		12
Resilience and vulnerability		14
Several assumptions		16
The central thesis		18
The material		20
The structure of the book		21

Part 1: Expanding protective networks   25

1. **The first attempts to protect oneself against shocking events**   27
1.1. Protection against natural catastrophes   27
1.2. The example of Sumer   33
1.3. The rise of the first big resilient network of relations   35
1.4. The stability of the network   38
1.5. The disintegration of the network   42
1.6. Concepts of pain and fear   44

2. **The emergence of a resilient network on a global scale**   54
2.1. Introduction   54
2.2. The dynamics in Central Asia and China   55
2.3. The dynamics in the Middle East   59
2.4. The dynamics in Europe   65
2.5. Hegemony within the network   68

2.6.	The vulnerability of the network: hunger and disease	72
2.7.	The role of religion as a way out of misery	73
2.8.	Monasteries and universities as engines of intellectual creativity	77
3.	**Protection by global interconnectedness**	**81**
3.1.	Global connections	81
3.2.	The global crisis of the seventeenth century	84
3.3.	The downfall of the Ming Dynasty	86
3.4.	The emergence of a global trading nation: the Netherlands 1600-1670	88
3.5.	The beginning of a global empire: England 1650-1750	90
3.6.	The Western European civilizing process	93
3.7.	The Atlantic Revolution	97
3.8.	The differences in resilience: center and periphery	101
Part 2:	**Recognizing unbearable suffering**	**105**
4.	**The discovery of the psychological trauma**	**107**
4.1.	Introduction	107
4.2.	The humanitarian revolution	108
4.3.	The focus on inner life	110
4.4.	Awareness of the risks of the first modern wars	111
4.5.	Awareness of the risks of industrialization	115
4.6.	The pioneers of the psychological trauma	119
4.7.	The confrontation with extreme violence	124
4.8.	The collective dealing with the memory	129
4.9.	The crucial role of the veterans movement in the USA	133
4.10.	The memory as a political programme	136

5.	**Awareness of the impact of modern warfare**	140
5.1.	Unimaginable horrors	140
5.2.	The role of the United States in recognition the suffering	141
5.3.	The initial reactions to the horrors	144
5.4.	"Hiroshima" as a national trauma	147
5.5.	Building a resilient society	151
5.6.	The memory of the horrors	153
5.7.	Genocide explained	159
6.	**The emancipation of the victim**	166
6.1.	The emancipation of emotions	166
6.2.	A wave of revelations	168
6.3.	The dynamics of recognition	172
6.4.	Medical recognition of post-traumatic stress disorder	174
6.5.	Similarities and differences	177
6.6.	Collective rituals	181
Part 3: Relieving trauma		185
7.	**The trauma regime**	187
7.1.	The rise of the trauma regime	187
7.2.	The function and stratification of the regime	190
7.3.	The extent and consequences of unbearable pain	193
7.4.	Victims and victim representatives	198
7.5.	The configuration of the parties	200
7.6.	Recognition and satisfaction	202
7.7.	The rivalry between the experts	204
7.8.	Interdependence as a booster	205
7.9.	Crisis management	207
8.	**The limits of the trauma regime**	211
8.1.	Complex traumas	211

8.2.	Medicalization	215
8.3.	Effectiveness	218
8.4.	Safety	220
8.5.	Victim culture	222
8.6.	Global humanity	225

Conclusion 231
Acknowledgements 233
Endnotes 235
Literature 255

Introduction

Shocking events, such as disasters, wars, mistreatment or abuse are serious attacks on the personal and social lives of human beings. The search for protection from these disruptive events is one of the major motives of mankind. It has made people more resilient against many of these events and empathy for the pain of other people has become the core of their civilization. This raises two intriguing questions. How have people and their societies managed to become more resilient and more sensitive to the pain of others? And are people with this capacity able to control the crises which the world is being confronted with now?

These questions are the subject of this book. The answers to the questions are searched for in changes in the networks that people form with each other and the mutual rivalry that drives the changes. The networks of experts, such as religious leaders, philosophers, psychiatrists and psychologists receive special attention. This is because the competition within their networks offers insight into the development of new ideas concerning the causes and consequences of shocking events to increase the resilience and relieve the suffering.

These developments cover the entire history of mankind and a large geographical area. The task is extensive, but the limitation lies in the focus on the big picture and the main stages in the development. The ultimate goal is to acquire insight into the development and effectiveness of the tools which humanity has invented to cope with shocking events and how it will be able to deal with the crises and suffering it is being faced with now.

The perspective
The term psychological trauma in the modern sense of the word was first used within a small circle of neurologists 150 years ago. They used this term to describe the far-reaching consequences of shocking events at the beginning of the industrial age. They laid the foundation for a comprehensive set of terms and manners with which people encourage each other to relieve the consequences of these events and to prevent them. This set puts a certain pressure on people to be patient, engaged and empathic. It is for that reason that in this book the set will be called a trauma regime.[1]

The trauma regime is the provisional culmination of a development which began with the first humans. The history of mankind can be regarded as an ongoing effort to protect people from the debilitating effects of shocking events. The list is long: earthquakes, volcanic eruptions, droughts, floods, epidemics, famine, wars, mass deportations, looting, serious mistreatment and abuse and substantial loss. In the western tradition we speak of the four horsemen of the Apocalypse: pestilence, war, famine and death.[2] They are huge destructive forces: suddenly with a bang or gradual and insidious. People play a major role in them either by intent or negligence. This role has increased with the extension of human influence on earth, man's settlement in risky places and the increasing impairment of the natural environment by man.[3]

The ongoing effort of people to protect themselves and their societies against shocking events is conceptualized in this book as an accumulation of abilities. By developing increasingly complex abilities people can strengthen their resilience and increase their sensitivity to the pain of others. Some examples are the ability to reduce hunger and epidemics with rational measures, such as food storage or improved hygiene, or to manage a big state which offers its citizens security and professional help to the victims. The trauma regime refers to very complex abilities of experts and is a social achievement, of which many people do not realize the scope, in a world where they are increasingly dependent on each other and disasters and violence affect more and more people.

The existence of this regime is wondrous and fascinating. In modern societies there are thousands of experts working together with victims, government agencies and the general public to control crises and to relieve or prevent psychological trauma. The experts who support the regime, try to incite themselves and others to self-control, by listening to the sad stories of the victims and to meet the world with less violence and destruction. The challenge to keep the planet livable with its billions of inhabitants is huge. The German philosopher Peter Sloterdijk even claims that the attempts at self-control in the past were no more than exercises for the challenges that humanity is being faced with now.[4]

This development has also evoked skepticism about abuse of the role of victim.[5] This abuse is made by people who use the term trauma for experiences that are part of normal life, but also by claiming draconian punishments for offenders, excessive compensation for the victims or to focus on trauma in the distant past to gain respect as a group. According to the skeptics, the competition for recognition between victims has increased inflation of the concept of trauma and provoked sentimentality. This has made it more difficult to distinguish between true suffering and experiencing some displeasure and this has resulted in a weaker position of experts. However, only the independent actions of honest, well-informed and incorruptible experts can be a counterforce against this inflation of the trauma concept.

Civilization and empathy
The profound identification with other people's destiny can be understood as a form of civilization. The German sociologist Norbert Elias, who wrote a standard book about the process of civilization, calls the development of sophisticated and controlled manners and the expansion of the circle of identification to people outside the circle of family and neighborhood, the main features of this process.[6]

This change in behavior and experience is caused by the social pressure that people exert on each other. This pressure is the result of the increasing interdependence of the network of relations between people. By specializing, this network extends and makes more people dependent on more other people for their livelihood, safety or information. In the long chains of dependency their behavior becomes more equable and stable, with fewer extremes and they become more aware of the effects of their behavior in the long term and the motives of others further away.

A civilization process may take centuries and may concern many people. In such a process not only their relation with nature will change, but also their relation with each other and with themselves. This can be described in three forms of dependence. To control nature they become dependent on more complex technology. This requires cooperation on a larger scale and makes them dependent on more other people. This, in turn, requires more self-control and makes them dependent on things like patience and empathy. Lack of self-control becomes a source of shame and self-control a source of pride.

In the civilization theory of Norbert Elias empathy takes up an important place. It is a quality that people possess and can develop further, but it is not exclusively human, and it may also fail in humans. According to primate researcher Frans de Waal empathy begins with emotional turmoil when you are affected by another person. It may change into concern which manifests itself in comforting and touching. It can deepen into taking over the perspective of the other, by examining how the other person experiences the situation and what he thinks, knows and wants. This is only possible if the empathic person can observe himself and look at himself from the outside, through the eyes of others. Human beings, but also chimpanzees and elephants, are able to do so. They recognize themselves in a mirror. This can be demonstrated by drawing a dot on their foreheads, which they want to touch when they look in the mirror.[7]

The capacity for empathy is not exclusively human, but human beings are certainly the most adept of all species. At the age of six a child can imagine what others think about what a third party thinks about what he thinks. However, empathy places high demands on people and will always be limited. To avoid being flooded by unbearable suffering, people turn away. If they become competitors, their identification will decrease. To protect themselves they often split themselves up, for example in an emphatic part at home and an insensitive part at work, or vice versa. In extreme cases they demarcate areas in which civilization is put overboard, such as in ghettos or concentration camps, whereas elsewhere normal life goes on. However, identification may be extended to strangers, even if they are only touched by images or messages. Then there is humanitarian sensitivity, a feeling for the suffering of others, such as Thomas Haskell calls it, or even stronger, the awareness that others who are suffering must be helped, of which Abram de Swaan speaks.[8]

Resilience and vulnerability

In the entire history of mankind the increase in the resilience of human societies against shocking events shows a constant factor: more resilience caused by increasing scale and complexity of the events evokes new forms of vulnerability, but also offers new possibilities to control them. This requires some explanation.

People made their societies resilient against many shocking events and relieved the pain caused by them. They achieved control over conflicts, famine and disease by cooperation and organization, new techniques, more exchange or by going to better places. But the measures they took, had a downside. The wealth of bigger and stronger units of cooperation attracted enemies, more exchange increased the risk of contamination and intensive use of energy resources caused pollution, erosion or depletion of the soil. More mutual dependence also increased the likelihood that they would share the same fate. Classicist Ian Morris calls the fact that the development evokes forces that undermine it the paradox of social development. Nevertheless, his conclusion is optimistic: "Larger and more complex core areas generate larger and more threatening problems, but they also offer more and more sophisticated ways to respond to them."

In his phenomenal study of the dominance of the West, Ian Morris presents four clear criteria for determining the resilience of societies: increased and more intensive use of energy, use of information technology, organizational capacity and military power. Organizational capacity is the ability to manage a stable state and a major city with the help of a tax and regulatory system. According to him, resilience may better develop in an extended network not only within, but especially between societies. Most information about the increase in human resilience can therefore be obtained by focusing research on the networks between societies.

In his book *Collapse* geographer Jared Diamond points out the risk of collapse after a period of decline by degradation of the natural environment, introduction of new species, overpopulation and climate change combined with hostile neighbors or loss of support of friendly neighbors. Downturn is reflected in food shortages, wars, diseases and decline in political, economic and cultural complexity. This decline is often gradual and conflicting interests and lack of leadership can encourage it. The collapse is usually unexpected.[9]

Both authors say little about the degree of suppression and sensitivity to the pain of others. Norbert Elias puts it on the agenda when he mentions two aspects of the civilization process: rationalization and psychologizing. The process of rationalization indicates detachment from emotions and attention for the long-term effects, the process of psychologizing indicates empathy for motives and feelings of others.[10]

Rationalization is a process that started in classical antiquity and the court societies in the early Middle Ages with reflection on ethical standards and tragic dilemmas – something that Martha Nussbaum has pointed out.

It continued in the late Middle Ages, when Christianity focused on a more intense experience of faith, long before the scientific revolution, which gave the process a final turn. The Canadian philosopher Charles Taylor pointed to changes in the Christian religion in his remarkable study of the secular times. Randall Collins described the social causes of the rationalization process in his masterpiece which was based on the history of philosophy.[11]

Psychologizing is a process that takes serious form in the French court culture of the seventeenth century, where knowledge of motives of influential courtiers was essential for preserving one's reputation. The process accelerated with the huge increase in interest for the inner life of individuals in the eighteenth and nineteenth centuries.

Several assumptions
One assumption in this book is that one process was decisive in the long-term development of the resilience of human societies and sensitivity to the pain of others: the increasing interdependence of networks that connect people. Growing interdependence, as is assumed, is a necessary condition for the increase in the resilience of societies and the level of distance and involvement when thinking about the people who are part of it.[12] Large differentiated networks are faced with shocking events with greater scope and intensity of experience, but they also provide more opportunities for experts, such as religious leaders, warriors, craftsmen and scientists, to increase resilience. Conversely, at a certain level of civilization and distance experts can improve it by their ideas, especially philosophers and mental health experts, such as psychiatrists or psychologists.[13] They form with likeminded people and in competition with opponents professional networks with

their own dynamics, in which humanistic ideals are developed, propagated and refined.[14] It is assumed that this development has a clear structure:

Increase in the scope of the events and the intensity of experience of it. This means that more people can be affected directly or indirectly and causes of the events are more difficult to trace. It also means that the messages have a larger range, that the intensity of the experience increases due to the more intense confrontation with those messages, such as intrusive images.[15] Crucial episodes occur when a remote connection is established between smaller more locally bound networks, such as the Mediterranean sea trade in ancient times between ports that separately served a smaller network, the Silk Road between previously relatively isolated areas in China and Europe or the Atlantic maritime trade after the discovery of America. Upscaling is often accompanied by the formation of larger states that provide security for their citizens in a large area, but may collide heavily with each other. Crucial episodes also occur when an extensive network collapses or contracts, such as the fall of the Roman Empire.

Increased scale and complexity of the reactions to shocking events This means that more people get involved in the recognition of the suffering and the provision of financial compensation, such as victims, experts, government agencies and the general public. They form a configuration with each other, a network in which they are mutually dependent to manage the consequences. Within this configuration each party tries to form coalitions with other parties and to compete with other coalitions to strengthen their own position. Because of the interconnectedness of the parties the outcome is often different from the intentions of each separate party.

Rationalization and psychologizing in thinking about causes and solutions. This means that people will consider the world more rationally and scientifically, that they will take into account the long-term effects of their decisions and empathize with the world of others more. In Antiquity and the Early Middle Ages there were, as I said, already circles of experts on human exchanges in major cities, with new ideas about nature and the role of man in it. According to Norbert Elias the pacification of warriors in Western Europe plays a major role in the further development and according to Abram de Swaan the process continued in the care for the poor and sick in the welfare state.

Professionalization in taking measures. This means that measures were increasingly taken by professional experts. They compete within a common professional field, a term derived from the work of the French sociologist Pierre Bourdieu.[16] Their main motive is to improve or maintain their position and reputation in relation to other experts. According to the American sociologist Randall Collins the personal contacts and mutual rivalry provide emotional energy and stimulate intellectual creativity. Personal contacts are always limited in number and therefore only a few well known thinkers will remain.

The central thesis
In every historical episode shocking events caused a lot of suffering, but in modern societies the scope of the events has greatly increased by the scale in which people have become connected, as described above. A disaster may now affect millions of people in different areas of their life and a relatively small incident can paralyze the vast network of trade, transport and communication. Modern societies are resilient against infant mortality, many diseases and

much violence and have a huge thinking capacity, mainly due to the increase in the capacity of computers, but they are vulnerable by depletion of natural resources, nuclear proliferation, environmental disasters and terrorism. The force of arms is bigger than ever and large groups of people can be persecuted, maimed or killed. Wars are relatively rare, but they are very destructive when they break out. Economically, they are vulnerable to debts, which now exceed the real economy fivefold.[17] But there is more.

In modern times the aftermath and settlement of shocking events is a complex interplay and counterplay between victims, experts and the general public. This is reinforced by a growing number of media that provide news that has become more personal, with pictures from all over the world. These are available in every living room and are widely distributed by the Internet or mobile phone. The intensity is strengthened by the importance that people attach to their personal world. They focus less on a deity, a saint, a priest, a ruler or master. The significance lies more in what they have built for themselves and less in the afterlife or in life as a continuation of somebody else. The world is experienced as being maintained and given meaning by humans themselves and the inner life is the source of identity. A shocking event is a violation of this personal world and evokes strong feelings and fears. It entails loss. Dealing with loss is particularly difficult in a society where death is far away and the living turn away from illness and incapacity. Victims of traumatic events are constantly trying to keep alive the memory of what has happened and to prevent repetition. They show that cohabitation can fail, despite its technical possibilities and without the help of gods or ghosts. This requires confidence in human progress. It draws upon a tradition, edits it and hands it down to future generations. This confidence is affected by the genocides of the past century, guilt towards countries with a colonial past and the flexibilization of work that supplanted craftsmanship and traditional skills.[18] It is possible to create a new empathic consciousness that extends to the whole of mankind. The problem is that this requires a more encompassing altruism that makes high demands on people.

The material
An obstacle to research and reflection is the tendency of people to turn away from everything that has to do with serious suffering and death. On the other hand, during the past forty years people have been inclined to reveal suffering sooner and to reflect more on their own emotions.[19] However, attention is strongly focused on dramatic incidents and sensational events. Disasters get more attention than traffic accidents, abuse more than maltreatment. Many disclosures have been dwelled upon in research reports and essays, which are used as material here. Studies on long-term trends and the history of psychiatry, psychology and professional trauma have also been consulted. By choosing a long-term perspective historical details may be underexposed and the study may be vulnerable to criticism from experts in specific areas. About the current state of affairs the author has conducted an additional 47 interviews with the most influential trauma experts in the Netherlands.

One challenge is to distinguish ideals from facts. The interests of the parties may make this difficult, such as the need to put offenders in a bad light, to downplay risks due to financial considerations or to emphasize victimhood in the struggle with other victims. In every culture ideas circulate about what trauma is and who is most affected.

Experiences are embedded in cultural traditions and the great diversity in these traditions is always shortchanged, especially when it concerns people who have been driven apart and massively persecuted. However, the material has mainly been derived from the Western tradition. This means that other nations and the way they give meaning to the experience in their stories are not fully addressed.

The structure of the book
The book consists of three parts. Part I deals with the increase in resilience due to the emergence of major networks in which people tried to protect themselves from shocking events. They were able to increase their resilience by intensive collaboration and new inventions, such as fire control and food storage, and with the help of new experts, such as priests and warriors. This development also involved new vulnerabilities caused by soil depletion, infectious diseases as a result of the more intensive contact and looting of the new wealth by hostile warriors. This is evident from the first networks and the networks surrounding the Mediterranean, culminating in the Roman Empire. Classical antiquity saw new ideas being developed about shocking events that were more realistic and placed the tragedy of life in perspective (chapter 1). Medieval court societies facilitated new connections and provided shelter to world religions which were spreading on a large scale then. The interconnectedness of the networks of people would eventually result in a world system with increasing resilience but also with new vulnerabilities, such as famine and epidemics on a large scale and a new role of religion in Europe by the rise of new religious orders, universities and ecclesial charity (chapter 2). The increasing interdependence resulted in the rise of great powers, such

as the Netherlands in the seventeenth century, the British Empire after 1650 and the United States in their Golden Age of Capitalism in the last part of the nineteenth century, offering security within their extensive domain. This facilitated a civilization process with a more rational view on shocking events and more sensitivity to the pain of others. More civilization implies more rationalizing and psychologizing, and new inventions resulted in the Atlantic revolution (chapter 3).

Part II deals with the recognition of unbearable suffering since 1850. In the nineteenth century major new risks occurred as a result of industrialization and the first industrial wars. In circles of experts they formed the impetus for the discovery of the psychological trauma in the modern meaning of the word. The first massive conflict of the twentieth century, the First World War was the first test for these new ideas about trauma (chapter 4). The Second World War was fought with industrial means resulting in new dynamics of recognition of unbearable suffering and the emotion management of countless people. This would lead to expansion and professionalization of the care for traumatized victims, emphasis on remembrance as a collective enterprise of modern societies (chapter 5) and the empowerment of victims (chapter 6).

Part III deals with the rise of the trauma regime as a result of management of modern risks and crises. It describes how risks increased and events culminated into crises in the early twenty-first century more easily and how trauma experts achieved a key role in delivering the terms and manners which people should impose on themselves to acquire the self-restraint necessary to cope with new threats in the protection of humanity. The trauma regime as a result of this development is thoroughly analyzed in its structure (chapter 7), its dynamics (chapter 8), its different manifestations (chapter 9) and its limits and challenges (chapter 10). In the conclusion the process which is dealt with in this book is placed in the perspective of the civilization process of humanity as a whole.

Part 1

Expanding protective networks

1 The first attempts to protect oneself against shocking events

1.1. Protection against natural catastrophes

Five million years ago the first hominids appeared in the hot and dry regions of Africa. They were small and vulnerable, but adapted themselves well, because they were able to walk great distances, communicate by means of language, use tools, gather animal fat food and master fire. To obtain and use the high-fat foods, they had to be able to hunt and save part of the loot. This required a long learning period, both in their common evolution and in each separate human life. When this learning process was successful, they started to live in a highly knowledge-intensive niche with high-quality food.

The first hominids were almost twice as large as chimpanzees, they lost their coat of hair, started to walk upright and divided the tasks of hunting and gathering between men and women. They learned to cooperate in large groups and they acquired brains that were almost three times larger than the brains of chimpanzees. The food was needed to survive, but also to feed their growing brains that used an increasing percentage of the energy demanded by the body (currently 20%). Quality food was the main energy source, but fairly soon it was joined by a second source of energy, crucial for the survival of the human species and its dominance over other species, namely fuel.[20]

The mastery of fire has been superbly described by sociologist Johan Goudsblom. He shows the importance of this energy source as a survival strategy at this stage of human existence, even though initially it could hardly be considered a deliberate strategy.[21] Fire occurred as a wild force of nature in forest and grass fires. Very likely attracted by the fire, groups of people discovered its many benefits. Initially it was the roasted meat that remained after a fire. They probably discovered that roasted meat was more tasty and could be preserved longer. When they were finally able to keep fire burning and to limit its range, they could exploit other benefits, such as heat and light, deterring wild animals, burning forest areas for hunting, and heating and cooking of food. Cooking helped digestion and also gave access to new sources of food. It stimulated the reduction of the intestinal tract and thus allowed the brain to grow. Fire also killed parasites.

The benefits of fire could only be used after great effort. It required the free use of hands and walking upright, mastering various skills and passing this knowledge on to future generations. It was not only a technical but also a mental challenge: to overcome recklessness and fear, which could only be successful by cooperating together. It is striking that no other animal has succeeded in mastering fire.

The lead in resilience compared to other hominids and species that could not control fire was getting bigger and bigger. Groups that controlled fire were larger and stronger because of their greater productivity and their ability to use fire for attack and defense. Eventually, only groups that were willing and able to control fire survived and no human being could live without fire anymore. Thousands of years later fuel as the main energy source would provide the basis for the agricultural and industrial regimes with their huge increase in energy use and food production.

The power to control fire was invaluable. Owing to this, mankind established dominance over other species and people could live in much larger and more resilient societies. This achievement stimulated cooperation and self-restraint, which in turn increased mutual understanding and sensitivity to each other. Fire gave people a means to exercise power. With fire they could defend themselves against all kinds of dangers and expand their technological skills and access to food. Fire played an important role in myths and stories, such as the acquisition of fire, or fire as punishment in representations of hell and at the stake. Fire would become indispensable for craftsmen, such as potters and blacksmiths, and particularly at times of war. However, the threat of fire had not gone. In domesticated form in human societies and in conflicts between and within societies it could manifest its destructive power even more intensively.

The settlement of the first human beings in fixed locations in the mountain ranges in the Middle East was made possible by the rising temperature on earth.[22] More sunlight and higher temperatures allowed more plants to grow and more animals to stay alive. This allowed people to survive in groups of forty to fifty in one place. Soon they were able to select larger seeds from wild grains and to plant them, so that the yield increased and the population grew.

The early settlements were faced with a major disaster: the melting of the ice caps in North America. Lake Agassiz, a lake of half a million square kilometers was formed. When the ice dams around the lake broke in 10,800 BC, the water flowed into the sea. The seawater cooled and the temperature on earth dropped. The cold period would last 1,200 years and many settlements fell apart. People died of malnutrition or had to learn to live from hunting again. In terms of scope and duration it was the greatest catastrophe in human history. All the disasters that would follow were dwarfed by this disaster. However, in the sparsely populated areas the number of victims was limited.

The settlements recovered when the climate improved, but many dangers remained. Dangers within the settlements were fires, diseases and lack of food. Outside the settlements there were attacks by wild animals, insect and snake bites, drowning, cold nights, forest fires or, as Jared Diamond pointed out, falling trees or falling from a tree. They did not always lead to death, but the lack of medical facilities caused many disabilities, injuries and infections resulting in permanent damage. This explains the very conservative, risk-averse behavior of hunters.[23]

Three horsemen of the Apocalypse were a constant threat: epidemics, famines and wars. Wars were accompanied by looting or had looting as a purpose. The warm areas – usually kept wet by irrigation – were hotbeds of infection and infectious diseases, and by the unstableness of the weather famines were a constant threat.[24] In those circumstances it was essential to keep stocks for hard times and protect them against pillage, gluttony or rot.

The people in these societies responded to the many dangers by establishing resilient, better organized units and smarter energy use. According to Johan Goudsblom one could not survive without specialized knowledge about sowing, harvesting, storage and distribution of food.[25] Gluttony, which is highly contagious, had to be curtailed by allowing it only at special festivities. One solution was to put the knowledge in the hands of priests, who claimed to have a special contact with the gods. By interpreting signs of the gods' wishes, they pretended to know when to sow and how the harvest should be divided. They allowed some of the food to be eaten at great sacrificial parties and kept the remainder under their supervision in the temples they built in honor of the gods and for the benefit of themselves.

The temptation to steal food was effectively punished in their eyes with divine intervention in the form of diseases and other calamities. The sacrificial rituals also offered the opportunity to immerse oneself in the intoxication of being together, without falling into chaos or ecstatic violence.[26]

Because of their need for grandeur priests and their temple households gathered luxury goods, which usually had to come from afar. However, the formation of a surplus for an elite evoked the problem of how to deal with those who could not share in the surplus. In other words, wealth created the problem of poverty. The poor could passively and humbly wait for their share, but also organize uprisings and demand their share. If they were banished, they could plunder or destroy surrounding fields. Every society with a surplus had to make arrangements for the poor in its community and to take care that this did not attract too many poor from elsewhere. According to Abram de Swaan, the contribution of the community had to be so big that the poor were satisfied with what they got, and did not weaken too much, so that they could be deployed as work force, if necessary.[27]

As human influence spread around the world, the chance of catastrophes caused by humans increased. Examples are erosion of areas that had been burned or exhausted by human activity resulting in famines, deforestation by burning and intensive use of wood as fuel or construction material, epidemics by dense population and pollution of the settlements, crop failures due to incorrect planning or defective protection against pests, spoiled stocks or stocks that were robbed, accidents within the settlements or on the roads between them and especially the wars and lootings. The farmers in the settlements became more and more dependent on warriors who could defend the settlement and surrounding land with weapons. They themselves did not have the time, resources or training for this and could not quickly enough mobilize an army. According to Goudsblom, farmers and warriors started a long symbiosis: farmers were productive and vulnerable, warriors destructive and resilient. Warriors could protect farmers, but could also subject, exploit, extort or enslave them.[28]

The warriors developed into a powerful class of violence specialists, experts in murder and arson, and their leaders into kings or military leaders. They acquired their skills by means of long-term physical and mental training. Mental training, focused on perseverance, discipline, self-control and courage, was just as important as physical training in agility, endurance and strength. The main threat to the king were his relatives or a competitive family clan who could murder him and take his place. Some kings killed their relatives or competing clans preventively to secure their reign and succession.

Kings consolidated their position with a display of power in the form of an extensive entourage, visible wealth, ceremonies and bodyguards. A king could force landowners to cede a portion of the proceeds or to join the army. For their services he could reward them with pieces of land or important positions in the realm. To collect regular income taxes he needed an organization that was staffed by people who could calculate and collect. With the money he employed craftsmen and experts in art and science. All this created an extensive network around the king, where new ideas could emerge, especially in experts who were in frequent contact with other cultures or tradesmen who travelled a lot.

According to psychologist and linguist Steven Pinker, in societies of hunters and gatherers and settlements without a centralized state, the proportion of people that died by violence was more than 15%.²⁹ This percentage is much higher than the figure of 0.7% in the centralized states of the twentieth century, which is considered a violent century. If all the people killed by man-made disasters in the twentieth century be taken into account, including famines by warfare, this is no more than 3% of the total population.

Much violence originated from honor and revenge killings, from theft, adultery, abduction of women and alleged enchantment. Torture was very cruel, such as cutting off limbs, heads, scalps and genitals or slowly skinning a captured enemy. Women who were married off frequently acted as spies to inform relatives of the tribe from which they came, about war plans of the tribe they lived with.

1.2. The example of Sumer

Around 5,000 BC human habitation had been extended to the basin of the Euphrates and the Tigris, now Iraq. It was a dry area with little rain, but where much water was available because both rivers flooded regularly. The technique of digging canals and ditches and building sites for food storage had developed so far at that time, that the residents were able to maintain a big city and build a civilization, the Sumerian civilization. Their system was much more productive than the agriculture in the hilly regions and it enabled a complex society with temples and priests.

In Sumer there was already a form of long-distance trade. Products have been found from Afghanistan (lapis lazuli), Anatolia (silver) and Iran (stone axes). In 3,000 BC, the Sumerians had already invented the wheel and they harnessed oxen in front of carts, but for long journeys they made use of pack mules and sailing vessels in the Persian Gulf. The remains of vessels with water buffalo inscriptions from the Indus valley have been found in the Persian Gulf. The ships met in Bahrain (Dilmun in Sumerian).[30] After 3,000 BC, increasing drought forced them to work under a central administration. By making obligatory the voluntary donations to the temple, the Sumerians invented the first system of taxation.

The temple household was the core of society. The territory of the temple was surrounded by privileged households employing agricultural laborers and slaves. According to the Gilgamesh epic the possessions of the temple included one third of the city of Uruk. From 3,500 BC Uruk on the Euphrates, the longest of the two rivers, was the center of a large network of relations. Around 3000 BC the city counted more than 50,000 inhabitants. The Sumerians called their land *ki and gir*, the land of the civilized rulers.

The people in the small villages came under the influence of this great network and they had to focus on it, by either the exchange of goods or by subjection, taxation, lease and robbery. Within the temple household specialized craftsmen could find work and luxury goods could be manufactured. From the perspective of the Sumerians, the gods could be pacified by bringing offerings which prevented famine, epidemics and robbery. However, the origin of the resilience lay in the connections between the towns and villages. With the exchange of goods, information, people and techniques, they could distinguish themselves from people who were not bound by such a close-knit network of relations. McNeill and Mc Neill point in their study of the development of the World Wide Web to the importance of the connecting network between societies, which gave the people who were part of it access to more resources and better weapons to protect themselves against raids of nomads.[31] In this respect more interdependence was accompanied with increased resilience.

In the elite's view the system of irrigation distinguished the Sumerians from "barbaric nomads" who "knew no barley" and it showed an "ordered world, a cosmos that had its origins in the gods at the dawn of history." Cane was used for roofing, flooring, drainage and boat building and clay as building material and as raw material for the famous clay tablet. As to irrigation, people depended on the spring flood and "its blessings always came back in omens, wishes and fate."[32] The water had to come in the right quantities and in time to prevent devastations. In Sumer, a creeping disaster occurred, caused by salinization. Even though the Sumerians replaced wheat with barley, which was salt-resistant, they could not stop the salinization because population pressure did not allow for leaving the land fallow, which was necessary for the soil to recover. This decline meant that the Akkadians could invade weakened Sumer in 2,370 BC.

1.3. The rise of the first big resilient network of relations

The rise of the first big resilient network of relations took place in the Mediterranean. According to Peregrine Horden and Nicholas Purcell, this area is highly varied and unstable. In a number of places, such as southern Italy, there is much volcanic activity and in Greece earthquakes are quite common. The area is prone to landslides, erosion, formation of sludge in estuaries, and fires. Some areas, such as the Syrian and Arabian deserts and parts of Egypt and Libya, are very inhospitable. The sea is dangerous because of unexpected storms and numerous rocks near the coasts. Rain usually comes unexpectedly and on land causes huge mudslides and fills crevices with swirling water masses. Because of the instability the landscape is constantly changing as to composition and fertility. In the long run ports could silt up and hinder access to the sea.

Volcanic eruptions were devastating, such as the eruptions in 1,628 BC at Thera (Santorini), and in 373 BC close to the cities of Helice and Bura. Those cities disappeared in the Corinthian Sea and the eruption of Vesuvius near Naples in 79 AD covered Pompeii and Herculaneum with a thick layer of ash. Both Horden and Purcell noted that there was a gap of hundreds of years between them and that the fertile land could often be exploited again shortly after the eruptions. Earthquakes have not affected the course of history fundamentally, although they could be devastating, such as in Lycia in 141 AD. According to Seneca, earthquakes and diseases could threaten cities, but they could not make them disappear.[33] In late antiquity, there were also major floods in Italy and Anatolia.

The capriciousness of nature and the special landscape around the Mediterrean Sea were reasons for the inhabitants to connect numerous meanings to them to make life more understandable and bearable.[34] In the course of time many rituals, religions and cults arose in which the natural environment played a crucial role. This was reflected in the respect for places that were considered sacred and where people from afar went to. Holy wells were important because of their cleansing and healing properties, but also mountains, road intersections or hazardous straits acquired a magical significance. The demons of the sea and the cliffs were feared and the devastating storms filled people with awe. It was assumed that in remote, inaccessible areas demons housed. Many people travelled to major religious festivals in special places.[35] The inhospitable Syrian and Arabic deserts especially appealed to the first Christians. In places where lightning had struck, shrines were built, such as on the Palatine Hill in Rome.

In the Mediterranean a vast trade network arose after the crisis, which lasted from 1,200 to 900 BC. This was a step forward in the resilience of people and their societies. The network allowed people to access to products that were scarce and it enabled them to exchange or sell surpluses. This resulted in a wider circle of contacts and in openness to new ideas and techniques which could spread rapidly. Within the network this exchange led to specialization and making products for other peoples. It forced people to empathize with the lives of other people and to respect their interests. An important advantage was the chance to build up immunity against infectious diseases within the network. Because of all the advantages, the people inside the network became richer and more powerful than the people who were not connected to each other that way.[36]

The main initiative came from a nation that has been designated by the Greeks as Phoenicians. Their capital city of Tyre was located in present-day Lebanon. The city traded mainly in luxury products, such as glass, cedar wood, ivory, copper, bronze, silver and purple robes – the color purple was extracted from the glands of specific seashells. From Tyre colonies were founded in Sardinia and Sicily, Africa and Spain. This was made possible by new inventions, such as the use of bitumen for finishing ships and the use of a very large sail.[37] The Phoenicians extended their trade network beyond the Strait of Gibraltar. They founded the colony of Gades (now Cadiz) at the mouth of the Guadalquivir, where large amounts of silver from Andalusia were traded.[38]

The initiatives of the Phoenicians were imitated by the Greeks, who settled in Southern Italy and Sicily. They came in larger numbers than the Phoenicians, and penetrated deeper inland and settled as farmers. Greek society consisted of dozens of independent city-states, where citizens were loyal to a temporary magistrate, who replaced both priest and king. The Greek city-states waged wars with the great and mighty Persian Empire. These wars united the fragmented archipelago of islands. A coalition of Greeks and Spartans drove back the Persians with a smart strategy which allowed the Persian fleet to be trapped and destroyed.

Warriors were faced with shocking events on the battlefield. Sadness, anger and revenge controlled their lives. Telling stories about wars and staging tragedies in which the experiences and dilemmas were represented, became part of the culture of the elites in these societies. Examples can be found in the Iliad and the Odyssey by Homer, which dealt with a glorious period of the past and served as models. In the Odyssey, Homer portrayed the blind singer Demodokos, whose job it was to tell stories about the war with Troy. These stories made the old warrior Odysseus cry time and again and he hid under his cloak out of shame.

1.4. The stability of the network

The largest network to be built around the Mediterranean was the Roman Empire. The organizational ability to govern this empire and to keep a great city such as Rome functioning was unprecedented. The capital was huge. At the beginning of the Christian era it had around one million inhabitants and in 400 AD still half a million. From 300 AD Constantinople arose as the second capital, which eventually would surpass Rome in size. The government in Rome saw a big city as the heart of the empire and to keep the city that big many poor had to be fed. Initially they had to pay for bread, but eventually it was provided for free. This ultimately cost the state a quarter of its budget.[39]

The organizational capacity was reflected in a sophisticated tax system which entailed about a thousand smaller cities. Each city had its own curia that quite independently controlled the city and maintained large buildings, such as the forum and the temple. The Roman Empire was a network of cities. The inland transport connections were ingenious. Every ten miles there was a stopping place for the horses and there were lodgings every 25 miles.[40] The roads were used for rapid communication of messages by couriers, for transport of troops and especially for trade. Trade was very extensive with the transport of metals from Western Europe, furs and cattle from Brittannia and Spain, wine and olive oil from Provence, wood, tar, and wax from South Russia, fruits from Syria, marble from the Aegean coast and grain from North Africa.[41] The cohesion of the empire was promoted by a common culture propagated by the elite, a good legal system, a common language – Latin was the main language in both parts of the empire up to 600 – and a large army.

The resilience of Roman society was mainly promoted by military power. A highly professional army fostered unity and security in the realm, the "Pax Romana". Around 400 at least half a million troops were stationed along the borders, especially along the Rhine, the Danube and the Persian border. The Navy, which was less respected than the army, guaranteed that the entire Mediterranean Sea was a safe transport route for the thousands of ships. The main function of the navy was to protect the supply of grain from Africa.

Another characteristic of resilient societies is their productivity thanks to the use of energy. With water mills that were connected – and there are remains – a power as high as 30 kilowatts could be generated. This can be compared with the use of 100 oxen. In one simple rubbish tip in Spain, the huge number of 25 million pots in which mainly olive oil had been transported, were found.[42] When the empire stopped expanding and looting stopped as well, it became increasingly dependent on intensive agriculture. When the temperature sank in the third century, agriculture would deplete the soil.[43] The Roman Empire was also characterized by information technology. There was a good system to inform all parts of the empire and to collect information on the revenues of the provinces for taxation purposes.

The Romans lived in unprecedented prosperity and on average they lived longer than before, despite the fact that half of the children died before the age of five, and few people lived beyond 50. Citizens from all parts of the empire could work their way up to high positions.[44] Security, however, was relative. Within the realm there was a lot of violence. The Jewish rebellion in 68 AD was bloodily beaten down and Jews were caught in the open field and driven back into their homes. The houses were set on fire and elderly people and infants were killed. More than 50,000 people were killed.[45] The Romans deported slaves on a large scale and slaves in the mines led miserable lives. During interrogation people could be tortured and severely maimed, especially if they had no friends in higher circles. Well known are the violent games with fake fights between prisoners of war or fights with animals, or the acting out of mythical stories, in which slaves and naked women were tied up and raped. Half a million people died a gruesome death at the games. Violence continued into the fifth century and public killing of wild animals into the sixth century.[46]

Rome and China maintained indirect contact via the Red Sea and India and via the route across the mainland, which in 1877 was renamed the Silk Road by a German geographer.[47] Alexander the Great had reached Bactria in northern Afghanistan, and from there the route went as far as China. (From 400 AD they went much further north). The expansion and climate changes drove people to migrate and increased the risk of invasions of nomads and the spread of contagious diseases.

The first contacts are difficult to trace. It is doubtful that Marcus Aurelius visited Luoyang. Part of his name is mentioned in Chinese sources. The empire of Parthia in Persia, was known in China as An Hsi and was visited by Chang Ch'ien after the conquest of Bactria and Sogdia in Central Asia in 126 BC. A return visit by the Parthians to China took place in 106 BC and lions and antelopes were donated. In 97 AD a Chinese expedition to the Roman Empire reached the Persian Gulf, but it was told there that travelling farther was dangerous. In 147 AD, the Parthian prince An Shih-kao, who had converted to Buddhism, arrived in China.[48]

Besides the official contacts there are less well documented trade contacts. Coins from Persia have been found along the Silk Road as well as letters from Sogdia in Central Asia about prices and products, such as silk, camphor and rice wine. There are reports about a Sogdanian trading post in the city of Luoyang. Genetic research on the remains of a man from the second century AD that were found during excavations in southern Italy, points to eastern ancestors. Pliny the Elder wrote about an annual trade expedition via the Red Sea to Sri Lanka. He knew that silk originated from the silk moth, whereas Seneca and Virgil still thought that it was a product from trees.[49] The purchase of silk cost the Romans much gold and the Senate, therefore, attempted to prohibit this. The Romans imported wood, ivory, silk and many other goods from India and this could only be paid for with coins, because they had nothing else to offer. Roman coins and pottery shards have been found in India.

The Silk Road ran through areas that were highly developed, such as Bactria and Sogdia, but also through empty steppes and deserts inhabited by nomads. The nomads already tamed horses in 3,500 BC and in 2,000 BC they put the horses in front of chariots. From 1,000 BC they were able to ride horses in a sitting position and armed with portable weapons during battles. Around 600 BC they threatened the Assyrians, the Medes and the Babylonians. Safety increased when around the beginning of the Christian era the Kushan empire arose between Persia and China. This empire had contacts with Persia and China, as well as with the Romans.

The biggest threat emerged when the Huns invaded the western part of Central Asia in 350 AD. The migrations had a domino effect: people that began to move, drove other people in front of them and it was difficult to stop this process. Driving people back was exhaustive given the state of their mobility. These migrations had disastrous consequences due to the spread of diseases.[50]

1.5. The disintegration of the network

From 160 to 500 AD, a crisis of a magnitude, depth and length which until then was unique in human history occurred. In 161 AD China was faced with an epidemic, which came back several times in the following twenty years and killed a third of the troops. The Roman Empire was faced with it, as already mentioned, in 165 AD. From 180 AD it kept returning. The epidemic came by sea, because the ships brought with them rats and fleas, the bearers of the bacillus. An infected rat could survive for several months, enough for a long voyage by ship. From the ancient descriptions it cannot be concluded that the epidemic was caused by the plague.[51]

The epidemic itself was catastrophic, but Rome had to endure even more. The average temperature dropped by almost two degrees between 200 and 500 AD and there was less rain. The ground was exhausted by intensive agriculture in many places and there was a lack of wood due to the large-scale cutting of trees. Threats at the borders forced the Romans to deploy more and more mercenaries in the army. In 350 AD the Huns moved west and German tribes invaded the realm. The Goths, who had arrived in the Balkans, defeated the Roman army there and moved westwards, when the Huns approached. In 410 AD, the Huns besieged Rome for three days. This led to large numbers of refugees and caused a huge shockwave in the empire.[52]

The shock wave aroused feelings of doom. It was the motive for the church father Augustine to present the Christian doctrine of salvation in his *De Civitatis Dei*, about the city of God, as an alternative. Both in the Chinese and the Roman Empire people increasingly relied on a doctrine that offered salvation in afterlife. The figures speak for themselves. In 65 AD, there was only a handful of Buddhists in China. In 400 AD this number had risen to one million and in 500 AD to ten million. In 32 AD, there was a handful of Christians in the Roman Empire, in 250 AD one million and in 400 AD thirty million. This despite big persecutions in 250 and 257 AD. The number of Buddhists doubled every thirty years, the number of Christians every twenty years.[53] Monasteries and ecclesiastical administrations attracted more and more people with qualities. Assistance for the poor and care for the pilgrims who came to spend the night came in the hands of the deacons. From 600 AD they appeared in Byzantium and Italy, and in 780 there were already 22 of them in Rome with increasingly stronger ties with the church. They took over the care for the poor from the Roman government.[54]

The city of Constantinople in the east of the empire vehemently protested against the downturn. The city had 800,000 inhabitants in 400, in 450 a quarter remained. In 700, the city had only 50,000 residents left. In 467 Admiral Basiliskos was sent from Constantinople to North Africa to recapture this rich province from the Vandals, who had been expelled from Spain by the Goths, who were now fighting on the side of the Romans. When the wind turned, his ships got stuck and were set fire to by the Vandals. Nine years later Odoacer would invade Rome.[55]

The fall of Rome is one of the most shocking events in the history of mankind. In his famous *Decline and Fall of the Roman Empire* Edward Gibbon calls it "the greatest, perhaps, and most awful scene in the history of mankind." It was a "triumph of religion and barbarism."[56] The level of prosperity of so many people and the resilience of such a large area would not be equalled for more than a thousand years.

1.6. Concepts of pain and fear

In an unsafe and frightening world people found an obvious explanation in unseen gods and spirits that were more powerful than they were. These gods and spirits offered them a way out in the form of immortality or gave them supernatural forces to control shocking events by means of powerful magic. Armed with this worldview, they responded to catastrophes, adversity, disease and death.[57] In the magical world, the natural environment is presented as "enchanted". Mountains and rivers, storms and tempests, and some animals, have magical powers. The world is populated by spirits who can take possession of humans. They manifest themselves in dreams, bedevilment, out of body experiences or special healings. The fear of bedevilment is great because a spirit can undermine a person's will. Death means that the spirit has left the body and lives on elsewhere. It may return or take possession of other bodies, images, animals or objects. In some cultures a taboo on showing grief at the death of a beloved one arose, caused by the fear that the spirit would return.[58]

The most remarkable thing about the magical world is the lack of an independent subject that takes autonomous decisions. The world outside the subject is supreme and inspired. Famines, plagues, storms and death at sea are seen as acts of gods and spirits. The fear of the wrath of God refrains them from doubting this world view. It is unthinkable. They do not want to change the world. People are embedded in a society that is part of a cosmos with a perpetual cycle.[59]

The sacrificial rituals led by priests, shamans, or medicine men hold society together and correct abnormal behavior that evokes forces that threaten the community. In his extensive and famous study into the roots of dynamic psychiatry, Henri Ellenberger claims that the first collective rituals had a healing effect, such as bringing back the soul, expelling ghosts or removing invisible causes of illness.[60] These rituals are related to modern psychotherapy, which deals with getting in touch with healthy parts of the person, reconstruction of the ego, the upward pull of invisible pathogenic secrets and gaining support from the surrounding community. The difference with our time is that it was thought that forces came to us from outside, whereas they are now perceived as being part of the inner world. We do not exorcise demons by hitting someone, according to philosopher Charles Taylor.

Views of people reflect the state of development of a society, but can also promote further development. These views can even evolve into theories or ideologies and act as driving forces in further development. In ancient times, the magical world view even developed into a series of rituals, cults and the emergence of entire religions. In ancient times cities and shrines were built on upland plains, such as on the Palatine where lightning had struck and emperor Augustus had a temple built to honor the gods and to strengthen his own reputation as benefactor of his city and his empire. The town of Delphi was situated high up, possessed sulfur springs and it was an important religious center dedicated to Apollo. Here the oracle resided. A priestess breathed in the fumes and spoke an incomprehensible language, containing hidden predictions. A big part of the mobility of people was religiously motivated, caused by the landscape that invited to travel over land and water. Pilgrims headed for holy places, festivities or oracles, priests and saints wandered and relics were distributed. The varied landscape with many barriers evoked a wide variety of rituals and cults. It is difficult to describe the enormous religious dynamics in this long period within the scope of this section, because it spans so many cultures and religions. The rivalry between the great world religions that arose, will be the subject of the next chapter, especially the rivalry between the religious centers of Rome, Jerusalem, Constantinople and Mecca.

Classical Antiquity was also a period in which radical suffering became the subject of philosophical and scientific reflection and new forms of human expression arose, such as the classical theater and classical literature. Both in tragedies and epics, suffering was shown in great depth. There were intrusive descriptions of moral dilemmas and attempts were made to explore reality with less fear and superstition. According to Randall Collins, three conditions must be met for the rise of a heyday in intellectual creativity. The first is sufficient support from a community to a circle of scholars. The second is sufficient density of the circuit to be able to meet each other and thus gather emotional energy to further develop ideas in isolation. The third is sufficient competition to stimulate innovative thinking, enough followers across multiple generations and thinkers making a synthesis of the ideas and pass it on to future generations. Eventually, there will always be only a few thinkers who become famous. They are the ones who are able to obtain a position in the centre of the circle of scholars in which ideas that were important then were exchanged. Verbal exchange is essential because it provides the emotional energy for concentration and innovation. Support of financiers and protectors is needed, since one cannot provide for oneself or guarantee one's own safety. Innovation is reflected in ideas with a higher level of abstraction with more distance from primitive fears and motives. Controversies propel its development.

In ancient Greece, the trade network was so dense that such a circle of scholars could form at Miletus around 600 BC. Miletus was the largest port on the Ionian coast of Asia Minor with more than 60,000 inhabitants. It was surrounded by many smaller towns from which the scholars came. These scholars detached themselves from the religious thinkers and claimed an independent area: philosophy. They controlled their immediate impulses and anxieties and looked for the reality underneath the surface, without invoking higher powers or spirits. The circle of Miletus consisted of great thinkers who later became famous, including Heraclitus, Parmenides, Pythagoras, Hippocrates and Anaximander.

Athens is the city in which the most famous circle of scholars formed. Socrates is widely regarded as the founder of this circle. He formulated the task which humanity would engage in from then on: the pursuit of truth by using all mental faculties. It was the duty of every individual to overcome illusion and superstition by means of knowledge and understanding. He assumed that truth would not show at once, but could only be obtained laboriously. He unmasked many apparent attempts at finding the truth. With his activities, he laid the foundation for philosophy as the enterprise of experts to teach people to rise above themselves by using ratio. This was a new task: in future the individual had to detach himself from group morality, rely on objective knowledge and be constantly aware of his integrity in his search for the truth and the welfare of mankind.

An example of a more rational view of catastrophes is the description of the Greek writer Thucydides of the major epidemic in Athens in 430 BC. As a general, he had been degraded after a defeat and exiled for twenty years. This enabled him to distance himself from everything and travel a lot. As cultural anthropologist Anton Blok writes:

> "Freed from social restrictions and without the need to please and by using two contemporary spiritual movements – the philosophers and tragedians – Thucydides could design a totally new approach that emphasized strict standards in order to gather evidence, to make an analysis in terms of cause and effect, to propagate political realism, to consider the relations between nations as based on power

relations rather than on law and to explain human behavior in extreme situations – plague epidemics and civil wars."[61]

His description of the danger of contact and immunity after having endured the epidemic that ravaged Athens, is evidence of this.

The disease began – as they say – in Ethiopia, and then gradually spread across Egypt and Libya, and across most of the empire of the Persian king. In the city of Athens, it suddenly broke out and first attacked the inhabitants of Piraeus, that claimed that the Peleponnesians had poisoned the reservoirs; at that time the sources were not there (...) No constitution, strong or weak, proved resistant to the disease which took down all people, even those who were treated with the greatest care. Worst of all was the despondency someone felt, when he noticed that he was ill (...) It was terrible to see those who died like sheep because one person was infected by the care of another person. This caused the majority of deaths. For if they did not want to visit each other out of fear, the sick would die in desolation and many families died out by lack of someone who nursed them (...) Those who had recovered from the disease felt more compassion for the sick and the dying; they knew what it was and they felt safe themselves; Because the disease did not grasp a person a second time, at least it was not fatal (...) The bodies were stacked and more dead than alive the sick dragged around on the streets and at the springs, gasping for water; the temples where they had sought shelter were full of the bodies of people who had died there (...) all the customs they would use at funerals, were neglected now.[62]

An attitude in which life's dilemmas may be overcome by accepting the vulnerability of humans is tragic awareness. The classic tragedies written by Aeschylus, Sophocles and Euripides take a special place. They invite us to empathize with people who often had to endure a lot of suffering. They show that other people are as vulnerable as we are, put in a perspective in which suffering evokes empathy, and a feeling that despite the terrible dilemmas, living in this world and accepting one's own life and that of others is valuable.

The main characters in the tragedies are hurt on a large scale which was hard to avoid. According to Philoctetes, this causes a strong desire to help in a tragedy of Sophocles. It also shows that such bad luck can also affect us. Martha Nussbaum puts it concisely:

> "Tragedies show us that calamity touches at the core of human action. It does not only cause superficial discomfort, but it is an obstacle to mobility, plans for the future, citizenship and even for life itself. If we see that human being is affected by such disaster, we also experience tragic compassion for we do not want humanity to be wasted, not even callously mishandled. Tragedies therefore demand from us to navigate laboriously. On the one hand we must recognize that the misery in life is a vicious blow and hits the very core of human dignity. On the other hand we have to trust that humanity does not disappear and the ability to do good remains when everything else has gone."[63]

Philosopher Jos de Mul indicates that the tragedies originated in Greece over a period of only fifty years, but they have been an inexhaustible source for European culture in later novels, plays and movies. The special feature of the tragedy is that it shows that human action is fundamentally ambivalent. The main characters in the tragedies are faced with insoluble dilemmas, such as Prometheus in a tragedy by Aeschylus. Prometheus steals fire and technique from the gods and shows that people with the possibilities of technology can escape their miserable lives and take fate in their own hands. This is praised by the choir in the tragedy. At the same time Prometheus is punished by the same technique when for the sake of revenge he is chained to a rock by the god Hephaestus under orders of Zeus. Every day an eagle tears apart his liver which then grows whole during the night. The tragic notion is that the technique is a way out of human misery, but it also turns itself against man at the same time.

The tragedy sharpens tragic notion. According to Aristotle, this awareness includes three beliefs: that the suffering is severe and not trivial, that the person does not deserve it and that he has the same possibilities as the one experiencing the suffering. Has someone caused the suffering himself, then there is less compassion. Therefore it is often emphasized in the tragedies that a person bears no blame for his suffering and nor does the spectator. Tragedy poets indicate that the onlookers may be affected themselves.

Greek society has also become known for the so-called Asklepia. After a sacrifice to the gods and ritual purification, the sick spent the night in a sacred bedroom, the *abaton*. In their dreams they were visited by Asclepius and these dreams were analyzed and interpreted by the priests. They suggested a form of therapy, consisting of a modified diet, relaxation and exercise, bathing and intellectual entertainment. The Asklepia were well attended, especially the Asklepion at Epidaurus, which was popular with the Romans.

Epicurus, who lived at the end of the fourth century BC, developed a doctrine in which peace of mind was central. In this doctrine he rejected the fear of gods and higher powers. According to him, nature had no higher purposes. The best was to lead a retired life. He was famous for his large garden, where he taught his disciples. According to the Roman poet Lucretius, a follower of Epicurus, the universe has no creator or designer. The world consists of particles that take certain forms on the basis of chance. There is an infinite number of combinations which may succeed or fail. Man has the choice to resist the forces or to yield to them, but he is not the center. It is not certain that humanity will survive, nor is there a paradisiacal beginning. The human soul disappears with the body and there is no afterlife. At death, the particles fall apart. This does not bother man, because he no longer exists. Religion is superstition, it is cruel and sows fear. There are no ghosts and demons.

According to the teachings of Epicurus, the ultimate goal is pleasure in life and avoiding or reducing pain. Militarism and violent sports are perverse. Fantasies of infinite joy or infinite pain, such as in religions, make people unhappy. However, understanding the nature of things gives peace of mind and evokes deeply felt amazement. Lucretius' poem was considered lost until 1417 AD when the papal secretary and humanist Poggio Bracciolini discovered a copy in a monastery in southern Germany. The ideas of Lucretius fitted the emerging humanism at that time. Epicurus and Lucretius were freethinkers, but their impact was limited and did not fit into the dominant worldview of the ancient world. Not until the fifteenth century when exclusive humanism without belief in gods or other forces became an alternative for many people, did the time come to accept the worldview of Epicurus and Lucretius This situation only occurred when Western culture began to abandon the idea of gods and demons. This required an evolution within Christianity and Jewish philosophy, such as Spinoza's, to a sense of self and individual responsibility.

2 The emergence of a resilient network on a global scale

2.1. Introduction

The development of a global network that could substantially provide better protection against catastrophes and serious suffering, gradually took off after the fall of the Roman Empire. It was characterized by a steady growth from 600 to 1200 that accelerated between 1200 and 1450. The first steps in the formation of this network occurred fairly independently of each other in three regions: Central and East Asia, the Middle East and Europe, but there were already direct connections between several empires in these regions: the Tang dynasty, the Byzantine Empire, the Islamic realm of the Abbasides and the Frankish empire. These empires were led by rulers with an extensive court life and located in cosmopolitan centers, where many scholars were active, such as Chang'an in China in 700, Baghdad, Constantinopel and Aachen in 800 and Cordoba in 1150. These centers were also the power bases of the world religions that spread on a large scale within the expanding network: Judaism, Christianity, Islam and Buddhism.

The development can be divided into three dimensions. The first dimension consisted of an increasing interconnectedness of the separate networks in each of the three regions driven by conquests, trade contacts, exchanges of knowledge (including ideological influences and conversions), migrations and new ways of production and warfare. The second dimension consisted of a growing scope of the effects of shocking events, which could hit more people and more areas simultaneously. This was due both to the growing interconnectedness of the networks and the increased complexity of the reactions to it, such as the increasing competition between the parties involved. The third dimension consisted of the emergence of new perceptions and insights concerning causes and consequences of catastrophes within circles of experts, such as religious leaders and scholars.

This stage in the development of the networks that connected people, was characterized by more differentiation and specialization. This was the case for the kind of connections between people, the organization of protection and the knowledge and exchange of knowledge about causes, consequences and remedies to alleviate the suffering. Not only could more people be affected by this larger interconnectedness, but the reactions could also be more intense and vehement in the form of hopelessness, retaliation and collective mourning.

It should be noted that the growing interconnectedness and as a result the larger scale of the networks could increase both the resilience and the protection against shocking events and the vulnerability for these events. In this period shocking events consisted mainly of epidemics, invasions of rulers from other regions, riots and famines.

2.2. The dynamics in Central Asia and China

From 300 AD, in poor South China an unprecedented prosperity had emerged by extensive rice cultivation. Buddhist monasteries delivered the capital to invest in costly mills to process the rice. The North had united after much fighting in the Sui Dynasty (589-618) in 589 AD and when the first Emperor Wendi had conquered the south, he had a large channel built between the Yangtze

Jiang and the Yellow River, thus creating an important connection over water. The channel was 2400 km in length and 40 meters in width.[64] The growing prosperity made it possible that the armies were expanded with horsemen and waged war against the looters and smaller kingdoms in the steppes. The Chinese rulers even reached the Caspian Sea. The taxes Wendi introduced weighed heavily on the realm. They were high due to the high costs of the channel, the extension of the Great Wall and military campaigns against Korea. Thus the Dynasty came to an end soon. This was not an obstacle to the continuing progress of China. After a major crisis and with the help of the Turks, China recovered under the Tang dynasty. It would even surpass the West during the next five centuries.

After the unification, the Chinese empire had more inhabitants than the Byzantine, Frankish and Islamic empire put together, i.e. over sixty million. The great prosperity during the Tang Dynasty (618-907) attracted many foreigners. There were a large number of Persian and Arabic speaking immigrants in the port cities and other religions were tolerated there.[65] The capital of Chang'an was a center of art and learning. There were 100 Buddhist monasteries, 16 Tao temples and a church for Nestorian Christians. It had more than one million inhabitants, including 100,000 soldiers, 50,000 monks and 7,000 students. There were four palaces, the largest of which was two kilometers long and one and a half kilometers wide and had 21 gates.[66]

In the capital, a new vision on fear and suffering was developed by the Buddhist scholar Fa-tsang (643-712) from Central Asia in the so-called Hua-yen (flower garland) school. He translated Buddhist scriptures from Sanskrit and wrote "the golden lion" in which he tried to explain Buddhism to Empress Wu. His vision consisted of exercises in silence and meditation, through which a state of consciousness of inner emptiness could be achieved.[67] According to his philosophy, reality, including shocking events, temporary and transitory, was based on mental constructs. Actual reality was empty and could only be found in natural phenomena. He used paradoxes to detach people from fixating on certain ways of thinking. According to him, the mystery was the individual himself and therefore one had to go back to daily life after meditation "to carry water and chop wood" because in the end they were "holy acts".[68] Fa Tsang limited his advice not to an elite of priests and monks, but he wanted to reach the entire nation. Such a programme for disciplining all people would not be formulated in the west until the rise of Protestantism.

In this period, Central Asia experienced a huge dynamic. The area stretched from the Caspian Sea to Gansu in China (5,000 km) and from south to north – from the Hindu Kush north of Kabul to the steppes of Mongolia (800 km). It was certainly not an empty area where only nomads lived, but it linked East and West and its influence was felt everywhere, both in the spread of religions, trade and science and in many bloody conflicts and uprisings. The route, which was renamed the Silk Road in the nineteenth century, flourished from 600 to 800 and again around 1200 under the Mongolian domination. In the sixth century, the Byzantine writer Cosmas Indicopleustus said that the land route for silk from China was already more important than the sea route to Ceylon (Sri Lanca) in the fifth century.[69]

The main link on the Silk Road was initially Bactria, north of Afghanistan, conquered by Alexander the Great, and later the more northern Sogdia, with the cities of Bukhara and Samarkand that became famous later. Irrigation was almost impossible with the raging rivers in this area and the country highly depended on trade and the local industry (carpets and glass). Traders from Sogdia could be found everywhere in the Turkish, Persian and Chinese empires. Many scholars from this region went to Bagdad after 750. Sogdia was supported by the Turkish empires, which controlled a large area between 550 and 750.[70] Sogdian temples, inns and stores flourished in China and the charm of the Sogdian women was praised in Chinese poems.[71]

Around 750 AD major uprisings and revolutions broke out. There was an Uighurian rebellion in the Turkish Empire under pressure of Sogdia and a rebellion in Byzantium by the Armenian General Artavasdos. There were also two revolutions, the revolution of the Abbasid, from Marw in Central Asia and the establishment of their empire in Baghdad and further west the Carolingian revolution that connected the trading routes to Central Asia of the Saxons and Avars with Europe. In China, there was an unprecedented bloody uprising unleashed by general An Lushan, who was of Sogdian origin and had a Turkish mother. An Lushan became the most important general in China, in spite of having been pardoned following a death sentence, but he was fat and sickly. Because he showed how little he understood of the court etiquette, being a so-called barbarian, he was appreciated by Emperor Xuangzong. Due to the rivalry among the generals he was expelled from the court, but he prepared an uprising in the north with an army of 164,000 men. Eventually, he conquered the cities of Luoyang and Chang'an. In a counteroffensive An Lushan was killed by his son. Turks and Sogdians were chased and killed during a great massacre.

According to Stephen Pinker, the rebellion of An Lushan was the conflict with the greatest death toll that mankind has ever known in relation to the size of the world population. There were proportionately more deadly victims than during the Mongol conquests or the slave trade, second and third place, or the Holocaust which takes up the ninth place. Two-thirds of the inhabitants of the empire, about a sixth of the world population at that time, were killed. These figures are controversial because sometimes refugees were counted as deaths, counting itself suffered from the conflicts and the borders of the empire shifted.

2.3. The dynamics in the Middle East

For a long time the Byzantine Empire had in fact been the continuation of the Roman Empire in greatly reduced form. The inhabitants spoke Greek, but in their hearts they remained Romans. In 330 AD emperor Constantine had inaugurated the city of Constantinople with great feasts. He had images of emperors, a serpent column from Delphi and an obelisk from Karnak transported to the city for the benefit of the Hippodrome, the place for cart and horse racing. Two hundred years later, Emperor Justinian was responsible for the construction of the Hagia Sofia and he codified Roman law. The empire had to cope with many shocking events, such as the wars with Persia, which at the time of Justinian had plundered large parts of Syria and an epidemic that resulted in hundreds of thousands of victims.[72] The epidemic was a huge drain on the empire. Procopius describes the plague as follows:

"At that time (542 AD) a plague that wiped out almost all of humanity raged. For all other scourges sent from Heaven, always had provided some explanation by audacious people (...) For this disaster, it is quite impossible to say or think of any explanation (...) It seemed with this disease that it did not matter how people differed from each other (...). By many people apparitions had been seen in various human forms (...) Those who cared for them were unceasingly close to exhaustion (...) It turned out that neither doctors nor others contracted the diseases through contact with sick or dead, for many people who were constantly busy burying the dead and nursing the sick could continue with it (...) If it happened that water was nearby, the sick wanted to throw themselves therein, but not for drinking (because most people walked into the sea) (...) Many died because no one was there that could care for them and therefore they died of starvation or plunged from a height down (...) In Byzantium the disease kept for four months and raged for three months at its fiercest (...) and the number of dead increased to five thousand per day, and later even to ten thousand and more. (...) When it appeared that all the existing cemeteries were full, one after another mass grave was dug all around the city, (...). Later, when the gravediggers could not keep up the supply of the number of deaths, they climbed the towers (...) took the roofs off and threw the bodies into it in a complete chaos. As a result, a terrible smell penetrated the city, which made the inhabitants even more desperate, especially when the wind blew from that quarter. (...) Everywhere you looked you could see mountains of seem that were thrown on the ships, which were left floating out to sea at a venture (...). In a city that had just flowed from all goods, an almost total famine prevailed. (...)."[73]

The plague would hit forty percent of the city's population, a quarter of the inhabitants of the empire. Especially the sixth and seventh centuries were disastrous. The number of shipwrecks in the Mediterranean, a measure for the volume of trade, was only ten percent of the number at the beginning of the era.[74] Many writings of the seventh century are about the end of times.[75] To increase the resilience of the empire the rulers chose to militarize the provinces headed by a general, to fortify the capital, to pay close attention to the glory of the classical antiquity and to found a common religious belief. By its location the city of Constantinople was eminently suitable to withstand major sieges and its inhabitants had a strong and secret weapon: the Greek fire. This was most likely a mixture of resin and crude oil that was sprayed over the water in case of enemy attacks and which set everything on fire. The Greek fire is a good example of a state secret with which a military power could persist for a long time. It has been compared with the Manhattan Project during World War II which entailed that the knowledge of the atomic bomb, as in Constantinople, was divided amongst different persons.[76]

The emperors paid great attention to education. It was secular in design with much attention for the liberal arts, classical literature, mathematics and astronomy. Scholars from many countries came to visit the city and Byzantine scholars went to other countries. The archives for study and research were widely known. In medical texts not the heart, but the brain was considered to be the center of mental activity and illness was a condition not associated with sin and guilt. The most visible legacy is the preservation and transmission of the classical heritage, the cultivation of behavior at the courts as an example of civilized behavior, which was imitated in many countries, and asceticism in the monasteries as an answer to suffering and pain.[77]

The Arabs were the greatest enemies of the Byzantines. Their chances grew when the many struggles had weakened the Persian Empire and the Byzantines had suffered much damage themselves. The Arabs lived in a region where life was hard and where loyalty to family and tribe and honor and revenge were all important. After a fierce power struggle, which Mohammed won, his tribe of the Quraysh focused on trade, protecting caravans and robbing infidels. Their religious zeal was combative caused by the chaos and militarism in the period in which it came into being. By focusing aggression on disbelievers Muhammad paved the way for the conquests of Persia and Egypt.[78]

The Islamist rulers tolerated other religions within the range of the "Dar al Islam", but were unforgiving if they did not conform to their laws. Outside the "Dar al Islam", people could be enslaved without limitation. Muslim rulers also bought slaves from the West for their armies, agriculture, mining, and their extended households. They controlled the two major trade routes between Europe and India via the Red Sea and the Persian Gulf, and extended their influence to the Mediterranean coast. The Islamic realms did not grow into one empire with a big navy, but despite this there was an enormous exchange of knowledge, culture, languages and products between Arabs, Syrians, Persians, Indians and Chinese.[79]

The Arabs traded in incense and myrrh which became very useful in cities that smelled of sweat, urine, excrement, offal, rotten fish and tanneries and where many people could not change their clothes regularly.[80] The products originated from plants that grew in Arabia and were transported in baskets (incense) and woolen bags (myrrh), on the backs of thousands of camels to the warehouses of Gaza.[81] In the expanding Muslim empire Baghdad became the new center. In the centre of the town there was the caliph's palace. He was the successor of the prophet and the religious leader. His power was always challenged by the "ulama", the religious experts united in the religious schools, and by powerful groups in his realm. The caliphs in Baghdad were strongly dependent on their bodyguards. The bodyguards were certainly no slaves, but independent and proud warriors, mostly from Central Asia. Only when they had killed three caliphs after 860 were they conscripted as slaves.[82]

The conquered Persian Empire was highly developed, both economically and culturally. Persian ships sailed directly from Persia to China and the Persians had trading posts along the Chinese coast. The second caliph of Baghdad, Al-Mansur, had to make every effort to keep the Persian faction in his administration satisfied. He managed to convince the faction that his Islamic empire was the successor of their great Persian Empire with the same mission to gather knowledge, which was a divine mission for the Persians. According to the teachings of Zoroaster, the main religion in Persia, all knowledge of the good god Ohrmard, was expressed in the Avesta, but it had become disseminated. The mission was to bring it together again. That was one of the reasons why he appointed many translators to translate the knowledge from other languages into Arabic, especially knowledge written in the Persian language, Pahlavi. The Syrian Christian Hunayn ibn Ishaq was the most famous translator, who with the help of his son translated almost everything that was available in Antiquity about medicine and half of Aristotle's works into Arabic.[83]

In literature, the House of Wisdom was mentioned as a center of knowledge under Caliph Al-Ma'mun, but it was no more than a library. The caliphs' purpose to support the scholars and to set up a translation programme from Persian and Greek was four-fold: (1) to show the mighty Persians within the Islamic empire that the Islamic empire was the successor of the Persian Empire and now had the task to bring together all the knowledge of the world, like the Persians used to do, (2) to present evidence for the only true doctrine towards other religions and dissidents within Islam (3) to show the enemy, Byzantium, that their kingdom was inferior to their predecessor, classic Greece. Byzantium was Christian and believed in the Trinity. This belief was considered inferior in Baghdad, especially since one of them (the Son) had to answer nature's needs, and (4) to gather practical knowledge to govern the realm, such as astrology to make predictions, geometry and algebra for land surveys and tax calculations, and knowledge of traditional medicine to fight disease.[84]

A major contribution to thinking was provided by some liberal theologians who presented their theology as a form of natural philosophy echoing the Greek natural philosophers. According to them, man could prove the existence of God by rational arguments. In their eyes life was a test to do good and to help those who suffered. Caliph Al Ma'mun saw this as the true doctrine and firmly tackled dissidents by means of an Inquisition. In 850, seventeen years after his death, however, orthodoxy prevailed.[85]

Medical knowledge within the Islamic empire was highly developed. The first hospital in Baghdad in the ninth century, was inspired by (Nestorian) Christian doctors from Gundashapur (Jundashipur) in Persia. How much influence they had on Baghdad is the subject of debate.[86] There was little theoretical innovation, but physicians greatly contributed to the knowledge of diet and psychological illnesses. The physician Abu Zayd al-Balkhi saw that depression sometimes had external causes, such as loss or setback, and that persuasive talk therapy could help. Al-Farabi saw loneliness as a threat to the psyche. Muhammad ibn Zakariyā Rāzī (Rhazes) from Rey, in Persia, had an eye for social conditions, such as poverty. He called religion based on revelation old wives' tales, based on dogmatism and ignorance.[87] These doctors paved the way for the great doctors of the eleventh century – Ibn Sina (Avicenna) also from Persia – and of the twelfth century – Ibn Rushd (Averroes) and Maimonides (Ram bam) from Cordoba. Ibn Sina wrote a medical encyclopedia (Canon) including three chapters on mental illnesses, which he placed in the centre of the brain. He acknowledged the role of fantasies, described the symptoms of melancholy and the relationship between pulse rate and inner feelings. Ibn Rushd and Maimonides were the bridges to Christian and Jewish philosophy. Cordoba was a center that attracted many scholars from Europe. A wave of translations into Latin, including the translation of seventy Arabic books by Gerard of Cremona, would usher in a whole new development in Western Europe, when these texts were introduced at the universities of Paris and Oxford.[88]

2.4. The dynamics in Europe

Beginning in the mid fifth century, many cities in Western Europe were abandoned, populations decreased and Roman roads were neglected. Trade and travel became difficult and the money economy collapsed. The export-oriented Roman agriculture disappeared and was replaced by smaller Germanic farms, aimed at self-sufficiency. This change was gradual and parts of the Roman form of government and law remained. The slow decline was not an obstacle for the rise of a large empire ruled by the Frankish kings from 750 AD. The attempt of Charlemagne, the greatest king among them, is particularly interesting, because he tried to gain unity by means of a strong moral message: the spread of Christianity as a form of spiritually noble behavior.

The empire of Charlemagne covered most of Europe, including the Balkans, and counted 20 million inhabitants. It consisted of 600 counties and 180 dioceses, which he could grant as a tribute for services rendered (both the land and the positions). He also needed to do this because there was little money in circulation.[89] He founded his own capital, Aachen. and was crowned emperor by the pope in 800 AD. The Byzantine church of San Vitale in Ravenna served as a model for the chapel in his palace, and he wore Byzantine clothes. To promote the unity of the empire, there were often big meetings in Aachen and the provinces. His most reliable aristocrats obtained key positions in counties and dioceses. Information about the empire was collected by sending so called "missi" to the areas. For planning he used a handbook, a libellus, written by Adalhard, his cousin and abbot of the Corbie monastery in Picardy.[90] Charlemagne had no advanced tax system and that was the weakness of his empire.

Charles saw himself as the representative of a nation chosen by God and was called David by the intellectuals in his circle. He could barely write, but found that good behavior and spiritual awareness were only possible after appropriate training. He wanted a new generation of educated Frankish scholars, for whom the Bible, the Church Fathers and classical literature were central.[91] They were often appointed abbot or bishop. The head of the palace school, Alcuin, was a monk from York. He developed a standard curriculum: the trivium (grammar, logic and rhetoric), as preparation for the quadrivium (geometry, arithmetic, astronomy and music). The Latin classics were in fact mostly saved by the monks of the Carolingian period. The monasteries, there were 550 in 700 AD, were rich sources of information. Since about 1900 AD, science has been calling it the Carolingian Renaissance.[92]

After several crises the connections in Charles's empire would become part of the global network and the foundation for European development. Christian thought would underpin thinking about fear and suffering, and the responses to the many catastrophes Europe would be faced with. Two centuries after Charles' death the land in western Europe between the Loire and the Elbe had changed into a carpet of wheat fields as a result of the increased agriculture. Horses were widely used and mills were built for power generation. Progress continued, despite the turmoil created by Viking migrations. European knights had gained more control over the landscape and missionaries had converted this part of the continent.[93] Around 1000 its network consisted of 200 million people. It stretched across most of Eurasia, including the northern areas of China, Japan and Korea and parts of Africa, such as Ethiopia, and ports along the East Coast and West Africa.

According to Immanuel Wallerstein, the cohesion, resilience and power of a network is not determined by its size, but by the regularity, speed and intensity of the exchange. According to him, when a network expands to different continents, the following developments occur: capital accumulation, division of labor and increasing differences between the centre and the periphery. There are cycles of progress and decline, associated with shifts in the hegemony of certain areas in the network. An upward cycle is characterized by population growth, increasing production, expanding trade and growth of cities.[94]

Between 1200 and 1450 the regularity, speed and intensity of the exchanges between the European, Asian and part of the African continents grew so strongly that it could be called the beginning of a world system. Abu Lughod points out that the connections extended from cities, such as Venice, Genoa, Troyes, Bruges, Alexandria, coastal towns in East Africa, Calicut in India to Samarkand and Bukhara on the Silk Road to Palembang in the Far East. Extensive arrangements had developed for business and storage and exchange of capital. Local markets around big cities started to focus more on the international markets of spices, textiles, porcelain, weapons, gold and silver.[95]

The world system in the making leaned heavily on three longstanding connections by land and by sea. In case of problems one could replace the other: two connections by sea – from the Persian Gulf and the Red Sea to the coast of India and – from there to the Far East, and a land route, the famous Silk Road. The route from the Persian Gulf ran from the ports on the eastern Mediterranean coast overland via Baghdad. Then you could sail from the Persian Gulf close along the coast to India. This became an important route when Baghdad flourished from 800 AD on. William Bernstein speaks of the Baghdad Canton express.[96] Due to subsequent conflicts it was replaced by the route via Alexandria overland to the Red Sea and via the open sea to the coast of India (Calicut). This route was more dangerous because of the monsoon winds.

The connections led to migrations and a change in spheres of influence. The Mongols and Turks migrated and Islam expanded its area: in 1300 AD to Sumatra and in 1500 to Java and the Moluccans. Between 1000 AD and 1500 AD the Islamic realm became twice as big. The Europeans were not familiar with the regions along the Silk Road. This started to change with the journeys of John van Ruubroek and Marco Polo in 1245 AD.[97]

2.5. Hegemony within the network

The Mongol leader Temujin, better known as Genghis Khan, was the first leader to be able to unite the tribes in the Asian steppes, making him a candidate for the hegemony in the world system. To overcome the contrasts between the tribes, he encouraged mixed marriages. His army was divided into inter-ethnic sections of ten men who had to live together like brothers. High military posts were allocated on the basis of merit. As a result, the Mongols had very capable officers, who also received a lot of freedom to employ their tactics. The Mongols lived in tents, until the son of Genghis Khan founded the city of Karakorum. The trading network they maintained, the yam, with every few hundred kilometers a trading post, very many bridges and ports around the Black Sea, and the peace they realized in Asia resulted in a huge trade.[98]

Genghis Kahn used the tactic of burning the villages, initiating a flow of refugees to the cities, where chaos, hunger and disease broke out. Farmers had to operate ram systems, dig ditches, or serve as human shields and craftsmen made fire-spitting devices. In Central Asia, the cities of Samarkand and Bukhara, which came off mildly, fell, but in the cities of Herat and Nisapur a massacre was created, killing millions of people by Tuli, Genghis Khan's youngest son.[99] China and the rich Muslim regions were the most coveted prize, but after several attacks on China the Mongols temporarily shifted to the west because of issues of succession. Genghis Khan's grandson Hulagu sacked Damascus and Baghdad and the Caliph of Baghdad was rolled into a carpet and pounded to death. The Mamluks from Egypt fought back and Hulagu went home when his brother died. This stopped the march to the west. Egypt, Venice and Genoa had been spared and the chances for hegemony of the world system were over for the Mongols.

Hegemony within the global network was initially destined to be obtained by the Chinese empire. In 960 this empire had reunited after the disintegration of the Tang Dynasty in 907. China's population grew slightly to nearly 100 million over a period of more than one hundred years. Hang Zhou with its ten square kilometers was the largest city. It had huge walls and canals for the water, at least ten markets and many tea shops and restaurants. In the north around Kaifeng there were large mines and iron workshops and it looked almost like an industrial revolution, with an iron production of 125,000 tons. However, in 1127 AD the city was overrun by the Jurchen from the north. The Chinese themselves welcomed their help in their struggle against the Khitan Empire.[100]

In 1215, the Mongols under Gengiz Khan attacked 90 Chinese cities, but because of family quarrels concerning Gengiz Kahn's succession they changed course to the West. A later attack in 1230, which coincided with floods, famine and epidemics, resulted in stagnation. When the last emperor of the Song dynasty was driven into the sea by the Mongols at the end of the century, the population had actually declined by a quarter. In the fourteenth century, a cold period accelerated the downturn because massive epidemics broke out.[101]

The exchange between East and West had now grown to such a degree that countless merchants, migrants and clergymen went along the Silk Road. Iron tools, paper, the compass and the first firearms from China reached the West. As in the second century, this was also true for diseases that came overland this time. The recovery under Emperor Yongle (1402-1424), who improved the Grand Canal and restored bridges, and the construction of the Forbidden City in Beijing by a million workmen yielded a lot of wealth, but this did not result in China's leadership. When in 1400 Zheng He moved west with 1700 warships and 400 cargo ships, his travels were broken off. In 1500 the death penalty was introduced for building a ship with more than two masts.[102] Why the Chinese withdrew, has been a subject for debate. Landes claims that the Chinese state was too powerful and controlled trade too much. Morris emphasizes the impossible task of the Chinese to cross the Pacific to America, a distance of 8000 kms, with the then existing vessels. Given the distance across the

Atlantic the West was able to do this though. Proof would come at the end of the century.[103]

In the West, the development started slowly, especially in the regions that had contacts with the East. Genoa boasted a well-located port that had been in use since ancient times. The city had declared itself independent around 1100. Thus the city was able to dominate trade in the Western Mediterranean. Venice had free access to the port of Constantinople and dominated trade in the eastern Mediterranean.[104]

Genoa and Venice were involved in the first crusade. The Crusaders acted like barbarians. During the invasion of Syria they even burned children on the spit. The access to the east offered both cities the chance to play a critical role in the trade between Europe and the countries of the Middle East. This trade consisted of the import of spices and the export of gold – often in the form of coins – and slaves. Between 1200 and 1500 the two towns were the largest suppliers of slaves for the armies of the Muslims.[105]

The volume of trade of Venice and Genoa with the Muslim world was huge. The spice trade was lucrative and Venice, Genoa and Egypt became very rich. Pepper and cinnamon from India and Sri Lanka were widely available, but nutmeg, mace and cloves from the Moluccas were scarce. Cotton came from Turkey, Syria and Egypt, silk from China. Many more goods were transported from the Muslim world to the West than the other way around. Venice and Genoa had to buy the goods with silver and gold coins, up to 1,000 kg of gold and 10,000 kg of silver annually. From 1360 to 1420, there was a great shortage of gold and silver. Much gold came from Sudan, where trade was under control of the kingdom of Mali. It was transported along dangerous routes through the Sahara. The gold mined in Europe, in Hungary and the Balkans, was far from sufficient. Around 1400 the shortage of gold and silver resulted in price increases and economic downturn.[106]

2.6. The vulnerability of the network: hunger and disease

The international network of the fourteenth century was vulnerable to disasters in economically weaker regions because of the increased interdependence. This was evident in Europe north of the Alps during the great famine of 1315-1317. Rainfall, which lasted until 1322, had resulted in poor harvests and dike breaches in England and the Low Countries. Large parts of Holland and Zealand were flooded. The famine caused mass mortality, crime and diseases among humans and animals. People saw hunger as a disaster that had been announced by a meteor, observed as far away as China, and a lunar eclipse, followed by earthquakes in France.[107]

The biggest disaster, the Black Death, occurred more than thirty years later. Up to 1300 AD, people in the four regions, Europe, America, the Far East, and the Middle East had lived quite separately from each other and they had built resistance to diseases that occurred within their own area, but not to diseases from other areas. An earlier epidemic, the plague of Justinian, was limited to the Mediterranean because Goths, Vandals and Huns blocked it and the black rat had insufficiently penetrated the rest of Europe. The plague probably began when the Mongols brought the disease to China. It would reach Kaffa on the Black Sea in 1348. One third of the European population, about twenty million people, would die within a few years. Many more people died until 1722, probably because not until then were sufficient, stone houses built in which fleas were less likely. However, medical practices barely changed. The best known rational measure was quarantining ships, a measure implemented in Italy and eventually applied to almost all ships that came from the East.[108]

The figures on the scale of the disaster in different cities and regions are shocking and they make clear how vulnerable the world system in the making was. In Paris there were 50,000 deaths, half of the population, 800 a day at its peak. England's population fell from more than 5.5 million people to 2 million within a century. Only in 1700 did it reach the level of 1300. Venice recovered and developed a trade route via Alexandria to China and India, which would remain the main route for 150 years. In the densely populated East, the epidemic also hit hard. Baghdad lost half a million people and China nearly a quarter of its 71 million inhabitants. Egypt was the most vulnerable country due to being an intersection and because there were no escape routes via the vast desert. The country recovered, although the population halved and in 1800 it amounted to only three of the original eight million people.[109]

2.7. The role of religion as a way out of misery

The development of thinking about shocking events in the context of a changing world system may best be illustrated in the light of the role of religion in Europe and the institutional structure of monasteries and universities, which ultimately enabled big innovations in thinking.

The main response to the catastrophic events between 1200 and 1450 in Europe was the escape to religion. According to Keith Thomas in his masterly description of magical thinking in England, conversions to Catholicism were traditionally associated with display of miracles and supernatural healings. In the twelfth and thirteenth centuries stories of the lives of saints became essential for propagating religion. Saints were able to predict the future, control the weather, provide protection against water and fire, move objects miraculously and heal the sick. After they died their power was transferred to images and holy places. Every church, city and institution boasted a protective saint, specialized in certain diseases or crafts.[110]

Pilgrimages played a major role in the cult of saints and were also a source of income for the community. Through prayer and moral behavior one could obtain the intercession of saints in averting disaster. Making the sign of the cross, praying and celebrating Holy Mass and funerals on hallowed ground all contributed to this. The more you prayed yourself or had others pray for you for a fee, the greater the chance of success. This does not mean that one should not actively contribute to improvement or healing oneself, but the help of God and the saints was indispensable and a god-fearing life brought salvation in the hereafter.

The ritual of the blessing of buildings, objects, people, animals, and special places with holy water offered protection and had healing powers. The Holy Mass was essential. None of the bread and wine should be wasted and stealing supplies for celebrating Mass was punished with illness and misery. Keith Thomas claims that the medieval church was seen as a vast reservoir of magical power which could be used for a variety of secular purposes.[111] Many pagan rituals were incorporated into the ecclesiastical practices and owing to this flexibility the Catholic faith could spread widely.

The veneration of saints fitted into a broader pattern of change within the church by means of which it tried to bind more people by new forms of devotion and to solve internal problems. An ever increasing problem in the church was the gap between the masses and the elite. Generally, little piety was expected from the masses. Real piety was the monopoly of priests, monks and nuns. This did not satisfy emerging groups in the cities, the new middle class in commerce, law and the councils of churches and cities. In the cities movements emerged, such as the mendicant orders, to bind people to the faith more. They travelled around and propagated a more personal faith. They focused directly on God, especially the suffering Christ and his mother and sought a personal relationship in prayer and devotion. An example is the stigmata of St. Francis of Assisi who carried the sufferings of Christ literally on his body. The new demands of faith included the duty of annual confession, prayer of intercession with which one could save another person and the purgatory that you could be saved from by confession and other people's prayers.[112]

The individual experience and the worship of Christ as an individual who as God had become man and had suffered for mankind was a first step towards individualization. It would, after many innovations, eventually lead to the idea that it was possible to detach yourself from the church as an institution and still later to detach oneself from faith itself as a form of magic. In this period it was rather a confirmation and strengthening of faith. The roots of the later secularization, which can be traced to this period, therefore consisted of a movement that strengthened faith as a more personal and authentic form of religious experience. This change in the faith was accompanied by a greater interest in nature. In the paintings of Giotto, the Lorenzetti brothers and some of their contemporaries a more realistic, lively and personal style becomes visible. It was the intention to depict nature in all its beauty and to portray people as living beings with emotions.[113]

The development of stricter requirements in the faith made the community stronger by allowing more people in its midst and by disciplining them. It was thus an impetus to economic development and enhancement of the economic and political resilience of a community. This impulse becomes explicitly evident in the ecclesiastical charity, which can also be seen as a form of capital accumulation, control over money flows and law enforcement. Ecclesiastical charity was propagated as a religious duty to help the poor and the sick. This motive not only originated from the feeling that people had been hit badly and deserved relief, but also from fear of rebellion, curse, or the idea that fate could affect anyone. The poor could be humble and accommodating, but also threatening and terrorizing by wandering in gangs and cutting off the supply lines of a city.[114]

Cities or regions which offered relatively much care, could be faced with an influx of the poor and the sick. They had to help the poor to deter them from rebellion and not to allow them to weaken, in case they were needed as laborers. To ensure that everyone within the community would participate, the contributions were made public by the Church in sermons or lists of benefactors. Freeloaders were put to shame. In this way the church functioned as moral conscience, but also as mediator in order for the system of charity to function. However, it could not be prevented that not all cities cooperated. Only with the introduction of state care in the nineteenth century was there an umbrella organization that could call profiteers to order.

The problem of itinerant poor people occurred mainly during an epidemic, especially an influenza epidemic. Influenza is the worst risk of infection for humans, because the virus circulating between birds, pigs and humans mutates all the time, spreads rapidly and makes throat and lungs susceptible to bacterial infections.[115] Rational measures were sometimes taken at random, such as shutting down homes where an infected person lived, so the whole family died and the contamination was nipped in the bud. Children were usually not sufficiently protected. They were the first victims, especially when they arrived as foundlings in orphanages which were often outright sources of infection.[116]

2.8. Monasteries and universities as engines of intellectual creativity

In medieval Christianity three institutions played a crucial role: the monasteries, the Pope and universities. Monasteries were initially founded in rural areas in cooperation with the local aristocracy, which usually sent some of its sons to a monastery. These monasteries depended on their gifts, but were able to acquire much autonomy by loosening family ties by celibacy and by employing lay brothers. From the twelfth century, the expansion of monasteries and churches had been huge. Between 1180 and 1270, only in France more than 80 cathedrals, 500 abbeys and more than 10,000 churches were built.[117]

The Cistercians are best known for their extensive land clearing, austere lifestyle and strong organization. In 1118 they owned seven monasteries, in 1200 already 525 and in 1300 even 694.[118] David Landes pointed to the role of lay brothers to relieve monks from time-consuming mundane affairs The monasteries possessed a lot of tools to generate hydropower and promote industry.[119] The Cistercian order can be regarded as an early example of rational behavior, a combination of self restraint and productivity. The order promoted an aggressive Christianity through its participation in the Crusades against Islam. The mendicant orders in the cities focused more on education, the fight against poverty and support in case of diseases. They derived their earnings from donations from the wealthy urban bourgeoisie. The Franciscans and Dominicans were the most famous orders. Around 1300, there were 28,000 active Franciscans.

The expansion of the monasteries and mediation in conflicts within the church gave the pope more power. The number of church lawyers in Rome rose sharply. The monastic schools and the pope were sometimes diametrically opposed. The teachers of the monastic schools received much independence in that struggle and organized themselves into universities. According to Randall Collins in his sociological study of the emergence and development of philosophy, the university, as it took shape in the West, is a unique institution in the history of mankind. Nowhere, not in China, India or the Islamic world, was there an institution where so many scholars could achieve so much autonomy and where so much intellectual progress was possible.[120]

The Franciscans came to control the universities. Paris with over 6,000 students became the center, together with Oxford with about half that number. In Paris the creative period lasted for more than a hundred years, from 1230 to 1360. Concepts from the Arab world were introduced and translations of Arabic texts on Greek science appeared in Latin. Philosophy was considered to be more important than revelation and this evoked fierce reactions. After this creative period the number of universities rose sharply but progress stagnated. This led to movements outside the universities, such as humanism in the sixteenth century.

Unlike in Islam, rational thought and classical philosophy had been part of Christian theology already from the early days, as illustrated by church father Augustine in 400 AD. In Islam this thinking remained separated from the mosques and limited to circles at the court. In later Christianity philosophy was supported by the aristocratic courts, whereas in Islam this support vanished. And also unlike in Islam, lawyers worked in separate schools focusing on the secular Roman law. In Christianity orthodoxy had therefore a much weaker institutional basis compared with Islam. Christianity could achieve more autonomy with its ecclesiastic organization, monasteries and universities. Islam always remained associated with the rulers, had no religious organization, universities or monasteries. In the madrassas, philosophy was a threat to orthodoxy and it became excluded.[121]

David Landes describes the late Middle Ages in Western Europe as a unique constellation of market relations and political divisions, making it impossible for the state to slow down the acceptance of innovations, as was the case in China or a religion that was supported by the state, as in Islam. Openness to innovation and extensive contacts in a growing trade network stimulated a series of inventions, which enforced each other and contributed to new discoveries. This created a big productivity and greater expansion of contacts. According to Landes, invention was actually invented.

Some examples of these inventions are new waterpower techniques, glasses, clocks, printing and gunpowder. Not all of these inventions were new, but their specific applications and refinements were unique. They laid the foundation for better utilization of energy with connected watermills, greater productivity of older workers by the use of reading glasses, better coordination by a fixed schedule and a huge production of books and pamphlets. Energy use, productivity, dissemination of information and better coordination gave a huge boost to the resilience of the society and the foundation was laid for the scientific revolution that took place shortly afterwards.[122]

3   Protection by global interconnectedness

3.1. Global connections

Between 1450 and 1900, the network protecting people against shocking events would spread around the world. The Atlantic world became the new center. This expansion and densification of the network of human relations was caused by an increasing division of labor and a growing number of trade contacts, but also by great conquests and migrations. It was supported by new inventions and exchange of knowledge and the formation of large companies and complex state bureaucracies. A civilization process that was connected with these developments led to a fundamentally different view of human ability, human cruelty and the emotional life of man. The shift of the center of the global network to the Atlantic world was accompanied by various crises. The process accelerated during the Atlantic Revolution between 1775 and 1830. It was followed in the nineteenth century by a radical transformation of the infrastructure of transport and production, the living standard and the international order. The system that protected people against shocking events became an extremely complex set of functions and positions.

In 1450 about 400 million people inhabited this planet. They were divided into numerous states and spoke thousands of languages. In the expanding network the larger states were better off thanks to expensive weapons and ships that only they could afford. Small isolated communities fell behind in all respects.[123] For some time, the Europeans had had the intention to break down the domination of the Islamic countries around the Indian Ocean. These countries did not have a strong naval force, but it was a problem for the Europeans to get there, since these countries controlled the approach routes through the Red Sea and the Persian Gulf. How the Europeans accomplished their dream is widely known. A few points that are important for our subject will be mentioned below.

First, the role of the Spaniards when they discovered America. Christopher Columbus departed from the Spanish Canary Islands in search of a route to Asia in the western direction, which resulted in him ending up in the Caribbean.[124] His discovery of America, which initially he did not even realize, was a big step forward in the extension of the network. From the Old World explorers brought viruses, which the original inhabitants of America had no resistance to. Flu, smallpox and measles were unknown and their genetic diversity was low.[125] As a result, the Spaniard Cortez could overthrow the Aztecs with a few hundred men, whereas his fellow countryman Pissarro conquered the empire of the Incas with 167 men. Half of the original population of America would die of infectious diseases between 1500 and 1600. It was one of the biggest disasters ever. The subsequent conquest of America by Europeans was quite a task. In 1700 no more than 250,000 people from Europe lived in America, in 1800 about five million. Large parts remained in the hands of the original inhabitants for a long time. From 1500 an extensive trade in slaves had developed. More than eleven million slaves were shipped from Africa to the Americas over a period of 350 years.[126]

Second, the role of the Portuguese concerning the breakthrough to the Indian Ocean. In 1498, a Portuguese expedition led by Vasco da Gama, succeeded in finding the route around the Cape and reached the Indian Ocean. Da Gama knew he could pass the Cape by making a large arc to the West after the equator in order to make maximum use of the wind. Despite his brutal approach only half of his 170 crew returned. After many conflicts with local leaders, Portugal conquered most ports on the east coast of Africa, but it did not gain access to the Red Sea. Two other Portuguese seafarers, Magelhaes and Serrao, reached Malakka and Serrao even reached the Moluccas. One of Magelhaes' five ships finished the journey around the earth in one of the most daring expeditions ever. Of the 265 crew, no more than 31 survived. The Portuguese settled in Macao after they had failed to conquer Canton. The cost of human lives to the local populations, crew and soldiers was high. Thousands died in the conflicts and of diseases like malaria, dengue, typhoid and cholera.[127]

On the Atlantic coast a whole new network emerged, led by Portugal and Spain, followed by the Netherlands, England and the United States. The latter three, which did not have absolutist regimes had the advantage.[128] The Atlantic trade acquired the same function as the trade around the Mediterranean in Antiquity, but on a much larger scale. New methods of production made products cheaper and a decrease in transport costs stimulated trade. More products came within the reach of more people. International companies stimulated consumption in order to sell the massive supply of coffee, sugar and textiles. In 1750 the Netherlands and England already boasted a consumer culture in large sections of the population.

An early example of the global reach of trade is the silver trade. Between 1540 and 1700, the Spaniards transported more than 50,000 tons of silver from South America to Europe. The king demanded 20% of the revenues. There was a lively trade between Malaysia, Japan and China. Japan had silver mines itself. China imported silver on a large scale and its taxation system was based on silver. Portuguese and Dutch traders dominated large parts of the trade thanks to their knowledge and because they protected their ships against pirates. Yet, much silver was intercepted by pirates. This happened to the French in Cuba and the English in Peru.

3.2. The global crisis of the seventeenth century

Between 1610 and 1670, there was a huge crisis in the global network. About every three years, a war broke out somewhere. The Ottoman Empire only had seven years of peace in that period. The Thirty Years' War between Protestants and Catholics in Germany was catastrophic with nearly two million deaths and countless more died of starvation and disease.[129] In China, more than 160 rebellions took place within twenty years involving one million people. In Japan, forty great uprisings and numerous riots took place over a fifty years' period. In the richest state, the Mughal Empire, there was a civil war that lasted for two years. In England thirty-six food riots broke out within ten years and in Germany there were twelve peasant uprisings. In Scotland, Ireland and the American colonies revolts broke out against the English king. The crisis also led to rebellions against the kings of France. And the Spanish monarchy was in big trouble as well. The Ming dynasty in China, the country with the largest population, perished because of bankruptcy, diseases and famines. In 1644 Beijing was occupied by rebels. The collapse of the empire cost an estimated 25 million people their lives.[130]

Many explanations were in circulation concerning the huge crisis. At that time, they were often of supernatural origin. A few people, one of them Francis Bacon, pointed to the weather as the major cause. Nevertheless, there are many descriptions from the era about cold and drought, including descriptions of the Bosporus, which had completely frozen over so that one could walk from Europe to Asia, and of the Little Belt between Jutland and Funen, which the King of Sweden could cross on horseback taking canons as well. A few years later, the French philosopher Voltaire would attribute the crisis to a period of extreme cold. Recent research on ice sheets, glaciers, pollen and tree rings confirms the picture of cold and drought. The solar activity had reached its lowest level in 2000 years. Between 1500 and 1600 real wages fell and hunger and poverty afflicted more and more people. The Chinese coast was dominated by pirates and smugglers. Charles V tried to unite Europe and the Ottomans tried to conquer it. Both failed.[131]

One solution was the commissioning of fallow or poor soils or, as in China, the commissioning of new crop. This happened on a large scale. The great expansion moves were not the result of the industrialization process, as is often claimed, but they preceded it. Larger countries added land. They colonized peoples, destroyed forests, reclaimed wet areas and damaged the game population. There was widespread deforestation in Japan, England and Scotland. In 1650 England took half of its energy from coal.[132] The Russians defeated part of the Mongols and moved with the help of the Cossacks who were armed with firearms and cannons. They moved into Siberia on riverboats to hunt for the millions of fur-bearing animals, such as sables, stoats, squirrels and foxes. In the seventeenth century, every year 200,000 pelts went to Russia, 10% of the revenues of the Russian state. Indigenous languages disappeared and Siberian peoples were converted to Orthodox Christianity.[133] Russians and Chinese met at the Amur River in eastern Siberia. Armed with firearms they were finally able to beat the steppe peoples. Two million Russians and five million Chinese went to the new land in the steppes.[134] In Europe and China invasions of nomads from the steppes and the spreading of illnesses as a result, were things of the past now. This was crucial. It made their societies resilient against two of the most shocking events of these days and it gave the West the opportunity to shift the center to the Atlantic world.

3.3. The downfall of the Ming Dynasty

The fall of the Ming Dynasty, the largest, most advanced and most powerful empire that the human race had known thus far, occurred in 1644. During that year, the Forbidden City was seized and the last emperor of the dynasty committed suicide. The wars, riots, epidemics, famines and the Inquisition with dozens of death sentences and the exile of the literary elite which accompanied the fall of the dynasty, lasted more than fifty years. The famine was partly caused by high taxes and rising food prices which caused people to sell their possessions and even family members.[135] The fall began with incursions from the north, the rebellion of Li Zicheng against the privileges of the 70,000 eunuchs, piracy from Japan, the closing down of the silver supply by the Spaniards and the execution of the most capable General.[136] It was accompanied by mass suicide of the elite. The fall of the empire has been documented in an intrusive ego document by a nineteen year old boy, Zhang Maozi, who was destined to follow in his grandfather's footsteps as Governor of a province. Especially the mental pain of the boy, being the sole survivor of a family that had committed suicide together with the entire staff – a total of 27 people – during the invasion of the conquerors, has been described in a most penetrating way.[137] Of course, the experiences and the way he interprets and remembers the events have been colored by his position and socio-cultural background, and the recovery phase in which he arranges and writes down the memories.

After his father's death, he and his mother were taken to his grandfather's, who was the governor of a southern province. His grandfather became suicidal and they lived in exile on some island. After the invasion of enemy forces in 1651, he saw how his family members committed suicide by hanging themselves by means of silk scarves and how the staff jumped into a well. He clang to his grandfather's coat and pulled at his mother's veil "...in complete loss of the world." He saw the blood spray from the heads and arms, was stripped by the soldiers and got clothes from one of them. He nearly drowned while crossing a river, got lost in the tall grass, was captured and so tightly tied on board a ship, that he could only move simultaneously with others. He only got pieces of meat, dripping with blood. Trapped in the dark, he could only sit on – as he thought – pieces of wood, which later turned out to be parts of skeletons. After some time, his situation improved, but he was only released after a hundred days and had to recuperate in total confusion for two months. "My body had become inured to a tragic existence, the painful disruption to my mind had become a fixed state, and whenever I thought or spoke of my (diseased) elders, I felt as though I would break apart."[138]

Zhang Maozi talked about his feelings of guilt towards his grandfather whom he had not been able to bury with the requisite rituals. He tried to describe his grandfather's noble character for posterity. He wanted to transfer his grandfather's remains to his current residence which was in line with the Confucian tradition, but he failed. He died shortly after, according to other sources. Much of what Zhang Maozi said, would later be referred to in the textbooks of experts as "psychological trauma" or "post-traumatic stress disorder." However, it was not the young man's intention to express his subjective feelings in such a modern way, even though he has succeeded quite well. He wanted to show how important his duties were in the line of succession and how hard he had tried to fulfill these duties in spite of all setbacks.

3.4. The emergence of a global trading nation: the Netherlands 1600-1670

Due to the events in China and the introvert elite in that country, Europe had a unique chance to develop further, but it was unable to unite under the Habsburg Empire. However, the disunity offered new opportunities which would benefit the Netherlands and England most. Between 1600 and 1670 the Netherlands, or more precisely the Republic of the Seven Provinces, was a society that derived its resilience from an urban market-oriented economy focused on global expansion. There was a good infrastructure, a literate population, a productive agriculture and a modern credit system. This system enabled the government to borrow a lot of money for the high costs of the army and expansion of the economy.[139]

The Republic was characterized by a far-reaching individualization with free partner choice, few children and few live-in servants. Groups from the bourgeoisie formed the elite and they propagated a strong sense of equality. The nobility, in the person of the stadholder, did not have much influence. The Republic emerged from the struggle for independence with Spain, which continued into its heyday and lasted (from 1568-1648). In 1622 Amsterdam was the largest city with more than 100,000 inhabitants and this number had grown to 200,000 in 1670.[140] In 1650 the entire population exceeded one million. Many immigrants lived in the Republic, mainly well-educated refugees from the South and Jewish refugees from Spain, but there were also many seasonal workers.

The land was mainly reclaimed from the sea. The focus was on the fight against water, with the construction of dikes, locks and bridges, combating salinization and silting up of rivers and harbors. With a new type of connected windmills up to 4 ½ meters deep waters could be milled dry. For the first time, natural energy was put to use. Much coal was imported from England, but the country had peat. Peatlands were dug, even if they were under water, and the peat was transported throughout the country across waterways. The connections in the country mainly consisted of a network of waterways, particularly barge canals. Between Haarlem and Amsterdam 300,000 passengers travelled by tow barge between 1660 and 1670. The toll rights of cities, which had obstructed transportation, were largely abolished.[141]

Dutch society, as so many other societies, reached its lead position by its location in a network of good connections and by the way they exploited this advantage. A merchant fleet sailed to all parts of the world. Most income was derived from the grain trade with the Baltic States ("the mother trade").[142] The Republic was strategically located between these States and Spain, which had a great need for grain. Between 1625 and 1700 more than 40,000 seaworthy ships were built. The wood was sawed in hundreds of sawmills. Many Dutch moved elsewhere.

The Dutch East India Company (VOC) carried more than 975,000 people, half of them foreigners, during its existence. Half of them did not return.[143] The VOC employed few slaves, but many private people had slaves. The VOC was a major innovation in international trade. It was the first corporation with shares. Amsterdam was not only the financial capital of Europe, but in the words of one of the freethinkers Pierre Bayle, also, "the great ark of outcasts."[144] The high level of education, the extended freedom of the press, the many publishers in Amsterdam and the greatest density of education at university level compared to other countries, stimulated its intellectual climate.[145]

Despite the huge costs of the uprisings and subsequent wars with England, there was little poverty and an abundance of food. There was enough money for social care, because many possessions of the monasteries had been seized by the cities and provinces. Social care and extensive literacy made possible the development of the nuclear family with plenty of freedom for women and children. However, maternal mortality was high and only half of the children reached adulthood.[146] From 1670 the economy stagnated and England would surpass the Republic in a fairly short time. The Republic was unique in that here a society flourished with great resilience against disasters, hunger and poverty at an unprecedented level of technical development, energy use, consumption and individual freedom.

3.5. The beginning of a global empire: England 1650-1750

In 1600 four million people were living in England and Wales, in 1750 the number had risen to five and a half million. The population of France was four times as big. But in 1900, after a huge growth spurt, England had almost overtaken France by 37 to 39 million inhabitants. This had been made possible England having experienced a tremendous development the basis of which was laid between 1650 and 1750.[147] The start of this process in England was painful. Life expectancy was thirty to forty years. Most people were chronically ill because of vitamin deficiency, poor food and poor hygiene. Between 1670 and 1690 thirty percent of London's population died during epidemics, including 30,000 cases of smallpox. In 1603, 30,000 Londoners died of the plague, in 1625 over 41,000, and in 1656 even 68,000. Epidemics caused famine and looting. Firefighting was bad, there was no fire insurance and the wooden houses with candle lights and open fires in the workplaces and homes posed a great danger. The Great Fire of London in 1666 destroyed 13,000 homes and 100,000 people became homeless. Yet there was no uncertainty on all fronts. The number of murders per 100,000 inhabitants decreased between 1400 and 1700 dramatically from 100 to 5. This was a development that was related to the process of state formation and it occurred in more European countries, but England was in the lead.[148]

The fear of shocking events initially refrained the population from rational solutions. Many people resorted to drinking. In 1684 people drank 182 liters of beer per person, subject to excise duties, and much illegally brewed beer. Tobacco use had not been established, but in 1700 consumption amounted to a kilo per person. Gambling was normal. Superstition was widespread. People's belief in witches could grow, because traditional charity was not adequate anymore. The fear of disasters and infection was projected on poor single women who, in the eyes of the population, had magical powers and could curse the community. Doctors could do little and their practices in the form of amputation, incising of abscesses, cutting open bladder stones and trepanation of the skull were feared. They were too expensive for the poor, who therefore relied on herbalists, witches or faith healers. Mental illnesses were attributed to melancholy or hysteria. Before Thomas Willis came up with his theory of the cerebral origin of hysteria around 1650, hysteria was seen as a disease of the uterus.[149]

The Protestant Church fought the Catholic faith which in the Middle Ages had become so widespread in the form of blessings, holy worship, sacraments and miracles. This was replaced by the belief in a divine plan. However, the common people continued to believe in doctors, astrology, fortune telling and witchcraft. Theologians claimed that one had better have a clear conscience than clean houses and streets.[150] Eighty percent of the population lived in rural areas. Only five percent of the population belonged to the rich top layer of landowners who enjoyed more than half of the national income.

The most important revolution was the Glorious Revolution in 1688 when. the Dutch stadholder William III (King Billy) and his English wife, daughter of the king of England, went to England with a large mercenary army of fifty-three warships and four hundred troopships.[151] He came at the invitation of the Protestants who wanted to free the country of their catholic king and the influence of the French. The English parliament won and the interest on state loans decreased. Many banks and trading houses moved to England.

The English profits of the Atlantic sea trade increased from £ 200,000 per year in 1600 to £ 900,000 in 1700.[152] In 1600 the tobacco trade with Virginia flourished as did the sugar trade with the Caribbean countries in 1640. By

1650 the British dominated the slave trade and by 1700 the coffee trade and trade in textiles. Coffee was originally from Mocha and Beit el Fakih in South Arabia. It was drunk widely in the Muslim world. After 1700 England got a grip on the market and the number of coffee houses in Europe strongly expanded. The Caribbeans were a kind of Wild West at that time, characterized by piracy and acts of violence. The English had a marginal position, but were able to create flourishing sugar plantations on the small island of Barbados and on Jamaica. The by-product was rum, which was very popular. There were not enough people for the labor-intensive and hard work on the sugar plantations, even though increasingly more prisoners were deployed.

Between 1519 and 1860 more than 11 million slaves were transported from Africa to America. Only 9.5 million arrived. Eighty percent of them went to the Caribbean and Brazil, the rest to the Spanish Americas. Only 400,000 slaves arrived in the British part of North America. Many people died in the cultivation of sugar due to malnutrition and hard work. In North American cotton farming life for the slaves was better.[153]

3.6. The West-European civilization process

In the confusion and chaos that had regularly held Europe in its grip from 1450, a long-term development is easily overlooked, namely the Western European civilization process. It is a change in the behaviour and self-consciousness of people. Norbert Elias, who wrote a standard work on the Western European civilization process, claims that by the increasing interdependence of the human network, the behavior of more and more people had to be synchronized and every person in the network had to regulate his/her behavior more.[154] The expansion of this network of interdependence was reflected in the formation of markets and states and it was closely united by the increasing division of labor. To force people to exert more self-restraint is not easy. Only with a state-monopoly of violence, with an army and police in the service of the state, can violence in society be reduced.

The formation of a state-monopoly of violence was enabled by the invention of the ship's gun, by field artillery and by the organization of the army. The army was intensively trained in fighting in strong units and individually. The supplies, new weapons and the intensive training could not be financed by looting, but only through taxes or loans. Only large countries could establish good tax systems. The local nobility did not have enough means to defend its domain. Their income from farming the land declined because there was more money in circulation owing to the growing trade. The impoverished local nobility went to the king's court to continue their luxury lives. They changed from warriors into courtiers with civilized manners. Army and police became a state matter. Trade and transport had less to fear from looting and robbery by local potentates.

This development occurred most explicitly in France. In Versailles an elaborate court life arose around a king who had almost absolute power. Civilization was synonymous with courtesy, good taste and table manners and French became the standard language of the upper classes. Building a good reputation and gaining the favors of the king and his courtiers was essential. The pressure to comply with the increasingly sophisticated court etiquette was so strong that it became a part of the conscience of people: automatic self-restraint with strong feelings of shame and pain. Violence and roughness were not only frowned upon, but people would not accept it anymore. Because the court was open to climbing citizens, they also adopted the manners to distinguish themselves from lower groups. Thus more controlled ways of dealing with the body and the use of force spread to large groups of people.[155]

The process of civilization manifested itself in two ways: as a process of rationalization and as a process of psychologizing. Rationalization implies increasing attention for the consequences of behavior in the long run and describing the world in less emotionally charged terms. Elias describes it as a gradual process in which people take more distance from their immediate impulses, making it easier to think about the long-term consequences of events and to observe the world around them in more objective and less emotionally charged terms. Natural disasters were considered disasters caused by nature itself. An example is the earthquake in Lisbon, which took place on 1 November 1755. Major fires broke out because the religious population had lit candles to celebrate the Catholic feast of All Saints. Two hours after the quake, a tidal wave swept across the city. Many people who had fled to the port, drowned. There were about 15,000 deaths. The Jesuit Malagrida saw the event as a punishment from God, but scholars, such as Voltaire, Jean-Jacques Rousseau and Immanuel Kant, pointed to natural causes and bad urban planning.[156]

Psychologizing implies increasing attention for inner motives and motivations, and more empathy for the feelings of others.[157] This is reflected in increasing public criticism of torture and punishment, slavery, despotic rulers, cruelties in wars and atrocities perpetrated against animals. Publicly enjoying breaking on the wheel, quartering, flogging, pillorying or burning at the stake evoked feelings of disgust and shame in more and more people. Between 1750 and 1850 torture became prohibited in almost all European countries.[158] Man was presented as an autonomous being.

He was no longer open to influences from ghosts and gods from the outside, but the spirit resided in the individual in his own private self, disconnected from the cosmos. The cosmos was empty and was perceived as an independent system with its own laws.[159]

The next step was to regard societies as autonomous systems, too. They consisted of an economy in which people formed a community (the market) motivated by self-interest and a public space where individuals could reach agreement by rational debate (public opinion, free press). The invention of the printing press made it possible for countless books and pamphlets to appear in print in Europe. In hundreds of universities scholars could exchange new ideas without many restrictions. The market for books and newspapers, and the protected space of the university were characteristic of the Christian world, where new ideas could spread more rapidly than elsewhere.[160] The university was gradually transformed into the modern research university with more autonomy than it had ever had before. From 1780, particularly in Germany, a fierce debate about education and the role of religion and accompanied by a burst of creativity, had started. This became possible because Frederick the Great had expanded the Prussian empire and strongly opposed the influence of religion.

The intention of the innovators was to get philosophy recognized as a core discipline. Immanuel Kant wanted to make philosophy leading in science by making rigorous demands on research and the creation of theories. The use of reason and independently conducted scientific research gained a central place in the curriculum. Fichte took it a step further than Kant. He claimed that intellectuals were the saviors of the nation, because they had no economic interests. The Prussian Minister of Education, Wilhelm von Humboldt, had listened to a speech by Fichte in 1808.

He applied his ideas by allowing professors much freedom in choosing their topics. He founded the University of Berlin, with Fichte as professor of philosophy and the first rector. Fichte was later succeeded by Hegel. For all senior posts in public service a university degree was needed. The Grammar school became the preparatory education and after 1820 a university degree was required for teachers in pre-university education. A large group of writers, including Goethe and Schiller, that worked in Weimar near Jena, adopted Kant's ideas and they worked hard to spread them. The German example became the standard for the modern university.[161]

3.7. The Atlantic Revolution

The development in the Netherlands and England shows what the first modern countries on the Atlantic coast were capable of. China had turned inward and the steppe peoples no longer posed a threat. But other things happened. The northern countries along the Atlantic coasts would enter a whole new era between 1775 and 1830. It would increase the resilience of the ever-growing network permanently, but at the same time increase its vulnerability in some respects. The revolution began with the battle that England had to fight with France for the leadership of Europe, which lasted more than a century until 1815, and with America in its struggle for independence of 1776. Thanks to a better system of lending, England could win the competition with France, but it lost its American colonies when England wanted to charge them for a part of the costs. France became embroiled in the French Revolution and could not defeat England despite Napoleon's efforts.

The English system of borrowing allowed large amounts of capital to be collected and invested in overseas expansion and domestic activities. However, for the development of an empire more was needed. It all began with the invention of the first primitive steam engine and its improvement in 1776 at the University of Glasgow by James Watt and funded by Matthew Boulton. This enabled them to pump away water in mines and greatly accelerate the spinning of cotton fibers. The production of cotton increased from 3,000 to 178,000 bales within twenty years' time. The iron foundry followed. Over a period of eighty years, the output power of the industry would reach the level of muscle strength of 40 million people. The high wages in England encouraged the shifts to mechanization and the use of energy stored in fossil fuels. Coal and steel would change the Atlantic world for ever.[162]

Cotton originated from India, but the English were able to cultivate it widely in North America, despite protests from their own farmers. Transport to England took only a few weeks, from India via the Cape of Good Hope it took six months. Sales were facilitated by the emergence of rapidly changing fashions. The English East India Company (EIC) had a good relationship with the English royal family and they tempted the king and his wife to ever new fashions. They were followed by the aristocracy and bourgeoisie, which strongly increased the sales of fabrics. Export of cotton from America had risen to two billion pounds on the eve of the U.S. Civil War.[163] From 1780 to 1830 the British population had doubled from seven to fourteen million people. Of those seven million people, six million people went to the cities. New York grew from 79,000 to 2.5 million between 1800 and 1890. Industrialization opened up new markets and brought mass consumption. The transport by means of steam trains narrowed the distances.[164]

The Atlantic network could evolve thanks to a massive expansion of the infrastructure of production, transportation and knowledge. Characteristic was the building of railways from 1830 and ports and steamships with intercontinental connections. In the US it offered employment to 100,000 Chinese. Thousands of kilometers of cables were laid on the ocean floor for telegraph connections. Characteristic were also the expansion of the press, the establishment of systems of knowledge storage, such as national libraries and archives and archaeological research – with which the memory was recorded on a large scale and the self-consciousness of the leading nations was propagated. Very important was the construction of an urban infrastructure of sewers and water supply, roads and undergrounds. Crucial for this was a worldwide standardization of the time in hours and minutes, the standardization of weights and measures and the introduction of a gold standard and a free-market system, which would replace silver as a currency and secured the reliability of international payments.[165] In this way, trade could be promoted, exchange simplified and the space on earth further explored by expeditions to inhospitable areas. New areas were given names and they were linked with the rest. States became the units, which together had to guard international order and coordinate the complex system of production, trade, transport, communication and exchange of knowledge.

The first major improvement in the transport system was the construction of the Erie Canal in 1830, connecting New York with the "Great Plains" via Albany. The grain production in the vast areas, which was much more efficient than in the eastern states and England, received a huge boost. In 1880 4.6 million tonnes of cargo were transported via the Erie channel. The railways enabled production to shift inland. In 1830 transport became even easier when refrigerated carriages and ships were introduced. The growing use of electricity in many fields made the distribution of energy from fossil fuels easier. The opening of the Suez Canal in 1869 shortened the routes from Europe to the East, especially to India, the jewel in the British crown. The distance from London to Bombay was reduced by half.[166]

The vast improvements in the transport system resulted in a completely new system of funding, which would make the United States the center of global capitalism. The United States achieved this unique position after the unification in 1865. It resulted in major investments in steamships, railroads and in products sold everywhere in the country and on the international market, often by fast transactions by telegraph. The construction of the railway in and around Manhattan, to the Mid-West, and especially the construction of the intercontinental railway to newly liberated California and five other transcontinental railroads involved massive investments. Railroad companies became large companies with professional managment and a large-scale administration to guarantee secure transport over long distances. Shortly before that, the gold rush had brought 200,000 fortune seekers to California. They had found $ 200 million in gold within five years. However, the railroads were a much better way of transportation than carts pulled by horses over roads that were often impassable due to bad weather. The journey from New York to San Francisco took six days. Before the construction of the first railway it took six months. In Pennsylvania a major oil recovery industry arose. Large trusts controlled the industrial chains of steel, oil, sugar, meat and machines and eliminated competitors.[167]

From 1875 to 1900 people, such as John Rockefeller, Cornelius Vanderbilt, JP Morgan, Andrew Carnegie, Daniel Drew and Jay Gould, the Colossi of capitalism the historian Brands called them, would amass huge fortunes. They made their profits in oil recovery, the steel industry and the construction of railroads. Some of them did so by speculation on Wall Street, which was booming in rapidly growing New York. The battle on Wall Street could rightly be called a titanic struggle. In 1830 31 railway shares a day were traded, in 1850 tens of thousands and in 1870 even hundreds of thousands of shares in railways and other industries. A large internal market developed in the vast country, which was rather densely populated – with a population of 40 million in 1870 and 76 million in 1900 – and attracted investors and immigrants from abroad. In 1865 four million slaves were set free in the South and this contributed to it, despite the fact that poverty in that area remained because of low prices for tobacco and cotton. In 1900 the United States was leader in industrial production with incomes that were twice as high as in France or Germany. To protect the industry and to pay for the construction of transport routes, high import tariffs were levied in the United States.[168]

3.8. The differences in resilience: center and periphery

The major changes that were brought about by the Atlantic revolution led to an integration of the different worlds around the Atlantic Ocean. This integration was mainly the result of a much better infrastructure and massive migrations from Europe to America. This resulted in strong commercial relationships and large-scale production in the center of the Atlantic world. Empty areas around the Atlantic coast and the hinterland were filled with new people. The original population had to adapt and became the major looser. The 300,000 Indians in California in 1769 had dwindled to a mere 30,000 in 1860 and they were forced back into enclaves.[169] Between 1820 and 1920, 33 million Europeans moved to the U.S. and 3.5 million to Argentina. Among the immigrants there were 2.5 million Jews from Eastern Europe. They emigrated to the U.S especially after the pogroms following the assassination of Tsar Alexander in 1881. Moreover, more than 2.5 million Europeans went to the colonies in North and South Africa.[170] The colonization of Siberia by Russia was only one side effect of the Atlantic revolution and it did not result in a thriving economy, such as in the United States with flourishing California. Siberia was partly a penal colony and place of exile. It had 400,000 exiles and prisoners in 1898 (7% of the population). This was also true for Australia with 162,000 convicts until 1868 and French Guiana and New Caledonia with tens of thousands of convicts.[171]

These large migrations and deportations to empty or undeveloped regions made nature vulnerable due to the large-scale hunt on whales, fur-bearing animals, bisons, tigers, elephants and leopards. Between 1820 and 1860, 50,000 whales were caught annually and between 1865 and 1880 15 million bisons were killed. Vast areas were mined, hunted, deforested and plundered. This increased vulnerability was partly compensated by the growing agricultural productivity in the Atlantic world thanks to the improvement of crops and mechanization. Initially mechanization was slow. The tractor was only widely introduced in Europe after 1918 and horses were still in use in agriculture as draft animals in 85% of the cases in 1950. Yet, in 1800 agriculture in England was twice as productive as in Russia. And in 1850 less than 50% of the working population worked in agriculture in Western and Northern Europe. Mainly due to the differences in productivity in agriculture, differences arose between precursors and laggards. For example, in 1900 agriculture in the United States was fifty times more effective than in India.[172] Not only productivity, but also trade in agricultural products grew enormously due to the competitiveness of new emerging agricultural areas.

The shifts in agriculture increased the world food production, but also made some areas vulnerable to famine. Other factors played a role, such as corruption and the bad functioning of the food storage and food distribution in China. The religiously inspired Taipeng uprising of 1850-1875 was the final blow with an estimated 30 million deaths.[173] After 1875, China experienced massive famines with another 9 to 13 million deaths. Outbreaks of diseases reinforced this. It happened in regions where there was little modern infrastructure and there are hardly any images of the disaster left. Famine also arose in Ireland, then a peripheral area, where after poor harvests and a typhoid outbreak one million people died between 1845 and 1849. Another one hundred thousand people died due to illnesses during and after the emigration.[174] Epidemics became less threatening in Europe, except cholera and tuberculosis, which initially even exacerbated by the poor living conditions in the cities. In the more remote regions in India, Australia and Oceania they would result in many deaths. In 1898 an outbreak of the plague occurred, killing 13.2 million people mainly in South Asia.[175]

The twentieth century shows, that global capitalism spread significantly. After 1945, on the initiative of the U.S., free trade was promoted in the so-called GATT negotiations. The volume of world trade increased explosively from 5.5 percent of the joint gross domestic product of the world in 1945 to 17 percent in 1998. The invention of the container made transport across big distances easier.[176] By expansion of the communication network via telephone and internet, a large amount of information became available everywhere on earth. Investments in ICT along with a wave of liberalization and an influx of capital led to an acceleration in the volume of capital transactions, but also to a fivefold increase of the joint debts of governments and individuals in relation to the real economy. This would substantially increase the risk of global economic crises, which became visible more than ever between 2008 and 2014.

Part 2

Recognizing unbearable suffering

4 The discovery of the psychological trauma

4.1. Introduction

In the second half of the nineteenth century all the ingredients for the professional and public recognition of the psychological trauma and its advance to a central place in modern life were available. The Atlantic Revolution had resulted in a fundamental change in social relations, the standard of living and life's risks. The Western civilizing process had created a completely new perspective on man and his environment. The risks and threats of modern life had become the subject of public debate and national interference. For the first time in history, public health care had become a central theme.[177]

The ongoing process of industrialization and the transformation of society that accompanied it, would accelerate the way in which one thought about human suffering and risk control and result in an entirely new perspective on human life and society. It was reflected in four ways: a humanitarian revolution, a focus on the inner emotional life of people, a growing awareness of the risks of modern warfare and awareness of the risks of industrialization in general. These four dimensions will be discussed in detail in the following four paragraphs. It shows how they created the conditions for the social recognition of the suffering and the central place it would occupy in modern life.

4.2. The humanitarian revolution

The first dimension of this change in thinking involved a revolution in the perception of atrocities. In the early nineteenth century, public executions and the display of tortured and mutilated bodies disappeared from public space and were replaced by the prison system. The prison was considered humane because it appealed to the conscience by means of quiet contemplation. In a so called "penitentiary civilization offensive" the upper classes brought this way of thinking to the common people, who had a strong preference for retaliation of crimes.[178] It was definitely an improvement, but there was also much criticism since prison included many inhumane features. It was thanks to writers, such as Heinrich Heine, Charles Dickens, Victor Hugo, Fyodor Dostoyevski, Anton Chekhov and Oscar Wilde, that people began to empathize with the suffering of prisoners. Charles Dickens claimed he could not sleep anymore if someone suffered in a silent cell because he had given permission. A director of a prison found that prisoners were completely unsettled at their release. They were unable to write their names in the register and could not even hold a pen with their trembling fingers. They did not seem to realize where they were and jumped from their seats all the time, sometimes twenty times a minute. Many doctors, however, interpreted these phenomena as simulation, innate disorders or a person's simple need of too much distraction. However, the protest led to the emancipation of prisoners and great attention for victims of deportation, torture, solitary confinement and totalitarian institutions in the twentieth century.[179]

The attention for atrocities extended to more areas. In the United States a movement arose against cruelty to children. Until that time virtually all children were beaten with sticks and whips, put on a hot stove, tied to beds, put into cold water or they had to kneel down for hours and were scared by tales about monsters and ogres. Belief in the innate depravity of children ratified these acts.[180] In 1693 John Locke claimed that the child is a blank slate and that its development depended on understanding the childlike helplessness, but this did not change practices. Only in 1874 was the "New York Society for the Prevention of Cruelty to Children" (SPCC) founded by the lawyer of an abused girl. Within thirty years, it would expand to more than 200 of such organizations in the USA. The organizations wanted to change the behavior of educators to prevent children from ending up as criminals. It was recognized that industrialization and immigration had worsened the living conditions for children of poor families.[181] There was major media attention for cruelties in dysfunctional families. The aversion to beating children came much later, after 1950. It started in Northern European countries and Democratic U.S. states. In Sweden in 1930 33% of the parents beat their children every day. In 1995 this was 4%. In 1979 the beating of children was prohibited in Sweden.[182]

The attitude towards psychiatric patients changed at the same time. In 1803, ten years after Pinel had freed forty mentally ill from their chains, Johan Christian Reil wrote in his *Rhapsodies* about a more humane form of psychiatry. He made a distinction between the doctor who was to deal with pharmaceutical methods and the psychologist who was to deal with the psychological healing of the (excited) soul.[183] This changed attitude towards atrocities also extended itself to animals. Animal protection organizations in England and the United States managed to achieve that fights between animals as a form of entertainment were reduced and the living conditions of pets and horses greatly improved.[184]

4.3. The focus on inner life

A second dimension of the change in thinking was reflected in the focus on the inner emotional life of people. Thinking about other people's motives had already been encouraged at the court of the King of France, where courtiers tried to acquire favors from superiors by putting themselves in their shoes. Count Saint Simon, an insider himself, provided a penetrating picture of such behavior.[185] However, the greatest stimulus came from scholars who were interested in special phenomena, such as epilepsy, fainting, telepathy and hysteria. These phenomena had already been demonstrated extensively at fairs and in theaters. Scholars, such as Whytt, Cheyne and Cullen of the University of Edinburgh, saw the phenomena as manifestations of illnesses of the nervous system. Metaphors based on electricity created a new vocabulary with terms, such as connection, stimulus, conduction and tension.[186]

An example of this way of thinking is animal magnetism or Mesmerism, named after Franz Anton Mesmer. He regarded nervous diseases as a disturbance in the distribution of the fluid, a medium that was present throughout the universe. Magnets could move this medium after swallowing a ferrous liquid. They caused a magnetic crisis which could relieve symptoms. His ideas were debated extensively in the western world.[187] In 1784 the Frenchman Marquis the Puységur provided the main impetus to this way of thinking by inducing a trance using concentration and calming techniques: the magnetic sleep or somnambulism. During this trance someone could listen, speak and act by order of the magnetizer and pain could be relieved. Between 1800 and 1820 animal magnetism was taught at more than ten universities in Germany. In England wandering French magnetizers acquainted English physicians with it. In 1842 the magnetic sleep was renamed hypnosis by James

Braid and thus made respectable. Charles Dickens used the method on Madame de la Rue and made her tell her secrets under hypnosis to relieve her pain.[188] James Esdaile performed many painless operations with the help of Mesmer's method in India. It was scientifically recognized in Nancy at Liébault's and in Paris at Charcot's. According to Ellenberger in his famous overview, hypnosis was the "royal road" to inner phenomena.[189]

Charles Beard, a neurologist from New York, is considered to be the father of neurasthenia. According to him, the tensions, the high pace of life and the mobility of the hard-working middle class in the United States expressed themselves in a new pattern of complaints with phenomena of exhaustion, insomnia, migraine and eating disorders.[190] The term neurasthenia was adopted in Europe and mixed with the old notion of decay and degeneration. Neurasthenia was the disease of civilization par excellence and could be cured by rest, physical exercise and good nutrition. Well-known was the Weir Mitchell cure, originally from Philadelphia and much followed in Europe. Psychiatrists could offer treatment to the upper class in private practices and raise the status of the profession. The diagnosis allowed pedagogues to avoid terms, such as guilt and sin, when treating problem children.[191] All this had major consequences. Much behaviour was not charged with guilt or dismissed as affectation anymore, but regarded as a problem that was located inside man.

4.4. Awareness of the risks of the first modern wars

The third dimension of the change in thinking was the growing awareness of the risks of modern warfare. After the Napoleonic wars a complex network of major powers had formed in Europe, consisting of France, the British Empire,

Prussia, Tsarist Russia, the Habsburg dual monarchy and the Ottoman Empire. From 1815 they tried to balance each other with a system of alliances which succeeded wonderfully for some decades. In Eastern Europe, however, a fervent nationalism arose, because some countries wished to free themselves from Poland, Russia and the Ottoman Empire. The relationship between Christian and Muslim peoples was precarious. In Crimea there were Muslim Tatars and in the Caucasus Islamic peoples as well as Christian Armenians and Georgians.[192]

The Ottomans were on the defensive. They had had to deal with erosion of their empire ever since the hey-days under Suleyman in the sixteenth century. They looked down on other religions, but tolerated them within a system of "live and let live", the millet system.[193] The ten million Orthodox Christians were the biggest millet. They were supported by the Russians. A Russian army of 60,000 men attacked the Balkans, but half of them then died of diseases. The Christians in the Ottoman empire became more and more trapped. The army including 40,000 conservative Janissaries, the sultan's infantry, blocked all attempts to change. According to the British, the Russians wanted to conquer Europe and Asia and acquire control of the burial church in Jerusalem. The city belonged to the Ottoman empire, but there were schools, hospitals and offices of different religions. At Easter tens of thousands of Russian pilgrims went to Jerusalem thanks to better travel options. The West offered Turkey help to contain Russian expansion and claims for the control of the burial church. This led to a major conflict, the Crimean War (1853-1856) in which France became involved with 300,000 soldiers and Great Britain with nearly 100,000 soldiers.

In the nineteenth century the Crimean War was regarded as the main conflict of the century. For the first time the home front was informed of the horrors via newspaper articles and pictures. There were more than 250,000 Russian victims (civilians and soldiers). The French lost 100,000 men, the British 20,000. At the Battle of Inkerman, the Russians lost 12,000 soldiers within four hours. The battlefield was littered with limbs and severed heads caused by shelling. The siege of Sebastopol lasted almost a year and resulted in 127,000 deaths among the defenders of the city. More than five million bombs and grenades and 150 million bullets were used. The horrors of industrial war had become visible for the first time.[194]

The Crimean War has become well-known thanks to Florence Nightingale. She was a woman from the English upper classes who wanted to reorganize the hospital of the British forces at Scutari. She succeeded only partially. The wounded English soldiers were taken there on crowded transport ships across hundreds of miles away from the front. Pirogov, a Russian doctor was more successful because he used chloroform and performed amputations carefully. In the English army numerous amputations were conducted and thousands of soldiers died of infections due to poor hygiene, alcohol abuse and the refusal to use chloroform. Among the British and Russians mainly, the horrors of the Crimean War became part of the collective memory. Due to the state of medicine at that time this did not result in professional psychological care. The main reason was that desertion and infectious diseases overshadowed the psychological problems. Not until ten years later would the first signs of mental health care for the victims appear, both in the American Civil War where hygiene was better, and following the first railway accidents in England where the victims could exercise much pressure on the general public and the experts.[195]

The American Civil War from 1861 to 1865 took place between the northern states, the Union with 21 million inhabitants, and the southern states, the Confederation, with 9 million inhabitants, 3.5 million of them slaves. The obvious reason was slavery, which the southern states considered necessary for their cotton plantations, and which the northern Union states rejected. There were also conflicts about free trade, which the Union wanted to limit. When Abraham Lincoln was elected in 1860, six states seceded and formed the Confederacy shortly before his inauguration. When in South Carolina the Union besieged Fort Wagner five more states seceded. There were 618,000 deaths, more than the American army suffered in World War II, although more soldiers were killed in battle and fewer due to diseases among the soldiers.[196] The biggest battle took place at Gettysburg in Pennsylvania. There were 51,000 casualties (including wounded and missing soldiers) within three days.[197] The horrors were big, e.g. in the actions of Bloody Bill in Missouri, Kansas and Tennessee and the Unionist retaliations led by General Sherman in Georgia and South Carolina.[198]

During the war the Union paid much attention to hygiene among the soldiers. There were official inspections of sanitary committees, staffed by volunteers and many doctors. The experiences of the British in the Crimean war served as a specter. Of every three deceased soldiers two died from diseases and one in battle. This ratio of 2:1 was a major advance compared to the Napoleonic wars in which the ratio was 8:1. For the first time, the mental problems of soldiers came into focus. In 1871 the cardiologist Jacob Mendes da Costa associated the many (functional) heart complaints, that soldiers on the battlefield displayed, with nervous irritation (*irritable heart*).[199] The most common mental complaint was homesickness, *nostalgia*. It became the second most frequent diagnosis in this war. The diagnosis was made 5,547 times and 74 deaths were attributed to it.[200]

Homesickness was a problem, because half of the soldiers was of peasant origin and had strong ties with their families and with the region where they lived. They had rarely been away from home. The army had quickly incorporated them, because they expected to have to wage war soon. The army attached great importance to contact with the home front to maintain morale. Emotional control was considered essential and families were recommended to cheer soldiers up. The soldiers themselves were encouraged by their superiors to keep their homesickness under control. By the way, the diagnosis *nostalgia* was limited to the U.S. Army. In the British Army it was called *melancholia*.[201]

4.5. Awareness of the risks of industrialization

The fourth and most crucial dimension of the change in thinking was caused by the process of industrialization itself. This process increased the awareness of the risks of accidents with mechanical transport, accidents in factories and infectious diseases in polluted cities, such as cholera and tuberculosis. These risks were certainly not small, and they were enhanced by settling in risky places, such as fault lines in the earth's crust or areas at risk of flooding. The eruption of Krakatoa and the tsunami that followed, which resulted in 36,000 deaths in 1883, the earthquake in San Francisco in 1906 and the 1908 earthquake in Messina all contributed to a growing risk awareness.[202] This awareness ensured that measures were taken, such as improving safety systems, prevention against toxic and explosive substances and much later the building of a welfare state that could protect people from the risks of illness, occupational disability or unemployment. These measures greatly contributed to a sense of security, but the awareness that industrial disasters and accidents with serious consequences could occur unexpectedly, was also established.

Industrialization also caused a big change in personal life. It started a process of individualization with scale reduction of households, empowerment of women and children and personal relationships based on free choice. People became more attached to their personal world and privacy. Sensitivity to violations of personal integrity increased. The violations could consist of abuse or mistreatment and severe attacks on their personal freedom in institutions, such as prisons, barracks, monasteries and boarding schools, sects or authoritarian families. In the highly individualized society of the late twentieth century, these violations would be very much the centre of attention.

In a more general sense, an expansion took place in the scope of shocking events and the intensity of experiencing them. This process would ultimately ensure that shocking events played a central role in the world of modern people and in their collective efforts to create a livable society. The reason was that in extensive networks, which were connected by a fragile infrastructure of information and transportation, small disruptions could have unforeseen consequences and an aftermath with many legal and political complications. In the "sociology of disasters", this is called an increased risk of "transsystem social disasters", disasters that exceed the limits of a social system. The perception of the threats intensified by the expansion of the mass media and the increased media attention for these threats. More experts were concerned with the impact, and the aftermath, including the search for the facts, compensation, recognition of the severity and rebuilding, took a lot of time and increased the intensity of the experience. When more media arose and the news became more personal, the shocking event even grew to be the core experience that media attention focused on. This was a development that had gradually taken place since 1850 and it culminated in the media age after World War II. The responses to the first railway accidents in England are good examples of the dynamics in the first phase of this development. To get an idea of this process, it will be described in terms of changes in the nature and perception of the events, the reactions of victims, experts, government and the public, and the interactions within the circle of experts.

The first railway between Manchester and Liverpool was opened in 1830. This was the beginning of a massive expansion of the railway network. Forty years later, in 1870, more than 20,000 kilometers of railway had been laid in England, Ireland, Wales and Scotland.[203] The railway was certainly not safe in its early years and railway accidents raised many concerns. This led to major changes in thinking about shocking events. The concern can be explained by both the nature and the perception of the accidents. Shocks can do much damage by their nature, but may not be experienced as intrusive and little damage can cause a lot of concern. Therefore, nature and experience are both important. In this case, the accidents were experienced as overwhelming, due to the enormous forces that were released in a collision with a steam locomotive. A railway accident also evoked a sense of arbitrariness when some carriages were hit much harder and people became victims, regardless of class or ethnicity. This was quite unique in England's class society, where the "better" circles always felt better protected. The extent of the accidents has been accurately recorded in the statistics of the Board of Trade. The number of passengers killed between 1843 and

1870 was on average 37 per year, the average number of wounded 524. Yet, mining and road accidents caused more victims.[204] The concerns people had about the railway companies were fueled by fraud, speculation with stocks and shares and destruction of historical heritage. The companies and their leadership, the "railway kings," had a bad reputation.[205]

The responses to the accidents occurred among five parties: victims, doctors, government, the public and the railway companies. The reactions were so intertwined that no party could determine the outcome. They become understandable in the context of the liberal English society of that time. Characteristic were the big class differences, little government control, fierce competition between railway companies and a critical public, well informed by newspapers and magazines The reactions were enhanced by the many lawsuits that had been filed against the companies. A strong impetus was Lord Campbell's Act of 1846 which offered victims and survivors the opportunity to get compensation in proportion to their income.[206] Of course, this was in favor of wealthy passengers. After a few cases, where a broad interpretation of the law set the tone, the number increased explosively. This was also due to the fact that most cases were won by the victims and the cases provided an important source of income for the lawyers.[207] The public sympathized intensely with the victims and wanted to punish the companies for their misdeeds.

The dynamic resulted in an unintentional involvement of doctors as expert witnesses in litigation. They had to revise their views on physical causes and hereditary degeneration, but their resistance was strong. Surgeon John Erichsen, expert witness in several lawsuits, claimed that railway accidents differed from other accidents due to their violent nature. At the time of the accident the victim was barely aware of its seriousness. Only after several days did phenomena occur, which he attributed to disruption of the nervous system by a severe mechanical shock.[208] Erichsen made a comparison with a magnet which lost its magnetic force because of a hard blow with a hammer and with a watch that became disrupted by a shock.[209] Herbert Page, who worked for a railway company, pointed to the helplessness of the traveler, the confusion and the cries of the injured. This could cause anxiety, depression and even hysterical attacks and memory loss.[210]

The diagnosis Page suggested, was attractive for victims from the middle and upper classes. It fitted a well-established tradition in the views about nervousness and it could be used without assigning the stigma of mental illness to the victims.[211] The accidents unleashed a fierce debate in the medical community in England, France, Germany and the United States. This led to a huge competition among neurologists, who wanted to improve their reputation.

4.6. The pioneers of the psychological trauma

The medical debate that was unleashed after 1860, fitted in with an older debate about nervous symptoms. In that debate, new diagnoses were developed, such as neurasthenia and old diagnoses obtained new meaning, such as hysteria. In the debate, the Parisian neurologist Jean Martin Charcot played a key role. Charcot had acquired his position by establishing his fame with great zeal. On Tuesdays he held demonstrations, on Fridays his famous lectures, to which he invited many foreign students and colleagues. During the demonstrations he caused attacks of hysteria in his female patients, that were accompanied by paralysis, fainting, and numbness. Famous was the so-called *arc de cercle*, the abdomen directed toward the ceiling, with only head and toes touching the floor.[212] Blanche Whitmann regularly figured as one of his patients. According to Charcot's colleague Pierre Janet, who had watched her for several months, she had largely learned the position by the many displays.[213]

Charcot became "the Napoleon of hysteria". He had contacts in the highest circles in France and had senior officials from various countries as his clients, including the son of a minister of the Tsar and members of the royal families of Spain and Brazil.[214] He corresponded with the famous German neurologist Hermann Oppenheim.[215] He made sure that the term hysteria and the relationship of this condition with traumatic experiences took a central place in the views of the international medical community. Charcot worked at the Salpêtrière, located next to the Gare d'Austerlitz. According to Ellenberger, it was a city in the city with 45 buildings, large gardens, streets and a church.[216] It was a famous place where Pinel used to work, where Louis XIV had established a shelter for beggars and prostitutes and during the French Revolution massacres had taken place. Charcot's main goal was to explain phenomena scientifically, such as being possessed, trance, ecstasy and heavenly apparitions.[217]

Charcot saw the psychological shock as the decisive cause for hysteria, a degenerative disease, according to him. He thought that the event was not the cause, but an "agent provocateur", the provocation.[218] The memory of the shocking event worked as a pathogenetic secret, a 'mental parasite'. Charcot tried to make visible the symptoms by hypnotizing his patients. He also wanted to associate the consequences of accidents and other traumatic events, such as fires, storms and war, with hysteria under the name of "neuroses traumatiques".[219] One of his opponents was the German neurologist Oppenheim who worked at the Charité in Berlin. He described 41 victims with nervous symptoms, mostly caused by accidents, sixteen of them by train accidents. He explained them by small fractures in the nervous system, but he also saw psychological causes. According to Oppenheim, some shocking events had such an impact that they justified a separate diagnosis: the *traumatic neurosis*, comparable to the now well-known diagnosis of post-traumatic stress disorder.[220] He fell into disrepute when colleagues thought that patients simulated and got benefits too easily. In Germany, hysteria stood for hypersensitivity and weakness of the will and the diagnosis of traumatic neurosis would not persist.[221]

The idea of a pathogenetic secret was adopted by Sigmund Freud after he had stayed with Charcot from October 1885 to February 1886. He opposed the idea of physical causes and hereditary degeneration and focused on the secret itself. The Dutch sociologist Christien Brinkgreve, who has written a lot about the history of psychoanalysis, describes this very aptly:

> "(He) realized he had to look not only at the female bodies that shook and trembled, but at human beings with a story that had to be heard. That was his discovery and that meant a radical change in the approach of women. They were no longer seen as animals or machines to be put on show, but as people who had experienced shocking things and had a story to tell. Or rather, the story had to be formed, and that happened together with him, the listening and interpreting doctor."[222]

The story pointed to a desire that had become trapped together with the accompanying feelings of shame, sadness, anger and fear. The body speaks in riddles and only a good listener who can watch and listen, understands them.[223] The wedged desires and feelings were the "mental parasites". The strange symptoms pointed the patient to repression of desires looking for a way out.[224] Realization did not mean recollection in a literal sense, but an image of what had happened. Freud's attention would increasingly focus on inner images and fantasies about what had happened. For treatment, he created a therapeutic setting with a fixed location (the doctor's office), fixed times and fixed reimbursement systems. In this neutral setting patients were able to become aware of inner conflicts and to develop a more realistic approach towards their own desires and feelings.[225] In the neutral setting the manifestations of the patients could not be attributed to suggestion or influenced by the therapist or a third party. The patient's behavior could only be understood from the patient's past experiences.

So Freud did not only cause a breakthrough in thinking, but also in therapeutic practice. This was his great merit, despite the sometimes dubious way in which he presented results, covered up failures and dealt with some followers. He rejected hypnosis, which he found exhausting. Concentration and free association were sufficient.[226] Freud also cleared the way for the study of the development of traumas in children. The disorders occurred, when the biological development of children, the permanent physical changes and the fear and shame that these evoked, were suppressed. Traumatic development could be just as painful as a single traumatic event, without any connection with abuse or mistreatment. Freud's discovery had other consequences as well. By focusing on the traumatic development in children, the importance of traumatic events in later life could be denied. The report of trauma in later life could even be seen as an expression of a neurotic imagination.

This caused much misunderstanding and even led to a professional blockade against reports of abuse. By focusing on the emotional development, Freud also paved the way for the study of "psychological sensitivity". The ability to empathize with others and to regard the other person as a thinking and feeling being is only rudimentary innate. It gradually develops relationships with other people, especially primary caregivers. In the current psychoanalysis this capability is referred to as "mentalizing" power. When the parent observes the inner mood of the child and guides it, the child's mentalizing capacity can develop. Mentalizing seems to be a critical factor in the psychological protection against transgenerational trauma. Empathy for the consequences of violence that is used towards others is impossible without mentalizing. Without this ability, one is able to harm others without remorse.[227]

In four volumes Pierre Janet described nearly 600 patients whose psychopathology was traumatic in origin in almost 50% of the cases.[228] He worked in Le Havre and later in Paris in the Salpetrière. According to him, very violent shocking experiences were disintegrating. Janet spoke of the loss of the synthesizing function of the various parts of consciousness. Consciousness becomes fragmented. The traumatic memory splits off so to speak. It manifests itself in paralysis, numbness, automatic movements or automatic talking.[229] Psychological automatisms occur when certain contents of consciousness can no longer be unified. Janet made a distinction between the narrative memory that enables people to tell the story of the past, and the traumatic memory, an emotionally charged state of experience of the trauma dissociated from the rest of the personality. Traumatic memories could be accessed and reproduced under hypnosis, because the person automatically wrote down the memories.[230]

The method Janet developed, was primarily aimed at restoring integration. The processing of the memory was not to express the memory and associated feelings in words, as Freud suggested, but to reconcile the separated parts. His methods became obscure when hypnosis fell into disrepute. It would take some time before Janet's ideas would be rediscovered. It is mainly with the rest cures and the classical Freudian analysis that the medical world enters the twentieth century when it is confronted with unimaginable shocks.[231] As a consequence, the dissociative nature of severe trauma – especially of individuals having experienced chronic traumatization, including sexual abuse, physical and emotional abuse, torture – was ill-understood. In particular, the trauma experts Bessel van der Kolk and Onno van der Hart made great efforts to rehabilitate Janets' important work and applied his neglected ideas to these victims.

4.7. The confrontation with extreme violence

Between 1914 and 1918, the world was confronted with the extreme horrors of the First World War. As many as 61 million soldiers were involved. Nine million people were killed and 21 million wounded.[232] New inventions, such as the telephone, the machine gun and – during the war – the tank, had changed the way of waging war forever. Within a few decades, firepower, rate of fire and range of the weapons had increased tenfold. Soldiers could be mobilized en masse by better administration and organization and the use of trains. The army had become much more mobile, and could stay in the field longer, making field battles last for months. The large range of weapons enabled soldiers to fight in small units on a larger and emptier battlefield. They heavily depended on one another and were continually harassed by snipers. Gas and flame throwers caused much panic.[233]

The psychological effects were unprecedented. First, there was the exhaustion caused by lack of sleep and stress due to the constant noise of the guns and the cries of the wounded, but also by standing in the mud in coats made heavy by rain, by poor sanitation, the nuisance of rats and insects and the lack of sufficient food and clean drinking water. Second, there were the atrocities, such as the sight of corpses of humans and animals and the wounded who could not be reached or due to a lack of stretcher bearers were left between the trenches. Many soldiers were hit by shells and teeth and bones penetrated the bodies of fellow soldiers. Nearly 300,000 soldiers were maimed in their faces by fighting upright in the trenches.[234]

Third, the long wait and the impossibility to flee. This was reinforced by the ongoing risk of the loss of a comrade from the small combat unit, in which soldiers were completely dependent on each other. Fourth, the inexperience of many soldiers, because one quickly had to form a large army when the war began. The British army in France, which consisted of 160,000 men, was even supplemented with volunteers to over one million men within a short time. For the first time, soldiers with mental problems outnumbered those with injuries or diseases in a war. Desertion had become more difficult, because the troops were guarded by superiors who stayed behind the lines. Formerly, the highest percentage of the loss of soldiers by far was due to epidemics and desertion.[235]

The victims had to find a way to survive. In case of dropping out due to psychological problems, they were sent back to the front after a short rest cure and in severe cases sent home. The families of returned British soldiers found it hard to prevent them from being registered as psychiatric patients.[236] Officers sent to England were better off. They stayed in private hospitals with separate bedrooms and facilities for billiards and croquet. An unknown number of victims never visited a doctor and fought to the death or was executed. Anthony Babington, a London judge, concluded after extensive file research, that hardly any medical examination took place before the executions. In 2006, 314 executed soldiers were rehabilitated by the British authorities after strong insistence of a number of families.[237] One solution was to make informal agreements with hostile troops to show mercy, but this was strongly opposed by the army leadership.[238]

From the trenches soldiers could send letters to the home front, thus mobilizing the public. In England the public pressure would only take effect after the war, with the major research into shell shock. According to the commission, which published its report in 1922, most military suffered from anxiety and exhaustion. Nearly one-third had never seen a doctor. Some doctors saw 400 soldiers a day. There was little coordination between the doctors and they worked under great pressure. Their main concern was to limit the drop-out numbers, to reassure the home front, counter financial claims and expose possible malingerers. A way out was to establish an organic disorder, so that the soldier could not be accused of cowardice or personal failure and army command was exculpated.

Despite the difficult circumstances important initiatives were taken. In 1915 the psychologist Charles Myers described a soldier's responses after a grenade blast in an article in the Lancet. He shook and cried and thought he was going blind. He called these reactions "shell shock", a term that became very popular among the British public.[239] Pretty soon Myers saw the diagnosis was wrong and the symptoms pointed to an emotional shock. To help the soldiers he pleaded for shelter close to the front (Forward Psychiatry). In the five centers that were established in 1916 after the Battle of the Somme, some physicians used psychotherapy, but most of them considered a rest cure adequate. Myers received little support from the army command, was transferred and left France in 1917. Only in 1940 was he capable of writing about the war.[240]

Myers did important pioneering work with his idea that severe trauma splits the person into a "normal" and an "emotional" personality. In the latter the traumatic experiences played up vehemently, whereas the normal personality was aimed at controlling the trauma. According to him, it was caused by the inability to integrate the traumatic experience.[241] William Rivers, a physician and anthropologist and a colleague of Myers' from Cambridge, helped officers that had been sent back to England by means of individual therapy. He became famous when treating the poets Siegfried Sassoon and Wilfried Owen. Sassoon, who had become a pacifist because of his experiences in the war, went back to the front at Rivers' insistence. Owen also returned, but was killed a week before the armistice.[242] In Germany the situation was dramatic for the 600,000 drop-outs with nervous disorders. They were accused of lack of willpower and were harshly treated by means of the so-called Kaufmann cure. This consisted of electric shocks, followed by exercise, until the symptoms disappeared. Some physicians used varieties of this treatment, such as prolonged punitive exercises, immersion in cold baths, sham surgery or isolation. Hermann Oppenheim, who had become head of a military hospital in Berlin, found that the symptoms were associated with the horrors and not caused by innate characteristics or lack of willpower. He received less and less acclaim. In France, there was a therapy called "torpillage", which resembled Kaufmann's treatment. The emphasis was on isolating the patient in order to prevent contamination with the incorrect behavior.[243]

In the Soviet Union there was a brief revival of individual therapy after the war by Preobrazhenskii (Red Star) in Yalta in the Crimea. The resources were inadequate and many patients had TB, syphilis or suffered from malnutrition or were addicted. After three years the clinic was closed. In Russia victims of war were treated extremely hard. Grief was a form of weakness and was called "egocentric". Remarkably, there were few people who dropped out. The question is whether they went underground, became homeless and addicted, or were exiled or placed in institutions. In 2005 Catherine Merridale asked a large panel of Russian experts this question. Her conclusion was that this was probably the case, but that many also held out by the strong collective bond. It was all about surviving, even if life offered little hope.[244]

In the United States, the situation was quite different. Here, psychiatrist Tom Salmon was in charge of psychological care. The historian Nathan Hale characterizes him as follows:

> "Six feet, four inches tall, with a warm sympathy for patients and the disadvantaged, Salmon suffered from migraines and had recovered from tuberculosis (...) an advocate of the expanding reformist role of psychiatry in schools and prisons."[245]

During a visit to England he had found that one-third of the drop-out rate in the English army was caused by psychological factors.[246] The severity of the problem was confirmed by the New York psychiatrist MacCurdy and the head of the psychiatric and neurological department of the Surgeon General, Pearce Bailey. The latter suggested the harsh treatment of the French, but Salmon rejected it as being too punitive. Based on Salmon's report, the Army decided to set up a facility for quick treatment at the front for every army unit, specialist treatment behind the front and to train personnel. The opportunities for experts and victims were much greater in the United States than in other countries.[247]

4.8. The collective dealing with the memory

Memories can be united into a collective memory which is recorded in writings, film images and monuments and can be experienced in commemorations and pilgrimages to places of remembrance. It provides the framework in which individual memory takes its place and is shared with others, but it can also be a limitation for the unique individual experience. Collective memory can strengthen the interconnectedness and identity of a group or country and can even become a myth. States play a central role in shaping a collective memory with large-scale assignments for monuments, commemorations and movies.

Before World War I, there was always sufficient consensus to connect the heroism of a country with the ideals of democracy, reason and progress.[248] The large-scale industrial war changed all this. A new group asserted itself, the veterans, who submitted claims to the state, not in terms of democracy and equal rights, but in terms of compensation for inflicted suffering. The state began to feel obliged to this special group. They had served the nation and people felt that they were entitled to compensation for the damage they had suffered. The recognition of the claims of veterans led to other groups in society also manifesting themselves as victims and showing that they had been severely hit.[249] Initially, the competition was still limited and a shared story was possible. In the course of the twentieth century, after several major wars, the claims of the various groups would grow into a broad emancipation movement of mutually competing victim groups for the favor of the public and the government.

In order to create a collective memory from the traumatic experiences a period of reflection and imagination was needed.[250] This period of time was also necessary to agree on the form of a common story. In the early twenties, reflection and struggle about the First World War had been completed and the memory could be recorded in poems and memoirs, monuments and films. After some hesitation of the army, but under the pressure of an eager audience and some celebrities in the film industry, the army permitted making film recordings during the war. The situation in France serves as an example here. Under strict control of the French army newsreels were made. The front could not be filmed. There was a lot of censorship on showing new weapons or gas. Damage caused by the Germans had to be shown extensively. The cathedral of Rheims served as the end of a film with the comment that it would never be taken. There were also shots of soldiers climbing out of the trenches with their bayonet forward, but what happened to the soldiers was not shown. This shot was often used in other films. Later, pictures from Hollywood movies were added. The American filmmaker Griffith had been to the front and was free to film everything, but he had to admit that making a film of the fighting was impossible. Later he made such a film in a studio. From 1916 British films were more realistic and sometimes showed the activities of the soldiers at the front. Because of their very imperfection and suggestiveness, the images have left a strong impression. They have inadvertently fuelled the opposition to the war and stimulated the support for the victims.[251]

The monuments not only emphasized the heroism, but also the suffering of the victims. An example is the monument of Käthe Kollwitz in Vladslo, in which she expresses her grief for her dead son. Another example is the Menin Gate in Ypres by the English architect Sir Reginald Blomfield with the names of 55,000 missing people.²⁵² The state used the monuments to emphasize that the loss had not been in vain, but had been a sacrifice for a good cause. The suffering was shown in a penetrating way in the vast numbers of graves on the former battlefields which are still carefully maintained. The English situation is an interesting example. At the suggestion of the architects Sir Edwin Lutyens, Herbert Baker and Fabian Ware, the founder of the British graves commission, Sir Frederick Kenyon, director of the British Museum, had insisted on graves on the spot without distinguishing between officers and soldiers. This was unique because ordinary soldiers had been laid in mass graves until then. He insisted on preserving and caring for all the graves in perpetuity. The only distinction between the graves, was the "badge" of the regiment. The scale was enormous: 410,000 identified and 152,000 unidentified graves spread over 2316 cemeteries.²⁵³ Luytjens would also design the empty tomb, the Cenotaph in Whitehall in London, and the monument at the Somme. He avoided all heroism. The cemeteries became an impressive whole, where numerous people still remember the "Great War".

The poems were very penetrating. They could, on the basis of a word or phrase in the poem – a punctum among literati – evoke a widely shared feeling. A short poem works like an image, a caricature or a symbol. In the theory on remembering this is called a mnemonic, a memory aid that can instantly evoke a memory. They were particularly penetrating if the poets themselves had been in the frontline.²⁵⁴ The poets did not want to be romantic and bombastic anymore, but in the words of the poet Owen "truthful".²⁵⁵ The best example is the well-known story of the experiences of a soldier in the trenches by Erich Maria Remarque titled *All Quiet on the Western Front*. Incidentally, the time was unique. Such literature on the even greater horrors of the Second World War was actually no longer possible.²⁵⁶

The English war poets Rudyard Kipling, Siegfried Sassoon, Robert Graves and Wilfred Owen have become very famous, but there were also American poets with a wide audience, which more than ever – and even more afterwards – was open to poetry. The English poet Charlotte Mew expressed her feelings of mourning and doubt very penetratingly, and she explored a new language. Being a woman among men who had been at the front, she was only recognized later. National newspapers received tens of thousands of poems made by amateurs and filled with expressions of patriotism, even though reports of the atrocities could already be read in these papers shortly after the beginning of the war.²⁵⁷ The English poet Rudyard Kipling, mourning the loss of his son John near Loos, speaks in his poems about the usefulness of monuments. He calls them a place where one can support each other in the shared pain, but he also claims that this could never take away the grief.²⁵⁸

More than one thousand memoirs have been published about the war. Robert Graves wrote *Goodbye to all that* and Ernst Jünger *the Steel Storm*.²⁵⁹ They both came from wealthy families and had fought at the front. Robert Graves served in an elite military unit, the Royal Welch Fusiliers. In the ironic style of a member of the upper class and with his comrades in mind, he described the horrors. Jünger received a very rare decoration for bravery. For him, will, a sense of duty and honor came first and with them he could handle his fears in the trenches and even enjoy the war intensely.

> "It was our luck to live in the invisible rays of a feeling that filled the heart, and of this inestimable treasure we can never be deprived (...) We stand in the memory of the dead who are holy to us, and we believe ourselves entrusted with the true and spiritual welfare of our people."[260]

He did not feel defeated because the honor of the German soldier remained intact. In France, Henri Barbusse had published his widely acclaimed novel Le Feu in 1916. That same year the surgeon George Duhamel described in the journal *Mercure de France* in detail what happened in a field hospital near the front.[261] According to the historian Jay Winter, all these forms of remembering received their strength from the many ways in which they created forms of expressing the terrible suffering for the citizens of Europe. They opened ways to mourn. That would become more problematic after Auschwitz and Hiroshima.[262]

4.9. The crucial role of the veterans movement in the USA

In 1918 the largest veterans' organization in modern history, the American Legion, was founded in Paris on the initiative of twenty officers. Within a year the Legion had 843,000 members and that would rise to nearly four million by the end of the twentieth century.[263] The Legion emphasized the abnormal conditions during war, which broke perfectly normal people emotionally. Its lobbying resulted in the foundation of the Veterans' Bureau in 1921, one of the main providers of psychological help.

The conditions for a strong veterans' organization were ideal in the United States at that time. The need for voluntary organizations was strong in a large country with scattered villages and farms.[264] After the civil war, many organizations had started to commit themselves to the preservation of national unity and the strengthening of national values. In 1890 more than 400,000 veterans of the Civil War had joined the Grand Army of the Republic (GAR). The GAR founded nursing homes, hospitals and orphanages, created a holiday for commemoration (later Memorial Day) and introduced saluting the flag at school. It organized many local meetings, camps, sporting events and activities against "un-American" developments and erected major monuments. In 1900 there were at least 600 GAR fraternities across the country.

The American Legion often referred to the GAR, which they wanted to surpass. The Legion tied the veterans, who were spread over a large area, together with a shared ideal. Its slogan was: "Keeping the Spirit of the Great War Alive". Due to the short participation in the war, relatively few Americans of the two million who had been sent to the war, were killed, "only" 50 thousand.[265] For many soldiers the war was the adventure of their lifetime. The Legion had a strong leader, Theodore Roosevelt Jr., eldest son of the 26th president of the United States and educated at Harvard. He provided much status to the Legion with his network.

Initially, the Legion was a conservative organization. It struggled with corruption and even regarded Mussolini as a hero. Its primary goal was to help people who had mentally and physically suffered from the war. In 1941 already 75,000 beds in ninety veterans' hospitals were occupied with veterans suffering from neuropsychiatric disorders. The costs ran up to hundreds of millions of dollars.[266]

More than ten years after the First World War, a quarter of the federal budget was still spent on facilities for veterans. In 1933 President Roosevelt made an attempt to cut the budget. He paid a visit to the national convention of the Legion and proclaimed the thesis that veterans could not take an exceptional position. He received little support.[267] The special position of veterans in American society may explain the focus on psychological trauma in this country.

This development offered opportunities to experts. After the war psychoanalysts of the second generation gave environmental stress and trauma an important place in their thinking. Due to the flight of nearly two hundred psychoanalysts from Europe to the USA in the thirties and forties the USA became the center of psychoanalysis.[268] One of the best-known experts was the psychoanalyst and cultural anthropologist Abraham Kardiner. In the 1920s Kardiner had observed and helped over a thousand traumatized soldiers in a veterans hospital in the Bronx in New York. According to him nearly two-thirds suffered from traumatic neurosis. The ego had been severely weakened by pain and fear and had had to operate in a hostile environment.[269] He did not write his report until 23 years after the war. This work, *The traumatic neuroses of war*, became famous after a career in cultural anthropology with studies on human adaptation to specific circumstances.[270]

Other well-known experts were Roy Grinker, who had been stationed at the front in Africa in World War II, and the brothers Karl and Will Menninger. Kardiner and Grinker enjoyed great respect. They had been in analysis with Freud for a short time and were supported by their mentor, the influential and unorthodox Hungarian Franz Alexander. He held the first chair in psychoanalysis at the University of Chicago. Psychologists profiled themselves by experimental research and testing, which had proved to be useful in the First World War.[271] On the initiative of professor of psychology at Harvard, Robert Yerkes, they profiled themselves as "human engineers" to acquire a place alongside technicians and scientists.[272] Psychologists were also involved in leadership training and research into the moral support of the population.

These developments were not lost on psychiatry. In the twenties and thirties, a reform movement had come under way in this field which on the basis of experience in the child guidance clinics was in favor of early treatment to prevent admission into psychiatric institutions. These institutions had become uninhabitable in the twentieth century and were mainly populated by chronic patients. The situation had worsened by budget cuts in the thirties and lack of personnel during the mobilization.[273] The supporters of the movement would get key positions at universities and within the American Psychiatric Association. The Second World War was therefore an important catalyst. The United States emerged from the war as the most powerful country and the center of science. This would greatly reinforce the movement in other countries in the Western world.

4.10. The memory as a political programme

For the United States the Second World War was a much greater challenge than the First World War. President Roosevelt had to overcome considerable resistance to find support for participation in the war. To gain support a programme was developed in which the memory of the American Civil War played a central role. To understand the meaning and scope of this programme, it is first of all necessary to consider the function that remembering has for a society and its individual inhabitants. An interesting article by the American sociologist and professor Barry Schwartz serves as a guideline.[274]

Collective memories within a society are not only a collection of information about the past. They are arranged in such a way that they reflect the problems and concerns of the present. The memories of a colonial past are an example. Initially they consist of pride and heroism. After the loss of the colony they change into sadness about a lost paradise. Eventually they often result in shame about white oppression of a foreign country. Depending on what goes on in the present, the colour and content of the memory will change. In other words, remembering is a social construction of a society or groups within it and depends on what is considered important in the present. It is the result of a conflict of interests between different groups that want to put a mark on the memory. A strong interest group is able to construct a memory in such a way that competing interpretations, such as reminders of oppressed minorities or memories of wrongdoing, are ignored. The construction is reflected in history books, speeches, commemorations, museums and monuments. This sociological theorizing shows to what a degree interests play a role in remembering, but it is also one-sided. History is not so malleable. There is a reality that limits the construction of memories. Indeed, there are facts in the past that cannot be ignored. On the other hand, they can be dramatized or more nicely colored to serve as an example for the present.

This use of memories as a kind of model or programme for the present constitutes another perspective to look at memories. People can be united under the banner of the great deeds of ancestors and can draw inspiration and learn from these deeds. In such a programme one can withstand a crisis or an impending war and bridge tensions and contradictions in a society. It is an enterprise that has a deep impact. It touches fundamental values that are stored in the cultural system of a country. It draws from great stories that everyone knows and which are provided with new meaning. The memory becomes a symbol with a strong emotional charge. According to Barry Schwartz, this happened in the United States in the run-up to and during World War II.[275]

President Lincoln had been chosen as a symbol of the past. He had successfully ended the American Civil War, but had been killed in the end. In his time he was controversial. This was less the case at the time when most Americans who had grown up in the run-up to World War II were born. Lincoln was a model for human dignity and justice. He had established democracy and abolished slavery. This image was now widely propagated in speeches, including President Roosevelt's speeches, newspaper articles, plays, films, posters, cartoons and songs. The New York Times published 215 articles on Lincoln between 1940 and 1944 (compared with 36 between 1990 and 1995). The American Civil War was presented as a real war of liberation, a Second Revolution, following the First War, when America broke away from the English. With the defense of democracy in the world that America had acquired with these Revolutions it entered a new war which required even greater sacrifices. The story of Lincoln and the Civil War was a sacred story, which embarked on a moral to persevere a new costly and protracted war. It was an idealization and dramatization of the facts. The programme could only succeed however, because the story of Lincoln and the Civil War represented profound American values. It was the legitimization of the power that Roosevelt claimed for himself. It was also a source of inspiration and a framework to inform the public about the importance of the war and the planned strategy. This example shows how the memory can serve as an anchor in times of crisis and war, and how it can control the mindset to make action possible. It is a cultural programme that makes bearable deep fears and traumas and thus goes beyond therapy.[276]

5 Becoming aware of the impact of modern warfare

5.1. Unimaginable horrors

The Second World War was the worst war in the history of mankind. It entailed massive bombings of cities and large-scale terror against the civilian population. The all-time low was the persecution and murder of millions of Jews and other minority groups.[277] In this war, the largest raid in history was the one executed on the Soviet Union by the German Army with more than five million troops over a 3,000 kilometers wide front. In the East, Japan conducted a brutal war against China and other countries around the Pacific. Within a few hours the two atomic bombs on Hiroshima and Nagasaki would claim tens of thousands of victims among the Japanese citizens. The greatest losses occurred in the Soviet Union with 23 million and in China with 19 million people killed. Calculated as a percentage of the population most victims fell in Poland and Lithuania (18% and 13% respectively).[278] The war was incredibly drastic. This was the case for the few survivors of the concentration and extermination camps, soldiers who had undergone, seen or committed atrocities and civilians who had been abused, had lost family members or had been severely affected by hardship and loss of possessions.

The war took place in a polarized international context in which more horrors had occurred. In the Soviet Union in 1932-33 and in China between 1958 and 1961 there were desperate attempts to collectivize agriculture as a result of the great famines in the third quarter of the nineteenth century in China and in the 1920s both in the Soviet Union and China. Between four and six million people died in the Soviet Union and 2.5 million in 1932-1933 in Ukraine only.[279] In China the collectivization of agriculture was accompanied by forced labor for industrial workers, poor farming methods and the departure of many Soviet experts. Between 1958 and 1961 this led to a famine resulting in millions of deaths.

5.2. The role of the United States in the recognition of the suffering

To get an idea of the recognition of the seriousness of the consequences of war the United States was central once again. The start was bad. The military leadership in the United States paid little attention to the extensive reports of Tom Salmon on the care for soldiers in the First World War. In 1941, the number of psychiatrists in the army had even be reduced. The focus was on the selection of the men. The army leadership wanted to keep the costs of drop-out and aftercare of troops low, since these had exploded after World War I.[280] More than one million recruits had been rejected on grounds of mental health. Nail biting or having sweaty hands was often sufficient.[281]

When the United States entered the war, the army leadership felt that other measures were needed. The focus shifted to large-scale prevention and care. Prevention consisted of promoting group cohesion and providing information to be able to recognize signs of anxiety and panic.[282] Army doctors and psychologists had little experience with psychological traumas. It was limited to severe psychiatric disorders including psychosis. Most psychiatrists had never worked with clinical psychologists.[283] The initiative of a key figure among the second generation of psychoanalysts resulted in a fundamental change. William Menninger, who had established a clinic together with his brother Karl and his father in Topeka, Kansas, which was widely known, was put in charge of psychiatric care in the army and became the first psychiatrist in the United States to be awarded the rank of Brigadier General. Under his leadership there would be a lot of attention for cooperation between different disciplines and psychologists were widely deployed to take care of the soldiers.

The change in the position of experts also occurred in the area of scientific research. In the army a dense network of scientifically trained researchers would be formed within the "Information and Education Division", headed by the sociologist Samuel Stouffer.[284] After the war many members of the network would acquire leading positions at major universities. The military leadership supported the largest study ever to be conducted in sociology, which was published under the title *The American Soldier* and headed by Stouffer in 1949. It showed that not ideology or patriotism, but the bond between the soldiers, along with the support of the home front and the public, was the main motivating factor for the soldiers.[285]

The public was informed in detail by experts, backed by the army leadership. In several pamphlets, which were distributed on a large scale, it was explained that traditional methods of discipline worked insufficiently in a modern combat unit and that psychological care was inevitable. On the vast battlefield with independently operating combat units an intelligent and motivational approach which encouraged personal initiative and where superiors did not limit themselves to drilling and shouting was required.[286] Thanks to this information, the public could form a picture of the combat conditions and the psychological burden in a modern army. Thanks to this information it was widely recognized that each soldier could drop out in a modern war with intensive bombings, unpredictable tactics and indescribable noise.[287] The drop-out rate was highest during the invasion of Normandy in 1944. Forty percent of the enrolled patients, was mentally ill. The First Army received more than 11,000 applications on account of mental illnesses within two months.[288] How strong the veterans' movement had settled in American society proves the GI Bill – the Servicemen's Readjustment Act – introduced in 1944. It was a comprehensive provision for veterans for joining courses, compensation for unemployment and cheap loans to buy a house or start a business.

The support of the army command to experts is best illustrated by the work of psychiatrist and psychoanalyst Roy Grinker and his younger colleague John Spiegel. They were encouraged by the army command to take the emotional problems of soldiers seriously. Their book *War neuroses* was written for a small circle of officers in 1943, and could be published almost without any changes in 1945. It is an account of the observations of hundreds of patients from the ground and air forces of the American and British armies in Tunisia in 1943.[289] In their clinic they allowed painful, suppressed experiences to be relived and processed with light doses of pentothal, combined with counseling therapy. According to them, the barbiturate pentothal was a good alternative for hypnosis.[290]

At that time, several agents with hallucinogenic effects were already known. The French psychiatrist Moreau de Tours had investigated the effects of hashish in the Salpetière in 1830. Mitchell – known from the Weir Mitchell treatment, a rest cure for neurasthenia – had swallowed the buds of the peyote cactus which were already familiar to the Aztecs. In 1897 he described in the British Medical Journal the wonderful and colorful experiences that the drug evoked. In that same year, the active substance of mescaline was isolated by Heffter and a synthetic version was produced in 1919. In 1938 Hofmann happened to discover another drug, LSD, in the pharmaceutical company Sandoz.[291]

Grinker and Spiegel put much emphasis on fear which could explain the helplessness and complete disintegration of the personality.[292] In case of extreme fear people could not talk, they trembled and suddenly laughed or cried without reason. They made meaningless gestures and ran or jumped around. Any sharp sound startled them. Fear could hide depression, which manifested itself on the impending return to family and friends. Mourning over lost comrades was often the cause, or the idea to be unable to adjust to normal life. The most common statement they noted, was: "I took it as long as I could; I cannot take it anymore."[293] In 1944 it was estimated that there was a maximum of 210 days. So they came up to a maximum tour of duty of the individual soldier, which resulted in many changes in the combat group in later wars and unintentionally undermined the cohesion of the troops.

5.3. The initial reactions to the horrors

The persecution and genocide during World War II was unique in history as to size and organization. Shortly after the war, it was very difficult to map the psychological damage. The survivors were accustomed to hiding their experiences and they were forced to go back to work The worst victims, the Jews, received little support. Society rather preferred the memory of the horrors and its own powerlessness to fade away. Most Jewish victims had been murdered. Others had lost many relatives. They could not make a fist and had to process their experiences in a small circle or alone. Attention only came after the trial of Adolf Eichmann, who had been kidnapped by the Israeli secret service in Argentina and brought to trial in Israel in 1961. According to the sociologist Norbert Elias, one could no longer ignore things. A state had brought to life the memory and put forward the facts in an authoritative manner.[294] However, soldiers and members of the resistance received a lot of attention immediately after the war, especially if they were well organized and there was a tradition of honoring veterans in the country. The attention for them was partly intended to emphasize the heroism of a country and hide its weaknesses.

In 1954, Thygesen, a doctor, used the term concentration camp syndrome in Denmark for the first time. In France, doctor Richet, who had returned from Buchenwald camp, gained much influence. Inspections around the "Wiedergutmachung" in 1956 contributed to the physicians' definition of the suffering.[295] A penetrating and profound description of his camp experiences was provided by the Dutch physician Elie Cohen, who had survived the Auschwitz extermination camp. He distinguished three stages: arrival, adaptation and resignation. Upon arrival nobody knew about the first selection, in which 80% of the transport including mothers and their children ended up in the gas chambers. During the phase of adaptation the inmate had to find his way in a life with few breaks, hard work and dirty food. He only had one set of clothes and was never alone. His self-image was affected by humiliations, contact with other peoples' feces, people who did not get out of bed to urinate, death as a constant companion, and not being able to express anger.[296] In the third phase, resignation, there was more space for relaxation, finding extra food and helping others. Cohen also described the extremely cruel methods of torture and killing:

"Starvation, abuse, exhaustion, shooting when flying, intravenous or intracardiac injections of phenol, gasoline or air into sick people, death marches to other camps and gas chambers and gassing cars." In addition, there were the various medical experiments on the prisoners: "freezing, contamination with typhoid fever, wound infections, drinking of seawater and altitude experiments, transplants, sterilization and euthanasia."[297]

According to another psychiatrist, Kaas, who had survived Buchenwald, the core element of surviving was the bond between people who spoke the same language and providing mutual care. The rules of the economy of giving and taking were carefully monitored. An offence was severely punished. Germans had the advantage, because they quickly understood the SS since they shared the same language and culture. They were the "prominent figures" and they decided on hospital admission, the distribution of medication and on who would participate in the best working commands. The first position also included political prisoners, mostly communists. Secrecy played a major role because of the presence of illegal weapons and radio transmitters and receivers.[298] Reports and analyses of camp experiences belong to the genre of camp literature. They are about a reality that outsiders find almost impossible to understand. The most poignant descriptions are written by victims with great literary skills, such as Robert Antelme, Primo Levi, and in a different context, Varlam Sjalomov after his seventeen year stay in Kolyma, a prison camp in Siberia. However, camp literature is selective, often written by prisoners in special positions in the camp and with special skills (eg. doctors or musicians). Each camp is different, each camp constantly changes and every position within a camp offers other sources of information.[299]

5.4. "Hiroshima" as a national trauma

In August 1945, the United States dropped two atomic bombs on the Japanese cities of Hiroshima and Nagasaki with an interval of several days. Only in Hiroshima an estimated 80,000 to 200,000 people were killed and there were numerous wounded and radiation victims. The terrible trauma of this act of violence has been given a special place in the collective memory of Japan. The formation of this memory eventually lasted twelve years, a fairly long time, but much shorter than the formation of the collective memory of the Holocaust in Europe and the United States. The sociologist Hiro Saito made a reconstruction of this process on the basis of a large amount of data.[300]

In the formation of a collective memory Saito distinguishes three periods. The first period runs up to 1951. Shortly after the bomb, national newspapers wrote about the disaster as a crime against civilization and humanity, a violation of the Hague Convention. Within a month, the Supreme Commander of the Allied Forces, General Mac Douglas, issued a press code which forbade all news about the damage. From then on survivors were only able to express their suffering locally. News about the bomb was expressed only in general terms, as a sacrifice for peace, without mentioning the Americans. The annual memorial ceremony in 1951 was also attended by several war orphans, but it had the character of a commemoration: the survivors remained invisible.

The second period runs from 1951 to 1954. In 1951, Japan regained sovereignty and censorship disappeared. The first essays, poems and photo reports appeared without political overtones. It was only about the evils of war and the need for peace. The magazine Asahi Graph published a photo report of the damage caused by the bomb. More than 520,000 copies were sold within one day. The power of the images in a magazine that reached so many people, was unprecedented. The Japanese people became spectator of an unimaginable suffering, but from a distance: one felt compassion, but the events were over. Especially the damaged young women became the topic of conversation. The public was confident that they could be helped with plastic surgery. However, there were already people who argued that America should not have used the bomb to save thousands of its own citizens.

The third period from 1954 to 1957 began with a major incident. A national newspaper reported that a Japanese fishing boat near the Bikini Islands had been exposed to radioactive fallout. When the load with tuna was spread throughout Japan, it appeared that the fish had been seriously contaminated with radioactive substances. Japan's national food was threatened by the remnants of nuclear weaponry. A national "tuna horror" arose. When a crew member died that same year, it was attributed to radioactivity. From that moment on the Japanese population felt they were victims of atomic weapons. In the various sub-Parliaments resolutions were adopted and 30 million signatures were collected against the atomic bomb. The Japanese population was not a distant spectator anymore, but a community of victims. Hiroshima became a national trauma. In 1954 the imperial family visited the memorial. In 1957 a law to help the survivors was passed unanimously. The emphasis on the Japanese victims pushed the Japanese aggression during the war to the background. The trauma, however, had now been widely shared and it became formative for the Japanese identity from that moment on.

A few years after the official recognition of the suffering of the survivors of the atomic bomb in Japan, the American psychiatrist Robert Jay Lifton conducted a thorough study of their experiences.[301] From a list of 90,000 survivors who had been registered at the hospital of the University of Hiroshima, he selected at random 33 survivors and 43 people who by virtue of their function as physician, director, writer or member of a victim organization were able to talk about the complex emotions and social problems which had accompanied the disaster. He spoke with them at least twice for two hours under Japanese supervision in Japanese and he recorded the interviews. He discovered three patterns.

The first pattern was the surprise effect and the feeling vacant afterwards. The victims had been completely unprepared and even relaxed after a cancelled air raid on the morning of 6 August at 8.15 am, when the bomb fell. Leaflets with the message to leave the town had been scattered by the Americans, but many had not seen them. Others saw them as a form of propaganda. They also found it weird that the city was still so intact, whereas it was strategically significant for the military operations. But they did not have an inkling of what was going to happen. Within a radius of five kilometers, two thirds of the city was destroyed. People who had seen the event from a distance, described the flash, the fireball, the heat and the mushroom cloud over the city. The most intense feeling was the confrontation with death that was omnipresent. Maimed people were spread over many kilometers. At night the dead bodies radiated a phosphor glow. The survivors could in no way be effective due to the absence of everything and the huge numbers of victims. The survivors spoke of a shutdown of emotional life, especially when they were busy cleaning up the countless corpses. They primarily remembered images that had been most intrusive, such as a maimed child or a child whose skin had partly gone. They felt guilty towards the many relatives who had not survived, which compromised an important value in Japan: the continuity of the generations.

The second pattern consisted of continuous concern about the victims' own health. Shortly after the disaster, the rumor spread that the city would remain uninhabitable for 75 years and that there would never again grow grass and trees (in Japanese culture nature is seen as the ultimate source of life) and that everyone would die within three years. A few weeks after the disaster, many people displayed symptoms of diarrhea, vomiting, blood in their urine, fever, purple spots, eye problems and hair loss. From 1948 the large number of cases of leukemia and the many deformities at birth became conspicuous. All this increased concern, even in healthy people. The third pattern was the burden to have to live with the stigma of atomic victim, especially after the recognition in 1957. The term of atomic victim was intended to get compensation, but was also a constant confrontation with the status of victim. All manners of behavior and symptoms were only seen in this light. The victims were discriminated against in marriage and job hunting. They felt research objects and victims of a senseless nuclear experiment. They argued that they were used by experts and by people who wanted to benefit from the disaster. Worst of all was the never-ending confrontation with the horrors in the press.

Robert Jay Lifton also tried to find out what was unique about this event. According to him, it was the confrontation with death caused by an ultimate man-made disaster in an impersonal form which one could not prepare for. It was experienced as the end of the world. The survivors felt they were the victims of a futile experiment that threatened all confidence in life. It resulted in a deep sense of shame and guilt towards the dead. With this research, Lifton was able to map the suffering of the victims in a special way and at an early stage.

5.5. Building a resilient society

After the Second World War the West became embroiled in a Cold War with the Soviet Union and China. The authorities in the United States had a strong interest in a resilient population that was not afraid. The veterans struggling with mental health problems were a heavy burden. In 1946, 60% of patients in veterans' hospitals suffered from mental disorders, 44,000 out of 74,000. In June 1947, half of the compensation payments was given to half a million veterans with mental disorders caused by the war.

In 1946 the American government adopted the National Mental Health Act. It was the start of a massive expansion of mental health care services outside the institutions. It was supported by the army. The budget of the National Institute of Mental Health (NIMH) increased from nearly nine million dollars in 1950 to $ 315 million in 1967. The number of psychiatrists in the United States increased from 4,000 in 1946 to 27,000 in 1976. Many clinical psychologists were trained and half of their study expenses was funded by the military. Among the general public and in many companies, psychotherapy, group dynamics and sensitivity training became very popular.[302]

One of the spokesmen of this movement for mental health care was the above mentioned psychoanalyst and psychiatrist in the American army during the war, William Menninger. In 1946 he became president of the professional association of psychiatrists, the APA. Under his leadership, people who had an army background would form a strong lobby group within the APA. Menninger received support from President Truman, who in his speeches, and at Menninger's advice, described psychiatry as indispensable for the health of the American people and the preservation of peace.[303] In 1948 William Menninger was proclaimed "psychiatry's US sales manager" by Time magazine. His picture was on the cover. At a later stage he advised President John Kennedy who saw the expansion of psychiatric services as a building block of his "New Frontier" strategy. His brother Karl played a key role with his clinic in Topeka, where he trained a third of all psychiatrists in the United States in 1947. The clinic would become a model for 69 new hospitals with a psychiatric unit and 16 new psychiatric hospitals for veterans. Karl was the only psychiatrist in the U.S. who received the highest award, the Medal of Freedom.[304]

Shortly after World War II, a movement against the dominance of psychoanalysis emerged based on a more biological model. Already in the 1940s the views of Walter Cannon on biological adaptation had been translated by Harold Wolff into a more general model of stress and illness. In 1944 Erich Lindemann wrote an article about the symptoms of reliving, avoidance and arousal caused by stress, thus anticipating the diagnosis of PTSD. In 1950 Hans Selye wrote about the adjustment of the organism to special circumstances (life stressors). The biological orientation gained more support by the introduction of new drugs, such as chlorpromazine, reserpine, librium and lithium. Especially the unrest and the violence in psychiatric hospitals could be controlled with them. Invasive interventions for chronic patients, such as electroshocks without anesthesia and lobotomy, were called into question. By 1948 the maiming lobotomy brain surgery had been applied more than 5,000 times. More than 10% of these operations occurred in hospitals for veterans between 1936 and 1951.[305]

5.6. The memory of the horrors

At the end of the twentieth century, Yehuda Bauer, a member of the Executive Committee of Yad Vashem, wrote an article about why the Holocaust in particular has had so much influence on the way in which people have come to experience the horrors of the twentieth century. According to him, the Holocaust stands for the denial of the value of human life.[306] This was caused first and foremost by the killers' motivation. For the first time in history the perpetrators saw the total destruction of a group of people as an almost religious mission, focusing not only on their own country, but on the whole world. Secondly, the Holocaust was a lethal combination of ideology, technology, bureaucracy and scientific knowledge acquired in the best universities and preached in many churches. Not only politicians but the intelligentsia as well participated in the project. Thirdly, the Holocaust was an expression of anti-Semitism which provides clues for the position of the Jews. They read the Bible in its original form and propagate the values of democracy and liberalism. Anti Semitism opposes this and therefore is the oldest form of group hatred. The Nazis provided a special meaning to this. They saw the Jews not only as a threat, but as a satanic force.

In the light of this analysis mapping all aspects of this large-scale murder project became crucial. This was also dangerous. By disconnecting the project from history as a completely unique event, it could acquire an almost sacred status. This was also the case with the victims. Comparison with other genocides became inappropriate and criticizing testimonies almost sacrilegious, since they – the Jews – had suffered enough. This raised a lot of resistance. In 1999 Peter Novick spoke of a Holocaust Industry in his *The Holocaust in American Life*.[307] He was accused of a cool tone, a lack of compassion and of anti-Semitism. That does not mean that the Holocaust differed from other genocides in many respects: it was unique in its selection of a particular group, it was an attempt at complete eradication, of erasing all traces, and involved intellectuals, bureaucratic precision and technical sophistication.

How difficult it was to shape and retain the memory of the events is to be seen in the film *Shoah* by Claude Lanzmann in 1987. Lanzmann wanted to capture the truth of the death camps and to examine the responsibility for the events. Shoshana Felman has thoroughly analysed this film and some points will be elaborated on here.[308] The film is explicitly not a report that can be told by someone else, or a story with archival footage, but only a sequence of personal testimonies. The film lasts nine and a half hours and was recorded between 1974 and 1985. It consists of very personal testimonies of the catastrophe. Lanzmann wants to show what it means to be a surviving victim, perpetrator or bystander. He shows in particular what they had not been able to see because so much had been kept hidden. The events had been made invisible, traces had been burned and words like victims and body had been avoided. With regard to transport the euphemism "special" had been used and planning had been done by officers from behind desks who had never seen the dead.

The witnesses describe the events not only from different perspectives, but also in different languages. This reinforces the effect of the hard to fathom facts. Lanzmann focuses on the details. He asks questions, such as: was it very cold? How long was the trip? What did the gas tanks look like? He encourages people to tell their story, even when it becomes difficult, to break the silence, "it must..." He frequently repeats what the witnesses say, which enhances the effect.

Lanzmann's film transfers no knowledge, tells no story, but only shows a series of fragments. It does not provide answers, it only breaks the silence. The witness the film begins with, is a man named Sbrenik, one of two survivors of the four hundred thousand people who have been killed in the extermination camp of Chelmno. In the film he is 47 and he was a 13 year old boy back then. He could survive because he won games between chained prisoners, games that were organized by the SS, and because he could sing well. He survived an execution because the bullet had missed his brainstem and people found him in time. Lanzmann found him in Israel after the war. This almost symbolic fact gives him a place at the start of the film.

> "The story begins in the present at Chelmno, on the Narew River, Poland. Fifty miles northwest of Lodz, in the heart of a region that once had a large Jewish population, Chelmno was the place in Poland where Jews were exterminated by gas for the first time. Extermination began on December 7, 1941. At Chelmno four hundred thousand Jews were murdered in two separate periods: December 1941 to Spring 1943 and June 1944 to January 1945. But the way in which death was administered remained the same throughout: the gas vans. Of the four hundred thousand men, women and children who went there, only two came out alive: Mordechai Podchlebnik and Simon Srebnik."[309]

Lanzmann and Sbrenik go to the scene of the crime in Poland. Near a church, where the Jews were gathered, he is confronted with some Poles. The silence, precisely what cannot be told, is shown here. This happens in a scene in which the bystanders try to silence the witness Sbrenik again by stating that it was the Jews' fault. They do not realize this. Lanzmann himself was aware that there were few traces left. He had to look for traces of traces. Almost nothing was left of the real destruction camps of Chelmno and Treblinka. Almost everyone who arrived there, was killed and the traces were obliterated by the Nazis. And Sbrenik touches the core there and then:

> "No one can describe it. No one can recreate what happened here. Impossible. And no one can understand it. Even I, here, now."[310]

Elie Wiesel once stated: "If the Greek invented the tragedy, the Romans the epistle and the Renaissance the sonnet, then our generation invented a new form of literature, the testimony".[311] The testimony mainly concerns the experience of terror in the camps. The terror of the Stalin regime takes a special place in this with tens of millions of deaths. One of the most poignant testimonies of this regime was made by the Russian writer Varlam Sjalamov. In the thirties and forties, he had been in the camps of the Gulag, including Kolyma in the North East of Siberia, for seventeen years. From 1966 on his Kolyma Tales were published in parts in the USA and only after his death in 1982 in the Soviet Union.

According to Sjalamov, the experience of the camps was unique in history, because the moral boundaries of the human soul were stretched to the extreme. He could only display it in a new kind of literature. According to him, the novel, the old form with an individual plot, had died and admonitions had become meaningless. There were no heroes, only testimonies of people who had gone through hell. He considered himself capable of this because he had trained his memory to the extreme in the camps and could deploy it as the highest creative force. Only medieval writers could do this, sincethey not only wrote books, but also passed on many texts orally and knew long texts by heart. They used to train their memory by links to places, metaphors and sounds and they edited it in new texts.

> "I'm able to resurrect in my memory the infinite number of pictures I have seen in all my sixty years – somewhere in my mind is preserved an endless reel with these bits of knowledge, and with an effort of will I can make myself recall everything that I have seen in my life, any day and any hour of my sixty years. Not just one day, but my whole life. In my brain, nothing is erased. This work is torturous, but not impossible. Everything depends on the effort of will, on the concentration of will."[312]

The memories come to mind and precede consciousness, before the tongue starts to work, even before thoughts arise. It is like a horse that finds its way into the darkness of the taiga and the path is only made later. The memories break from the brain in a physical movement and that causes pain. Only then the headaches become milder. Silence and isolation, not a quiet place, but inner peace and meditation are needed for concentration to make the memory work. Someone who works with memories has to select locations and mental representations of facts and store the images in those locations. Sjalamov did this with the North Siberian landscape, the taiga: the mountains, the water, the caves, the rocks and the tracks, the flowers, the trees, the cold desert, the frozen mist, white clouds and the endless snowfields. He saw those as "markers" for the memory, for the journey of remembrance. The biggest threat was to forget, which he also compares with the landscape, such as when the wind quickly erases traces of human activity in the snow.

Sjalamov tells his hands were so cramped in the camp that they could barely hold a pencil. It was a physical need, like his throat craved for poems. His hands had become rough, his fingers become crooked around the handle of a shovel or pickaxe. The word book had been removed from his memory, but it referred to something very important. A pencil was essential since ink pens were forbidden, because with them documents could be falsified and playing cards be made. Sjalamov did not want to create a general picture of the camps, like the author Solzjenitzin had done in his Gulag Archipelago. He goes much further by letting people feel what life in the camp meant to people in the smallest of details. Hence that his stories are so close to the perception of the body and the physical need.[313] He describes cold as follows:

> "The workers did not get to see the thermometer: that was not necessary because they had to work at every temperature. Moreover, the old prisoners were able to determine almost exactly how hard it froze without a thermometer: if there is an icy mist it means it is forty degrees below zero outside; when exhaling air can be heard but breathing is easy, it is forty-five degrees; if breathing is hard and accompanied by shortness of breath, it's fifty degrees below zero. If temperatures are below – 55, your saliva freezes as soon as you spit it out. That had been the case for two weeks."[314]

He also writes about the relentless hunger, the pleasure of urination, the incontinence and the hoisting up of your pants at a temperature of fifty degrees below zero. It is a moment to catch your breath and to smuggle time when the body takes over the mind.

When the totalitarian power system has taken away everything and a man has been reduced to a spineless thing, there is still a spark of vitality left. The bottom is not indifference, but resentment, which is the last human feeling, the feeling that is closest to the bone.[315] Sjalamov tries to show the exceptional within the exceptional: real distress and sadness in which people do not have any solidarity left, but are only able to get moral force from themselves. The fact that a man can do this, means that he is stronger than an animal. What is special is that Sjalamov does not want to be pedantic in any way or use big words as inconceivable, but he wants to make the reader feel the basis of details, which he describes as accurately and penetratingly as possible. When commenting on others, he also shows that small things are crucial.

At the end of the century there were more impressive attempts to capture the past so long as there were witnesses. One example is the "Survivors of the Shoah History Foundation" by Stephen Spielberg. Between 1994 and 1999 the foundation interviewed 52,000 survivors in 56 countries and 33 languages. Two other examples are the archives of Yale University with 14,000 reports and the Holocaust Memorial Museum in the United States which interviewed living witnesses. In Stephen Spielberg's project, the interviews were conducted throughout the world, usually in two sessions. In the second recording session the personal experiences were discussed. Simon Wiesenthal was interviewed for four days.[316]

5.7. Genocide explained

In his article *Murder and the State* Abram de Swaan argues that states are the most comprehensive and most effective organizations mankind knows:

> "The state organizes taxation, law enforcement, justice and imprisonment on a large scale and with a huge machine;

the state regulates economic transactions and monitors the quality of goods and the preservation of the environment; the state also guarantees education and care of its citizens. And the state is the greatest destroyer of human life: occasionally by executing the death penalty, sometimes by suppressing riots and unrest, at times of war by fighting armed opponents. But more destructive states act against unarmed and defenseless people time and again. Many thousands, hundreds of thousands, sometimes millions, tens of millions of people were killed by this (...) In the past century, four regimes have killed more than ten million people. Between 1917 and 1987 62 million people were killed by execution, beatings, torture, exhaustion or starvation in the Soviet Union (...) Communist China comes closest to that with over thirty-five million murdered civilians between 1949 and 1987 (...). The Nazi regime is in third place with twenty-one million murders. The fourth (...) Nationalist China (with) ten million unarmed people (...) between 1928 and 1949."[317]

These examples show what states can mean for the welfare of the population, but also how destructive they can be and what they have done to unarmed, defenseless civilians. Modern times were exceptional by the use of mass propaganda and mass organization by means of press and radio and an efficient administration with a disciplined army of civil servants. This does not mean that it was not barbaric, bloody and filthy as well. The Nazi regime was the most murderous one.[318]

The question is whether these events indicate a collapse of civilization, as Norbert Elias claims, or that they are characteristic of modern civilization, as Zygmunt Bauman claims. According to De Swaan it is both. He speaks of dyscivilization. For most people, murder is repulsive. An order is needed to carry it out, if one is not a sadist. But that is not enough. Therefore, two processes must be put in motion as necessary conditions to make genocide possible. First, a process of disidentification: a group of people needs to be presented as inferior and be hated. Second, a process of compartmentalization in which the group is isolated, invisible to society, delimited in time and place where the dirty work can take place. Special units are trained to perform the work of registration, isolation, rounding up and destruction. In these secluded places, the executioner can do his job in marked periods of time. Before and after and in other places he is a normal human being. Other people make it happen or turn away from the secluded group, and sham ignorance. Ordinary life can continue outside the compartments and the citizens enjoy all the protection they need.[319]

Such control by compartmentalization characterizes the genocides in the twentieth century, even more than the extent of the violence. The civilization process is not broken down or reversed, but groups are excluded, the civilization process follows a dysfunctional route. The state has the means to monopolize the exercise of violence, but society is not entirely steeped in civilized relations. Certain places and certain groups are excluded and they are the target of state violence. This explains the combination of rational planning and irrational violence and the fact that a large part of society has little notion of what is going on.

The question De Swaan does not answer, is whether certain types of people are more likely to develop into mass murderers and executioners. The Amsterdam psychologist and psychoanalyst Wouter Gomperts has an answer. He applied some modern ideas on the psychological development of children to the emergence of the psychic structure of a man who is willing to kill massively.[320] According to him, people are able to see themselves and others as thinking and feeling beings. They can see that the thoughts and feelings of others may be different from what they think and feel. This is called mentalizing ability. It is not the same as self-reflection and introspection, because it largely operates unconsciously. This ability is formed in childhood. After eight months, a baby can feel a parent's mood and adapt to it. After a year, a toddler can understand other people's intentions in a game. At the age of three, a toddler can exclude someone else from a secret. At the age of six, a child can think what others think about what a third party thinks about what he thinks. In this way the awareness of different viewpoints in different situations arises and thus an awareness of subjectivity. At the age of twelve a child can even recognize unconscious processes, such as the tendency to hide something intolerable from himself.

The development of the mentalizing ability depends on the quality of the attachment with the primary caregiver and his or her mentalizing ability. Essential is the period before the age of four, before the explicit memory has developed. Parents with this ability are more likely to have securely attached children. These kids have enough confidence in themselves and others and can imagine other people's thoughts and feelings. Mentalizing is a critical factor in the protection against transgenerational trauma. Decisive here are the reactions of the parent to pain, fear and sorrow. With sufficient protection, the child learns to distinguish between their own mental states and those of others and not to be overwhelmed by their own mental states or to react by taking immediate action. Extreme traumatization without a sufficient mentalizing primary caregiver stagnates the development of the mentalizing ability in the child. This may be due to abandonment, absentee parents, illness or death of the parent. The child turns away and only seems to adapt.

The aggression that the child develops in the absence of secure attachment is not well thought out, for the mentalizing capacity is disabled. So it is not sadism which requires empathy. The child simply cannot identify with the other person, there is no compassion and concern. The other is either good or bad. Thinking is unbearable. On a large scale this may occur if parents are not present because of nature or war. This is a cause of blind aggression. It does not mean that all mass murderers lack the ability to mentalize. The lack of it may trigger this behavior, especially towards groups that have long been slandered. The killers can consciously develop into well-adjusted citizens. However, they may unknowingly have developed a tendency to aggression. This aggression is given free rein in secluded areas.

In 2001 the Dutch sociologist Ton Zwaan published a dissertation in which he describes the backgrounds of several genocides in the twentieth century.[321] The first thing that strikes him in three major genocides in Turkey, Germany and former Yugoslavia is that they occurred within just a few years, the murder of the Jews primarily even within one year. In all three cases it is about a process that takes place in stages and that is driven by very strong collective images and feelings. In the first phase, the monopoly of violence in a particular state is threatened. The state loses power in a process of realignment of power relations between states. Elites within the state feel the loss of power. Political entrepreneurs seize their chance. They mobilize their supporters by recalling images that take up a central place in the collective memory and reinforce them. Others unite in their turn, because they feel threatened by the entrepreneurs and their supporters and by the reduced protection of the state. It is possible that parts of the monopoly of violence are maintained and entrepreneurs use state violence to isolate the other group.

In the second phase, the attacked group organizes itself better. This is regarded as a provocation by the entrepreneurs and their supporters. The state is no longer able to control it and violence between the two groups increases. Kindred spirits find each other more and more often. The process of identification and disidentification accelerates and increasingly laden fantasies about each other arise. When the attacked group is defenseless and entrepreneurs can make use of the still partly intact monopoly of violence of the state, they use this violence against the defenseless group and prosecution will start. In the third phase this degenerates into the opponent's expropriation of homes, jobs, shops, land and livestock, and dishonoring and even rape of the most precious possessions: wives and daughters. The other sees his fears confirmed and tries to strike back with the same means, if he is able to. Incidents are magnified and violence is widespread. Intervention of neighboring states or the threat of it can strengthen the process and is often seen as an act of aggression by one of the parties. The conflict ends when people get tired of fighting or when in a fourth phase, another state or agency intervenes with a lot of violence. Peace returns within the state or the state is divided up with a high risk of recidivism.[322] It should be noted that In case of persecution and genocide, the persecuted group usually cannot fight back. In an ethnic conflict polarization is intensified by unrecognized humiliation and shame. In that case, revenge and vengeance will play a major role.

A question that has not been answered is whether any human being can develop into a mass murderer. The Belgian psychologist Jan de Laender has tried to answer this question by identifying all possible conditions which provoke human aggression or remove all inhibitions. According to him, people are unique in that they can hate, because consciousness itself extends to past hurts and humiliations with extraordinary vividness. They can recall the experiences as if they have just occurred or they teach others to hate on the basis of what they only hear.[323] Aggression is strongly fuelled by fear of the unknown. Due to all these factors, and especially when people have other people completely in their power, aggression can escalate into mass murder. The restraints on aggression disappear under peer pressure, when being anonymous in a crowd or when the responsible people are high up in an organization.

The American psychiatrist Robert Jay Lifton points to another aspect in an article in *World Policy Journal* in 2001. He claims that human psychological circuits are not suitable for nuclear weapons. The mind can no longer connect with the dangers. The apocalyptic scale and technological distance stun the imagination. The danger of a new nuclear era after the disappearance of the Cold War is far from imaginary. The danger of this is evident from the confrontation between India and Pakistan. The population in these countries supports, even with celebrations and dance, the confrontation and escalation of the conflict.

The danger is even greater, because more and more groups consider devastating weapons as a means to make a big impact. They even see them as a means to heal the world by destroying it. Healing by killing is a dangerous way of thinking. Lifton here indicates a psychological deficiency that all people possess. Lifton concludes his article with a quote from Seneca:

> "Power over life and death – do not be proud of it. What people fear from you, will eventually threaten you."[324]

6 The emancipation of the victim

6.1. The emancipation of emotions

Since 1965, twenty years after World War II, the freedom to express emotions has strongly increased in many Western countries.[325] In the sociological literature on this subject, this is explained by changes in the relationships between men, women and children, and between superiors and inferiors. These changes are related to growing prosperity, expansion of the welfare state and the emergence of a class of professionals in the services of this welfare state who propagate more flexible and informal manners. It has lowered the threshold for victims to express themselves, both in public and during therapy. The political support for the victims had a significant momentum: the trial of the war criminal Eichmann in Israel in 1961. Thanks to this authoritative process in a state that was safe for the persecuted Jews, politicians and governments could no longer look away.

The sociologist Abram de Swaan has described the changes in behavior and the rise of a class of professionals in his standard work on the rise of the welfare state. His thesis is that before the Second World War, an administrative apparatus had been developed to steer the bureaucracy of the state in the right direction. They had acquired experience with extensive administration and major campaigns and facilities for education, health care and social security were in place. The state apparatus could now be deployed to transform this system into a welfare state. Workers could be protected from succumbing to the temptations of communism. Due to experiences with the war economy the business world had reconciled itself with state interference and small traders ceased their opposition when they could benefit from this system.[326]

The provisions of the welfare state, such as care for the elderly, sick and disabled, child care and the invention of the pill improved the position of women. Women had fewer duties at home and expanded their horizons by means of work and education. This gave a boost to the feminist movement, which in turn then reinforced the process. The growth of the facilities also promoted the growth of the number of professionals, such as teachers, psychotherapists, doctors, nurses and social workers. Under their leadership, manners became more informal, open and equal. People demanded more rights, including the right to a personal life style. An example of the increased openness is the changed attitude toward dying and death. Strict rituals and silence were replaced by speaking openly about fears and emotions. However, medical treatment remained an important framework to resist fears of dying and death, even if there was no hope.

This far-reaching social development can be described as an acceleration in the process of informalization, psychologizing and individualization. In that process strict rules became more negotiable and emphasizing status differences was experienced as painful: a process of informalization. Empathy with the emotions of others and sensitivity to their suffering increased: a process of psychologizing. People broke away from family and neighbourhood and chose their own way: a process of individualization. This was accompanied by a greater sensitivity to humiliation and inequality in relationships. The world of the individual and his inner feelings became more important and, as stated earlier, violations of this private life were experienced as a traumatic violation of someone's personal and physical integrity.

This greater openness to emotions gave many victims a voice. Those who previously could not express their emotions, now sought recognition. Public recognition was an incentive for other victims to reveal their suffering. These revelations provoked new demands for recognition, giving rise to other disclosures. Thanks to more collective resources, governments were able to translate recognition in subsidized care. These developments would strongly change the balance of power between victims, experts, governments and the general public.

6.2. A wave of revelations

The first wave of revelations occurred in the late fifties in the United States. It was triggered by a strong movement among psychologists, sociologists and social workers. They protested against the violation of personal and physical integrity in "total institutions", such as mental hospitals, monasteries, camps, boarding schools, prisons and barracks. The movement committed itself to combat infringement of privacy and humiliation in these institutions. The sociologist Erving Goffman showed how shocking it was to undergo rituals which took away someone's sense of self-determination.[327] The result of the protests became most visible in the transformation of the asylum, with psychiatric patients in large halls, into a therapeutic community. This community consisted of small residential groups, characterized by emotional openness and equality and a focus on healing through psychotherapy and rehabilitation. Uniforms were abolished. Nurses were given more training, psychologists were introduced and the care, if possible, moved to the community outside the institutions.[328]

A second wave of revelations was related to abuse and neglect of children. Around 1900 legislation had been designed to combat child labor and to prevent children from following the path of crime. Now, the vulnerable child itself came center stage. In 1964 the pediatrician Kempe and a few other doctors published an article on the "battered child syndrome."[329] This attracted much publicity. About three percent of children up to 18 had to deal with abuse and neglect, or had witnessed abuse by violent and often alcoholic parents. The violence was mostly chronic and accompanied with secrecy. This resulted in bonding and learning difficulties and feelings of betrayal, which the child stored in the body.[330] The effect of the publicity was not visible until 1985, when the extent of physical violence against children had dropped to 1.9% in the United States. The overt approval for a "deserved" beating decreased and emotional neglect was noticed earlier, due to the higher demands for affection in the family. Physical neglect persisted in the lower strata of society caused by running up debts, expensive intoxicants and living on limited benefits. Domestic violence remained problematic. The interests of the perpetrators to hide abuse, the protection of privacy and the lack of witnesses impeded major improvements.[331]

A third set of disclosures was related to Nazi terror. Shortly after the war, many victims, including some doctors, showed what the Nazis had inflicted. The breakthrough among experts occurred at a psychoanalytic conference in 1967. William Niederland mentioned chronic anxiety and depression, sleeping disorders and nightmares with vivid images from the past. There was also a lot of apathy, anger, numbness and inability to speak about the experiences. According to him, they pointed to unresolved grief and feelings of guilt towards the dead, a "survivor syndrome with survivor guilt." Henri Krystal spoke of robotlike rigidity caused by external danger or inner feelings, when escape was impossible. These experts spoke of massive trauma.[332] The revelations of the psychological effects of the war would result in huge involvement of the general public and government agencies, and the establishment of numerous facilities.

A fourth wave of revelations in all western countries was related to sexual abuse and arose with the help of the feminist movement, especially in the eighties of the twentieth century. A central theme was the male domination of women, resulting in abuse.[333] In the cases of child abuse people tried to prevent the intervention of justice, but in the case of sexual abuse this intervention was perceived as recognition. There was a great distrust towards professionals who did not take women with complaints seriously. The feminist movement spoke of behavior which had been denied for a long time. Continuously, new culprits were designated, such as fathers, brothers and uncles, professionals in healthcare, education and leisure, leaders of cults, church officials and child porn networks. For the media the revelations were grounds to search for ever new facts, so that issues grew into scandals faster.[334]

A fifth series of revelations was related to crimes that harmed people personally. These were very diverse; they ranged from burglaries, robberies and shootings or serious accidents caused by a drunk driver, to hostage taking, rape, aggravated assault or disaster by human error.[335] Thanks to the increased security in modern societies and the increased importance of privacy, the confrontation with sudden violence was experienced as painful and shocking sooner. The victim asked the state for redress in the form of punishment and money. The rule of law in Western countries, however, could not put an end to the suffering of the victim. It could not undermine itself with higher penalties and more flexible rules of evidence to accommodate victims. This raised grievances over low penalties.

A sixth series of revelations was related to the suffering caused by serious loss. It was recognized that loss was part of ordinary life, but that it could also be extreme and very shocking. Examples were: the loss of a child, loss by murder or suicide, a sudden accident or a medical error. The revelations showed that the grieving process could be fierce and proceed with bewilderment, numbness, intense longing, despair, loneliness and anger. Sometimes it was impossible to allow the pain and grief became chronic. The lack of opportunities to say goodbye or to anticipate on the situation, made the shock unbearable. Due to lack of public attention, processing traffic accidents was even more difficult. The loss of a child, sibling or parents at a young age had more impact due to scale reduction of households, greater emotional investment within these households, the decrease of social support and religious consolation and the expectation of a long life. The loss of a child placed kin relations under serious threat. Many diseases and inexplicable behaviour turned out to be symptoms of grief.

The growing openness and empowerment of different groups of victims coincided with major changes in the public arena with the advent of television. With revelations in a medium that was available in every living room, a new world arose. The public was mobilized with penetrating images and these images could support claims for help and compensation. With dramatic images the victims were able to show how they suffered, how bad it was that they had to keep secret their suffering and how their lives were disrupted due to grief.

The presentation of the suffering showed two patterns. The first pattern consisted of expressions of ordinary citizens who had suddenly been faced with something horrible. The focus of this presentation was on the unexpected and traumatic nature of the events in a world that was deemed safe. The second pattern occurred with prolonged abuse or experiences in a concentration camp. Here it was shown how in an uphill battle shame had been overcome. They longed for protection, restoration of their sense of justice and ultimately the right to be. It was feared that the government could offer no real protection and at best left the problem to aid workers. It was also feared that people would drop out because the problems were too bad to bear. The fear for a society full of threats and risks grew stronger. In this jumble of emotions doctors had to judge on the degree of work capacity or legal accountability. However, they lacked a clear diagnostic system and a set of science-based therapies.

6.3. The dynamics of recognition

The world wars were not only traumatic for the countless victims, but also for the societies that participated in it. The feeling of invulnerability had disappeared. In the United States after Pearl Harbor and in Europe the question how it was possible that groups of people had been deported, humiliated and murdered on a large scale remained unanswered. It was a social and cultural trauma. The problem was not just how to cope with the loss, but also to find a new meaning for life after the horrors. The identity of the West and many other countries had fundamentally changed after Auschwitz and Hiroshima.

The recovery was chaotic, with stories about what had happened, trials of war criminals and all kinds of collective commemoration, such as museums, memorials, monuments, films and writings. Offenders, who remained in high positions, hindered the process, but also research into the causes had yet to take shape. The competition for who could claim most of the credit or should receive most compensation, made the coping process complex.

The complex recovery is particularly evident in the way in which the history of the Holocaust is presented in the present. Such a drastic and unimaginable event turned the forming of a collective memory into a permanent struggle between remembering and forgetting, and between reality and myth. In 1953 the control of the memory of the Holocaust had already been determined by law in the Knesset. It was assigned to a special government agency: Mosad Yad Vashem as part of the Zionist story, which outlines a way of life in the diaspora (galut), to redemption (Geula), the Holocaust (Shoah) and resurrection (tekuma).

The two best-known commentators and witnesses of the Holocaust, Primo Levi and Eli Wiesel, wanted the world to know what had happened and to continue remembering. However, they differed in their interpretation of the events. Eli Wiesel saw a divine plan, Primo Levi rejected the term of Holocaust because of the association with holiness. According to him God had nothing to do with Auschwitz. The danger was that the victims would be seen as icons and that the story of the events would be elevated to a myth. Anne Frank was such an icon. Her story has been read infinite times and told in many forms and in regularly adapted versions. Even her name was changed from Anna to Anne.[336]

The learning process showed how sensitive many issues were for those involved. It showed how important independent studies were, as well as official recognition, atonement and excuses and how difficult it was to face suffering.

The version of a history of the events, which not only talked of honour and heroism, but also of mistakes, powerlessness, fear and cowardice, only emerged after many years. So this period could not be closed, not even when the generations of perpetrators and victims had mostly died.

In this discussion, a very well-researched contribution of the psychiatrist Hans Keilson is striking.[337] He described his experiences with the treatment of Jewish orphans in 1979. He distinguished several sequences in their traumatization. The first sequence consisted of the erosion of the rights, wearing the Star of David, the destruction of the economic existence, isolation from the non-Jewish environment and the disappearance of relatives. The second sequence consisted of deportation or hiding, in which the children were often separated from their parents. The development of the children in the form of playing, learning and going to school was stopped and they were handed over to strangers. When in hiding, there was the constant tension of discovery.

The third traumatic sequence, which began on their return, put children into a world different from the world they had left. This created new tensions by being confronted with the death of parents or family, difficulties with the care and guardianship, the need to overcome learning disadvantages and the confrontation with the suffering of people who had been damaged themselves. This description of the sequences and the problems children encountered, made it very clear what the persecution had caused.

6.4. Medical recognition of post-traumatic stress disorder

In 1980 post-traumatic stress disorder was included in the classification system of the APA, the American Psychiatric

Association. This was a crucial moment in the history of the care for mental trauma.[338] This medical recognition enabled coordination between experts, because from that moment on they could work with uniform diagnoses that were used worldwide. Traumatic disorders could be studied for causes and effects in the same terms all over the world and could be tested according to medical standards. The diagnosis enabled a connection between the suffering of different kinds of victims: victims of war, victims of domestic violence, victims of crime, disasters or accidents and victims of serious loss. This promoted their emancipation. However, the diagnosis of PTSD was too limited because complex trauma could not be described with it.[339]

The main reason for medical recognition was the war in Vietnam. Within a period of nine years nearly three million American soldiers had served in Vietnam. 300,000 soldiers had been injured and 58,000 soldiers killed, 47,000 of them hit by enemy fire. Initially there were few psychological problems. This was attributed to the good information about combat stress, good facilities for recreation, the brief "tour of duty" and the direct contact with the homefront.[340] The limited duration of a "tour of duty" meant that many changes took place in a unit, because the soldiers ended this period at different times. When the images of the atrocities were shown on television and the home front expressed its doubts to the soldiers, problems arose.[341]

The doubts were fed by a small action group "Vietnam Veterans Against the War", supported by the psychiatrists Robert Jay Lifton and Chaim Shatan.[342] They gathered testimonies from soldiers about atrocities that these soldiers had committed or witnessed. People with several military awards, including the later presidential candidate John Kerry, played a prominent role. They denounced the discipline of the army and the heroism in war movies. The effect was enhanced by two events: the death of four students at the University of Kent in Ohio during a demonstration against the invasion of Cambodia and the death of Sergeant Dwight Johnson, who had received the highest award and was shot when committing an armed robbery. A publication of Shatan's in the New York Times, who coined the term "Post-Vietnam Syndrome", provoked a storm of reactions.[343]

The adjustment to normal life was severely hampered by the return to a world hostile to the war and with less homely wives than after previous wars. Furthermore, the image was created of a heroin epidemic in the United States Army, which on return of the soldiers would have spread to the homeland. It was an image that was not consistent with the facts: whereas an estimated one-quarter of the soldiers had used hard drugs during the war, most of them had ceased upon return.[344] The poor reception of the Vietnam Veterans was an important issue. However, the position of the veterans was not so bad. More soldiers had made use of the G.I. Bill than in previous wars. In 1975 president Ford declared the Vietnam era closed and it became quieter in the media.

In 1975 under the direction of Spitzer, the preparations for DSM III, which was introduced in 1980, had started. Lifton and Shatan approached Spitzer to place the complaints of Vietnam Veterans under the title of "post-Vietnam syndrome".[345] A committee was formed consisting of people of the Task Force for DSM, including Lifton and Shatan. A connection with the ideas of the stress expert Mardi Horowitz proved to be very successful. Horowitz distinguished several phases in the response to a distressing life event: outcry, denial, intrusion, working-through and completion.[346] However, the recognition of the syndrome evoked much resistance from the side of Veterans Administration which feared large claims. In 1977 they changed their position, when President Carter appointed a new board and the Congress provided new grants.[347]

The post-traumatic stress disorder was defined on the basis of three symptoms: reliving, avoidance behavior and increased vigilance. The primary issue was whether these symptoms were both specific and comprehensive.[348] According to the critics, dissociation, depression and substance abuse after severe and prolonged trauma were ignored. This criticism would lead to revisions in DSM III.

6.5. Unbearable pain

The agreement on the diagnosis of PTSD was the reason for international research on experiences of victims. Unbearable pain was a lead to express the common experiences. Unbearable pain after a shocking event was penetratingly described by the American psychologist John Allan.

Allan describes how one is haunted by the memory of a terrible event day and night, a war of attrition that can last for weeks, months and even years.[349] The event returns in flashbacks, with clear images in which the event repeats itself in vivid detail. Flashbacks can be activated by so-called "triggers" and can only partially be controlled by avoiding them. The information is stored at a lower level than the verbally accessible autobiographical memory. Victims organize their lives in such a way that the images remain outside the conscious mind by avoiding certain situations or by using drugs and alcohol. This causes a chronic feeling of hopelessness.[350] All energy is spent on "not thinking" and this reinforces the fixation on the past. Advice such as "put it out of your head," or "get over it" do not work because the body continues to call up sensations. The reactions may eventually lead to loss of trust in other people and a feeling of extreme loneliness and emptiness. "Emotional aloneness makes pain more painful and fear more terrifying."[351]

What is striking is the overwhelming power of the event and the uncontrollable reactions afterwards. The pain is similar to a natural phenomenon, which you virtually have no control of. Apparently it does not help to avoid situations or ignore the experience. There should be more attention for the exhaustion and the extreme tension. According to Allan, this is possible if one recognizes that the event touches the deepest feelings of attachment and connection with other people.

So in Allan's perspective pain is unbearable, because the familiar world is lost. The victim looses the idea that he means something to this world. According to the philosopher Richard Rorty, the worst pain that you can inflict on someone is to treat him in such a way that his own personal story loses meaning. There is no world that someone can see himself living in. He has lost the vocabulary with which he can tell a coherent story about himself. According to Janoff Bullman, it disturbs the feeling of living in a meaningful world that is benevolent to people.[352]

The pain is particularly unbearable when it is caused by humans in so called "man made disasters". Most radical are abuse and mistreatment for a longer period of time by people somebody depends on, such as educators, but camp guards as well. The pain originates not only from the usurpation by the event, but mainly from humiliation and degradation of the inner life. The attachment to familiar people is disturbed. Attachment regulates stress and protects against danger, but also ensures the development of self-awareness, which enables someone to develop a mental representation of feelings in himself and other people. He is no longer at the mercy of his emotions, but learns to reflect on them. He can be angry without beating someone or being afraid of being beaten and learns to recognize what is going on in others. In the case of extremely shocking experiences, this ability is affected, resulting in a lack of control of impulses, problems in relationships and loss of self-confidence.[353]

According to experts, mistreatment and abuse of children have the most significant and long lasting effects, which are transferred to future generations. Abused children show extreme adjustment mechanisms. They seek safety in shelters, exhibit inconspicuous behavior or become immobile while being hyper alert at the same time, a state of "rigid vigilance". In this atmosphere a child needs to comfort itself, develop intimacy and master bodily functions. The tortures that a child may undergo in the form of imprisonment, being burned, hit or kicked, threats to loved ones or objects, refusal of food or forced-feeding show many similarities with the torture of political prisoners according to these experts. In the absence of opportunities to escape, self-blame, vengeful fantasies or the belief that the perpetrator means well, arise. The atmosphere of silence and denial allow the abuse to be continued and makes processing more difficult. Loyalty problems towards the parents lead to feelings of guilt and shame. The lack of a mother's support is the most painful problem.[354]

According to the British psychiatrist David Healy, the damage to mental health caused by child mistreatment and abuse is comparable to the damage to physical health caused by smoking.[355] Many children are in a situation of increased risk of abuse, such as premature children, chronically ill children, children of addicted parents, adopted children, children of refugees or illegal immigrants, parents with mental disorders, long-term unemployed or disabled parents and children in vulnerable single-parent families.

Unbearable pain can also occur in war veterans. In war, soldiers can be challenged to such a degree that they lose self-control and end up in a state of blind fury, without fear, pity or sorrow. They feel invulnerable, are not hungry or in pain, and behave like animals. The horizon is limited to their unit with a strong bond with some comrades. The randomness of army command when deploying people in dangerous situations puts soldiers to the test. A slain comrade calls up indescribable anger and killing enemies is a way out.[356]

The sociologist Randall Collins pointed out that in World War II three-quarters of the soldiers were too scared to aim their weapons at the enemy and fire.[357] The psychiatrist Jonathan Shay points to examples from classical antiquity. He calls guilt at the loss of a comrade, especially if chance plays a major role and one has to contend with the question of "why him and not me?" When the dead body is removed quickly, or the unit does not stay together to mourn when retreating, feelings of sadness, anger and guilt may persist. Robert Jay Lifton, one of the most famous psychiatrists, spoke of moral collapse, which one can hardly recover from. This is especially true in a modern war with mines and roadside bombs, a hidden enemy that randomly shoots and when danger is omnipotent. Often this need for recognition is expressed in the call for punishment of the perpetrators or financial compensation for the suffering inflicted. However, it is primarily not about compensation, but about recognition. Many people do not want to be reminded of their own pain and vulnerability. Moreover, experts have started to focus more on rapid forms of professional help. There is less time and money to search for the core of the problem and the story behind the visible suffering.

From the moment that the harmful effects of the prolonged use of Librium and Valium became visible, the industry has focused on antidepressants. Patients began lawsuits against doctors out of resistance to talk therapy, without getting fast acting medications.[358] Mourning became a private matter and state funerals became more sober. This changed at the end of the century, especially when Princess Diana died in 1997 and when Internet sites emerged where people started to share their sorrow. Research revealed that victims felt a need for respectful treatment, access to information, knowledge of the facts, excuses, accountability and measures to prevent recurrence. These basic things are often withheld from them, not without reason. Admitting to bearing responsibility often leads to the claim for damages and claims can be considerable. With all these revelations and discoveries, victims had gained a pretty strong position during a complex and long emancipation process. It was the start of a new era in the management of psychological trauma caused by shocking events in modern societies.

6.6. Collective rituals

The recognition of psychological trauma covers a wide area of commemorating and remembering in the form of meetings, monuments, memorial places, cemeteries, films, diaries, poems and novels. Shaping the collective memory of major events, such as disasters and wars, is not without a struggle. Various interest groups try to leave their mark on the memory and to color it from their perspective. They try to determine what should remain prominent in the memory and what should be put away or ignored.

National states play a big role in determining whether the past will be remembered as heroic or shameful. They provide funds for monuments, commemorations, cemeteries, research and chronicles. Minority groups often struggle to keep alive their version of the memory. For example, the Jews in Europe have had little influence on the memory of the Second World War for a long time. It was determined by the proud resistance, whereas the persecution of the Jews was allowed to fade away. Only fifteen years after the war did the trial of the war criminal Eichmann in Israel change the way in which people regarded the war.

The memory of the First World War was strongly influenced by poetry and short films about the horrors of the trenches and by the monuments and well-maintained cemeteries in northern France and Belgium. The experiences of the camps in World War II have been expressed in numerous journals and through descriptions by psychiatrists and famous writers who had stayed in the camps themselves. Films, such as *Shoah* of the aforementioned Claude Lanzmann, showed the fragmentation of the memory. The thousands of testimonies are more systematically recorded in the also already mentioned major scientific projects at Yale University and in the works of the famous film director Steven Spielberg.

Memories can be used to alleviate the suffering, but also to mobilize people for a new war. President Roosevelt used the memory of the hero Lincoln in the American Civil War to mobilize people for the Second World War, as described above. Another use is to alert people in order to prevent violence. The memory expressed in the terms of Auschwitz and Hiroshima is an example of this. Atoha station in Madrid, the images of the Twin Towers in New York or the image of Bin Laden evoke people's memories of the horrors of modern terrorism and keep people alert. In the trauma regime these types of memories and commemorations are important tools to deter people or to reduce dangers. It also shows how important tangible symbols and rituals are in the support of victims and to evoke sympathy. The big collective efforts are signs of recognition and show that people do not forget the horrors.

Nowadays the memories of the common past of a society mainly consist of the major traumas that have shaped its history. In the flood of memories it is the fractures that are prominent in the imagination, such as the World Wars, and in the European memory the Thirty Years' War or the Lisbon earthquake. Competition between victim groups may obscure good intentions. The fundraising, the memorial events, the silent marches and the monuments point to a strong need for compassion. Compared with the disasters that happened more than half a century ago, the compassion with the suffering of the victims has greatly increased.

Part 3

Relieving trauma

7   The trauma regime

7.1.   The rise of the trauma regime

At the end of the twentieth century a great variety of institutions became involved in the care and handling of shocking events accompanied by unprecedented media attention. Guided by experts, people made great efforts to relieve or prevent the pain by stimulating each other to more compassion and less risky or irresponsible behavior. Since that time relieving or preventing psychological trauma seems to be the most important incentive of the collective efforts to create a safe society, to control crises and conflicts and to ensure quality of life.

To capture this state of affairs in one phrase, sociology offers a solution. In sociology, the term regime is used for people who present themselves as experts in a particular area and whose rules and habits are adopted by people in their vicinity. The concept does not refer to oppression or dictatorship, but to a set of terms, rules of conduct and practices. For example, a medical regime consists of medical terms (e.g. illness), rules of conduct (e.g. hygiene) and practices (e.g. therapy). Doctors as experts in the regime try to achieve that their recommendations are followed. Chances of success are better in the center of the regime, in hospitals, than at the edges of the regime, such as in campaigns for healthy behavior, where doctors have to wait and see whether their advice is followed. The concept of regime has affinity with the concept of system, but it is more open. The regime can expand or lose influence and within the regime there is a constant struggle for power.[359]

The regime concerning this subject can be understood as a trauma regime. The trauma regime is a set of terms, rules of conduct and practices under the guidance of trauma experts, which exerts a certain pressure on self-restraint: empathy for the victims and containment of violence, recklessness and indifference. This pressure is not imposed top down, but people force themselves and each other, encouraged by the experts who play a leading role in the regime. The trauma regime is a response to the shocks of the modern era, especially the horrors of the past century and it is continuously expanding. In terms of an evolutionary perspective, the trauma regime is adaptive and has started to play a key role in the survival of modern societies. Terms such as reliving, extreme anxiety, posttraumatic stress, unbearable suffering, inner tension or attachment disorder have become commonplace in modern societies.

Trauma experts generally think that their ideas and practices are almost exclusively created within a scientific community of rational people. That is a limited view. In the trauma regime competition is the engine that drives the behavior and the ideas of experts. Experts compete not only with each other but also with many other parties, including authorities, victims and the general public. They are driven by many more reasons than scientific precision, including the prevention of loss of reputation, securing money, resisting pressure from victims or preventing public outcry. The outcome of the interactions is not always rational and planned, but often unintentional. Not only experts but also victims frequently have a limited view of the context in which they act. They consider their experiences to be as unique and thereby overlook how these perceptions are created in interaction with others.

The trauma regime arose from the pressure victims exerted on the general public, the government and experts such as psychologists and psychiatrists. The big push came from the veterans of the First and Second World War and the Vietnam War. The psychic dropout rate was so high and the number of dropouts as a result of infectious diseases and death from injuries declined so much, that the psychological effects could no longer be ignored. In the seventies and eighties of the previous century, the veterans were joined by other victims, such as victims of mass persecution in World War II and maltreatment and abuse of women and children. They asked experts to commit themselves to their causes. This meant that a wide field of experts was formed which would engage with psychological trauma. The range of these experts is great because they are involved in many kinds of shocking events and many manifestations of trauma.

The trauma regime can be seen as being part of mental health care, but this does not do justice to the regime. It is about much more, including crisis management, restitution, shaping the collective memory, commemoration, parent support and the prevention of violence. It is a comprehensive system that includes various professions and certainly overlaps existing fields, such as physical health care, child welfare and criminal justice. It also covers the whole field of damage repair after stressful life events, insofar as it relates to psychological consequences. The entire system can be interpreted as a large-scale social exercise in empathy and self-control. It is thus related to the medical regime that also goes beyond treatment and focuses on following medical prescriptions and awareness of physical well-being as well. There is always the danger that a regime expands to questionable areas too much. This provokes criticism formulated in terms of "victim culture" or "inflation of the trauma concept". There are always people who are not reached, who are not aware of or turn away from the complex problems. It often involves culprits or people who can be indirectly blamed for what happens to people and who want to evade responsibility.

Many people who are within the scope of the regime may still feel troubled with the patience and empathy for the victims or are only able to hold on to this self-control temporarily. Empathy and self-control are limited, even in experienced therapists. Real support includes the difficult social recognition and reparation of the victims, in which the required commitment goes beyond the consulting room. Few experts are committed to the interests of the victims in addition to their therapeutic work.

7.2. The function and stratification of the regime

The function of the trauma regime is to relieve and prevent psychological trauma. This function is embedded in a national society which has an interest in the management of crises and conflicts and help for the victims; crises and conflicts which threaten the productivity and health of that society. The regime has many international branches that transcend national interests. The parties involved in a disaster, calamity or any other dramatic event have also become players for a large audience. As a result of the dissemination of numerous media this audience closely monitors the events. In other words, a disaster is a dramatic event in an imaginary theater for a large audience, sometimes millions of people.

The audience is not a passive spectator, but more and more often plays an active role and it can join the discussion, transmit messages and images and influence other people's opinions thanks to social media. It can release its own pictures, which many people can transmit and comment upon. The presentation can be personalized with the help of photo shop and be enhanced in the groups in which one participates. A person can have multiple identities and present himself in different ways depending on the audience he wants to reach and influence. With a different identity in social media he can do things that would not be tolerated in a normal public discussion. The public is increasingly becoming aware of this. In turn, contact on the internet can lead to mass visits to the disaster site or to people one actually wants to see and sometimes wants to intimidate.

The sociologist Erving Goffman already elaborated on this dramaturgical perspective in the sixties. In this perspective, people play a role in public on a front stage where one is visible and a back stage which one keeps hidden from others.[360] This perspective has become commonplace and every individual has become his own director and choreographer. Receiving attention and keeping it, is vital and having as many followers and obtaining as many likes as possible has become an obsession. According to the American researcher Jeremy Rifkin whose analysis has been used, this essentially implies a strong expansion of the human imagination and strengthening of human connectedness.[361] However, it does raise the question of authenticity: what is real and what is not?

A special feature of the trauma regime is its stratification. The most influential trauma experts within the regime try to increase the number of supporters and users of their terms, rules of conduct and practices. Other people adopt the terms and act in accordance with the rules and practices. As a result, terms, rules and practices related to empathy, violence control and introspection spread across large groups of people. They find their way in the field of crisis management, justice, care and treatment and in collective rituals of compassion, remembrance and commemoration. The layering takes the form of a pyramid.

The elite of influential experts and expert organizations are at the top with an underlying layer of other academic and non-academic experts, whether or not organized and specialized in kinds of traumas and various forms of care, treatment and research. The third layer consists of the other parties, such as victims, government agencies and the public directly involved. Below them the parties that play a role in the regulation of crises, disasters and conflicts from a greater distance, such as lawyers, judges, administrators, policymakers and aid workers. The base of the pyramid is formed by the general public that adopts terms, manners and practices and passes them on to others and in that sense, though in a somewhat derivative way, it is also part of the regime.

The pyramidal structure allows influential experts to be leading in the way the psychological trauma is dealt with and how it can be prevented. The stratification ensures that people lower in the pyramid adopt terms, rules of conduct and practices. At the base there is at least a vague sense of how bad shocking events can be and how complex the coping process is. The pyramid model is an ideal representation of reality. The reality is more erratic. For example, the demarcation of the regime is not always clear. There are many skirmishes on the "outskirts" of the regime between experts and charlatans who are moving into this loaded, but to them attractive field. Experts who operate in the periphery may deviate considerably from the guidelines of influential experts. The model reflects the wide variety of rules and practices which gives rise to many controversies. The picture of the range is not always clear, because much of what is thought and done is not visible to the outside world.

To obtain a more accurate picture of the range is not easy. Researchers struggle to find a balance between commitment to the horrors and sufficient distance. They are blamed for lack of commitment when they look at the many problems in the regime from a distance. This is a problem, because the suffering of the victims does not leave them unmoved. But, being constantly aware of this commitment and its pitfalls, makes it possible to portray the regime in a more objective way.

7.3. The extent and consequences of unbearable pain

To determine how often psychological traumas occur in a population or in a human life is not easy in this tangle of reactions. Measurements of the extent are typically done when it concerns overt disorders, such as post-traumatic stress disorder. This provides some indication, but does not cover all the consequences that impact the immediate environment, such as absenteeism, labor productivity, overall confidence, the cost of repairs, memorials or monuments, and compensation for suffering. To give an idea here are some numbers.

The U.S. National Comorbidity Study provides an indication of the magnitude of PTSD. It was published in 1995 and repeated in 2005. It shows that almost seven percent of the American population develops PTSD during his or her lifetime.[362] According to a survey in the PTSD Research Quarterly of 2013, 25% of the population in the United States has been exposed to a traumatic event by age 18, and more than 50% by the age of 45. On an annual basis PTSD occurs in 6.3 million people, more than 3% of the population in the US. Thirty percent of the people who have stayed in war zones develops serious complaints. The number of people that has been exposed to combat and that develop full PTSD, ranges from 31% in Vietnam veterans, to 18% from Iraq and 12% from Afghanistan.[363] Other studies show that forty per cent of the people with PTSD develop chronic symptoms and half of those a depressive disorder one or more times. More than three quarters of people with post-traumatic stress disorder also suffer from another mental disorder. Victims have an increased risk of coronary disease, chronic pain and metabolic problems and often suffer from relationship problems, excessive alcohol and drug abuse, financial problems and an increased risk of suicide. The costs of the disorder due to absenteeism, stress on the family, unhealthy lifestyle or risky behavior in traffic are very extensive.[364]

The number of cases of child abuse in the Netherlands with its population of 17 million was estimated at 119,000 in 2010. This means that in a safe small country hundreds of thousands of children are abused in the course of a few years, often with serious consequences. A third of the adopted children and children in foster care, two-thirds of the children from foreign orphanages and 15% of the other children display disorganized attachment. Nearly a quarter of adopted children is anxiously ambivalent or fearfully avoidant. Therefore, in half of the adoption and foster children attachment problems occur. Soldiers, policemen, firemen, ambulance and security personnel (risky occupations) have an increased chance of getting PTSD, even up to 20%. There are also many people who suffer from sleeping problems and physical symptoms. PTSD is the most commonly reported occupational disease in policemen. And there are thousands of robberies in workplaces and shops. These figures indicate substantial risks of acute or chronic traumatization in modern societies.[365]

The extent and intrusiveness of psychological trauma ensure that the social effects of trauma are enormous. This is perhaps the biggest challenge. Especially in case of big shocking events an entire society can become disrupted. Confidence can be severely damaged if the events are caused by negligence or malicious intent. The search for the culprits may keep society intensively involved and widely divided. Especially shortly after major events or great revelations of abuse the collective stress is huge. When society has failed, the recognition of the suffering is laborious and the trajectory of compensation and reparation for the victims is long. There is always a risk that people wrongly behave as victims or want to settle a score by suing others. Very serious events remain etched in the collective memory and processed in commemorations, monuments and meeting places. This may ignite a fierce battle, in which groups of victims quickly feel subordinated or misunderstood. Costs may rise enormously. Media attention may enhance the conflict and give victims the idea they had better withdraw.

Psychological traumas have a lasting impact on the health and productivity of a society due to their massive extent and long duration. The symptoms, disorders, learning and relationship problems, physical symptoms and the gradual exhaustion have a major impact on society and lead to enormous costs. At the same time, society is confronted with its vulnerability and everyday life must return to normal. Victims might feel that they have been left in the lurch.

The emotional impact of shocking events in the form of psychological trauma is sometimes very visible, but more often it leads a hidden life. One example is the most common form of violence, domestic violence. Domestic violence is widespread, if we rely on investigations into the extent. It is a major problem that is well known among researchers and social workers in child care, but rarely comes out in the form of reports to the police. The indirect effects are visible in concentration and learning disorders, relationship problems or physical symptoms but they are often not recognized as being the result of abuse or neglect.

Another category of hidden problems is formed by shocking events that often occur but are isolated, such as traffic accidents. They attract little public attention. There is too little social disruption associated with it and the victims are not an identifiable group. There is little recognition for the psychological suffering, even if the isolated victims try to unite themselves. However, it concerns hundreds of thousands of victims. Therefore, it is a hidden trauma.

Hidden psychological traumas often manifest themselves as mental disorders so that the traumatic background is not immediately noticed. In 2006 British researchers reviewed forty studies of inpatients and patients with psychotic disorders. Almost seventy per cent of this sample had experienced serious physical or sexual violence in their lives. In mental disorders, especially anxiety disorders and depression, a traumatic background is common. These disorders are an important part of the burden of disease, because the quality of life is low, often for an extended period of time. More than 23% of the disease burden is caused by mental disorders. In addition, the indirect costs of mental disorders in terms of lost productivity, inappropriate use of somatic care and crime surpass the direct costs by an estimated factor of 3 to 5.[366]

Secrecy is a strategy that can make life bearable and it fits with the social suppression that encourages this secrecy.

At the same time it increases the problems, because there is no recognition. However, a victim can keep a secret for a long time if required by circumstances and if revealing the secret comes at a high price. In all revelations there is always the question of what is still concealed. Disclosure, in other words, has many layers. Secrets may persist for a very long time and usually other people are hardly aware of it. It characterizes the complexity of the challenge of psychological trauma.

Agony caused by prolonged abuse, mistreatment or neglect is stored in the victim's body and it will not disappear by talking or by therapies that only change cognitions or behaviors. They can temporarily relieve pain, but the real pain, however, is stored deeper and cannot be reached.[367] Gradual reliving and yoga exercises may be a solution, but under strict supervision, because it is accompanied with strong feelings and physical reactions. Most therapies do not reach that level and they leave many victims in the lurch. Carefulness is required here and any incident can make people retreat to distrust and silence. Impatient media with a short attention span are unsuitable to help reveal the secrets and to describe the painstaking process of disclosure. Breaking the process of secrecy in the victims is only possible if the actual pain has been reached. Many therapies are too superficial and often enhance repression and are only effective temporarily.

Stimulating the social imagination in literature, film and the visual arts is often the only way to show the public what is going on. It is also the way to train experts to develop the right sense for the complex experiences and the social context of the victim. Unfortunately, the training of experts does not usually focus on this broader cultural, social and literary education. This is the greatest challenge. The numerous people that were severely traumatized in their childhood or were faced with extreme conditions as adults, suffer horribly and often do not get the long-term help that is needed. This long-term care requires thorough training, much supervision and a great amount of patience and endurance, and society will not or cannot do that for both emotional and financial reasons. However, people often forget that perpetuating the damage will cost even more, especially in the long run.

7.4. Victims and victim representatives

To gain recognition in a crowded public arena one exerts organized pressure on people and agencies that can provide recognition. It often helps to get experts to endorse the cause of the victims. They become representatives who stand up for the victims. One example is the American psychiatrist Robert Jay Lifton who, after having talked with veterans from the Vietnam War, testified about their suffering for the United States Senate. He then participated in the Task Force, which was responsible for the medical recognition of post-traumatic stress disorder.[368]

To be recognized, the victim also depends on the response to his suffering. The suffering can be too bad for a layman to delve into for a long time. It can also evoke disgust, as is the case with severely mutilated victims or the serious abuse and humiliation which occur in countless families. More often still, people feel ashamed, because they have been negligent or did not oppose the wrongdoing when it occurred. Many acts of violence in history have never been punished, because the victims were unable to exert sufficient pressure to show the suffering, evoke compassion and sue the perpetrators.

Despite the limitations mentioned, most people are perfectly able to understand that traumatized victims may struggle with what they have experienced for a long time and that patience and support are needed to overcome this. It is less well known that many patterns of behaviour, such as the use of drugs and alcohol, have to do with mitigating the intense feelings that the event generates. It is also less well known that psychological trauma may result in severe mental disorders such as psychoses, personality disorders and depressions, but also in violent crimes after which there is little understanding for the traumas of the perpetrators. Therefore it is difficult to gain recognition for the fact that trauma, especially when it takes place in childhood, is one of the greatest threats to public health and society in general.[369]

The most radical aspect of psychological trauma is that it affects the existential dimension of life. Victims have doubts about the meaning of life, people who have disappointed them, relationships that have been disturbed and the horrors they have had to endure. They often feel insecure, live their lives in such a way that their unsafe world view is confirmed and they exclude people who do not cooperate. Because that is not satisfactory, resentment persists and new people have to be excluded again and again. Victims especially struggle with the extreme things that have happened to them. Robert Jay Lifton mentions the following characteristics of an extreme situation: an indelible feeling of guilt that one is still alive, whereas others have not made it; not being able to feel, because the pain is too bad; a desire for help and at the same time rejecting it, because the renewed confrontation with one's own vulnerability is too much and an intense search for the meaning of what has happened.

7.5. The configuration of the parties

The trauma regime is a set of parties which together (and certainly sometimes against each other) try to solve the problems that cause psychological trauma. The main parties are victims, experts, government agencies and the general public. The interests of the parties differ and may collide. Thus, the victim may demand recognition of a new therapy, whereas experts prefer to do more research into its effectiveness out of fear of loss of reputation. Public authorities may be reluctant out of fear of claims, whereas the general public wants the victims to be helped. Each party has supporters who in turn can be divided among themselves. Within the government there are numerous conflicts of interest between the various government agencies and departments. Often views of experts vary widely. Some views become leading, whereas others are banished to the periphery. The conflict of interests between the victims is reflected in the competition for attention which may lead to exaggeration.

The intensity in the perception of shocking events increases when ever more parties are involved in the events and the aftermath. Each party tries to increase its influence and improve its reputation, alone or in coalition with others. With every disaster or calamity, one struggles with errors and unsettled accounts from the previous disaster. This quickly creates an atmosphere of crisis with scandals and hypes and involvement of interest groups, which make themselves heard at any error in the settlement of the disaster. All this means that crisis management and the regulation of massive commotion after shocking events have become core functions of modern societies.

To increase their influence several parties form coalitions with each other. An example is a coalition of experts and a group of victims that try to gain public support to influence the government in a threefold coalition. Competition between various coalitions can develop into controversies which leave deep traces. Much commotion may also arise when citizens or victims designate certain organizations or experts as scapegoats. The complicated dynamics result in none of the parties being able to influence the course of events positively and there are always unintended consequences. It also means that every event is part of a series of events in which earlier events have shaped the world of experience and memories of the respective parties. The competition as to who is right and as a result obtains a prominent place in the memory is what drives people. It makes the settlement of shocking events extremely difficult and costly.

The trauma regime is always connected with the wider society, such as the world of science with its own laws, or with the legal world in which victims have a marginal position. The regime is also connected with the world of the uniformed professions with their own culture of courage and hierarchy. For some players, the completion of the event is their main activity, for others it is a troublesome side effect in their daily work. The character of the place of the event may greatly vary: a close-knit community or the casual scene of an accident with stakeholders from everywhere.

A separate issue is the struggle to keep alive the memory in the form of memorials, monuments and places of remembrance. Again, each group has its own interests and may feel disadvantaged compared to other groups. States often play an active role in shaping the memory. Especially after wars, the design of the memorial and the way the events will be remembered, is essential.

7.6. Recognition and satisfaction

The struggle of a victim of a shocking event is the struggle against himself. Constantly being flooded with images, bodily sensations, fear of recurrence and a sense of numbness because it is unbearable to think about the events, is a war of attrition. The basic sense of security and the bond with others is often damaged in such a way that the suffering can only take place in silence. In this situation victims cause much suffering to others, such as distrust towards the partner, arguments that seem to come from nowhere, alcohol abuse which can damage other people, or acting out on their own children. Social life is always at stake.

That is the personal situation of many people who have been affected by this fate. But there is more. Someone needs to seek help and to recognize the seriousness of what he or she is experiencing. Inwardly experiencing so many problems makes this search emotionally charged. The problem is that many victims are engaged in this quest. Moreover, every situation is unique and no one wants to be seen as only one of many others. Nowhere is there so much strife and jealousy as in victim groups, despite the support and recognition that victims experience with each other as fellow sufferers. There is always the feeling that the other person does not really understand the inner struggle, and there is always the danger that others will surpass the suffering.

When the victim has found peace with some buddies, the next step is for social recognition. The problem is credibility. There is always the question whether the victim is not exaggerating, is not trying to obtain benefits or is damaging others by putting them down as perpetrators. Society also prefers not to be confronted with too much suffering and not to be faced with its own vulnerability continually. The road to recognition often comes by way of compensation. One feels recognized when compensation is paid. Money is often a visible sign that others care about him, even if the victim prefers emotional support. Sometimes draconian punishments are demanded, which is bad for recovery, because the victim remains fixed on his victimization. The various media can reinforce all of this by allowing the event to grow into a scandal.

Satisfaction in the form of penalties for offenders is a first step, but it does not take the pain away. Extreme punishments do not fit in a constitutional state in which every citizen receives a proportional punishment and a chance of rehabilitation. Therefore, satisfaction often takes the form of excuses, damage repair and monetary compensation. This usually ignites a fierce battle. Authorities do not dare to admit their mistakes for fear of claims. For monetary compensation there are funds, but often the government has to supplement these funds. As a rule this only happens after careful examination and that takes a long time. Meanwhile, the fight may become more intense and more parties may get involved in the conflict.

To acquire sufficient attention, the organization of peers is not enough. Support from influential people who stand up for the group, such as authoritative experts, is required. However, these experts are always apprehensive of committing to a case that will place their authority at stake. In psychological trauma this is problematic, because it is difficult to demonstrate what the traumatic event has caused and what is related to a person's past or his life after the event. Authorities are not generous with financial compensation, because it can cost them a lot of money and acknowledgment may provoke new claims. Anyway, they try to avoid a compensation culture in which dubious victims claim money. The dynamics may also lead to witch hunts for perpetrators, resulting in withdrawal of victims who do not want this.

Leading experts are keen to resist the temptations of dramatization by victims and to combat fixation on the role of patient. Due to the strong mobilization of citizens and the media, the mayor plays an important role at local level. In a crisis he must quickly coordinate and prevent panic or rumors. He must restore trust by his personal presence at the scene of the disaster and provide an outlet for emotions in silent marches and commemorations. Important in such a case is adequate information at press conferences at fixed times and weighing dilemmas with a knowledgeable staff, in which contradiction is permitted.

7.7. The rivalry between the experts

The experts in the trauma regime represent a wide field of expertise. Their insights are derived from psychiatry, psychology, neurobiology, sociology, legal science and communication theory. The knowledge of the experts ranges from the human body under extreme stress, mental processes, such as inner conflicts and the operation of cognitions from fear to social processes, such as collective processing and commemorating of traumatic events.

The rivalry between experts encourages the discovery of ever new areas of trauma, which in turn elicit disclosures of victim groups and new claims for recognition. This dynamic is exacerbated by the elasticity of the concept of trauma and the fact that trauma is surrounded by shame and revelations that may lead to public outrage One important factor in the dynamics of the field is the growing number of psychiatrists, psychologists and other professionals who are trained to assist people in processing stressful life events. More and more psychologists and social workers use therapies or derivative methods, that consist of some form of imaginary exposure or desensitizing.

The field attracts quite a lot of dubious practitioners who want to get their share of the market of victims with profound experiences in vulnerable positions. Experts are constantly exposed to criticism from people who feel they exaggerate, seek publicity for their own gain and have made victimization attractive. Their credibility is regularly questioned when controversies erupt, as happened in the 1990'-s with the debate about recovered memories.

The subject of trauma itself provokes controversy. There is rarely a straightforward and simple link between a particular traumatic event or series of events and the current condition. The particular meaning that is given to the event, social support as well as personality factors all play a role in the outcome and these are difficult to separate from the event itself. The shocking event may trigger a trauma, but also by itself increase the sorrow already existing. In many cases a shocking event does not lead to complaints and if there are complaints, they are very diverse: from mild discomfort and vague physical symptoms to PTSD, and even to complex psychopathology, such as depression, addiction, psychosis and personality disorders.

7.8. Interdependence as a booster

The trauma regime in modern societies has a wide range. Even in peaceful countries the number of victims of shocking events which experiences the traumatic consequences is enormous. Deployed soldiers, refugees, service providers, victims of violent attacks, abuse and assault, major accidents, serious medical errors or severe loss frequently suffer from the consequences. Experts have tried to make these consequences measurable and manageable by dividing them in symptom clusters, such as PTSD, depression, dissociative disorder, psychosis or personality disorder. This has further enhanced the expert's awareness of the enormous extent.[370] There are several reasons for this.

The main reason is that people are more connected with each other through trade relationships, travel and the Internet and therefore are more likely to be faced with shocks. Modern societies have to deal with new threats due to the globalization of the economy, increased migration and settlement of people in risky areas. The infrastructures of transport, energy supply and communication are fragile so that even a small disturbance can have major consequences. An epidemic may also spread more quickly through the worldwide intensification of contacts. Disruptions are also more difficult to predict, such as an accident at a nuclear power plant. Production and trade chains are longer and less clear and narrow sea passages are more often located in conflict areas. Resources become scarcer by global population growth and increasing prosperity of emerging countries. Capital is scarcer by increasing debts of governments and individuals. Productive people in western countries are becoming scarcer by decreasing growth of the labor force.

The intensified international competition causes impoverished and traumatized populations and regions by retreating industries. The problem is further exacerbated by cross-border crime and terrorism. Despite protective measures the degradation of the environment increases by leaps and bounds, resulting in famines, conflicts and migrations. In addition, there is political instability in many regions resulting in collisions between ethnic groups and religious movements. The wide spread of weapons increasingly culminates in terrorism and civil wars.

A second reason is that threats are perceived more intensely by the already mentioned expansion of the media and the increased media attention for these threats. The news includes powerful images, which are available everywhere. The suffering is shown immediately and the images are often repeated. The intensity of the experience increases, because more and more parties are involved in the event and its aftermath. This quickly creates an atmosphere of crisis with scandals and involvement of interest groups. There is also a decline in satisfaction with the functioning of the government and greater pressure for public accountability. Conflicts in the legal sphere are considered more from the perspective of what was done to the victim so that the psychological damage is discovered earlier.

A third reason is that violence in the relationships between men, women and children has not increased, but is experienced more intensely. Many people do not know how to deal with violence in their daily lives. Men cannot fight anymore because there is no need and it is strongly disapproved of. However, the news about violence has greatly increased and has become more intense.

A fourth reason is that many somatic problems are preceded by serious stress. Hiding this stress is less common in a society in which openness about emotions is paramount. Psychological damage also greatly influences the productivity of the individual and may lead to sick leave and has major implications for the environment of the person who feels regularly swamped.

7.9. Crisis management

An explicit manifestation of the trauma regime in modern societies is crisis management. Crisis management should be considered in the context of the threat that shocking events have come to form for the functioning of modern societies. In this context the trauma regime has acquired a crucial function at the intersection of three areas: crisis management, legal conflict resolution and health care. Firstly, in modern societies, as already mentioned, more and more shocking events develop into a crisis involving many parties with large social costs as a result. Crisis management has become a core function of modern governments. Secondly, legal conflicts are increasingly dominated by what has been done to the victims. Recognition and satisfaction of victims have increasingly become the motives in resolving conflicts and providing legal security. Thirdly, the quality of health care is increasingly determined by the quality of life. In the matter of losing quality of life, the role of psychological problems with a traumatic background is becoming more and more important. Solving problems in these three areas, therefore, requires the expertise of trauma experts.

This development has fundamentally changed the character of the field of crisis management. In disasters, the focus is now on preventing psychological damage and restoring the sense of security. Immediately after a disaster, victims often long for a support center they can go to with their complaints, problems and questions for information day and night, often for many years. Immediately after a disaster, victims do not feel the need for processing and reflecting, but they need security and help with practical problems. More and more incidents, such as disasters, major accidents, outbreaks of infectious diseases, unexpected public violence, family dramas or sexual abuse cases develop into crises resulting in confidence in authorities and fear of recurrence. The sense of crisis is magnified by lack of clarity concerning responsibility, conflicting information, poor coordination between agencies and a lengthy claim settlement. Emotions may run high by false impressions, awkward leadership of authorities and an ongoing stream of rumors. In case of disasters people may desperately search for the truth and tensions may rise until finally the victims have been identified. This dynamic is reinforced by the chaos on the site of the disaster and poor availability of support options. As a result, crises become more complex and more difficult to manage.

Experts in the field of support, crisis communication, compensation and assistance in the aftermath play a key role. Concerns about the risks of diseases can be reduced by performing systematic health research using control groups that are not affected. For a quick judicial process it is necessary that victims can claim damages collectively or that one party can litigate on behalf of others.

Nowadays the general public has an almost insatiable need for information and visible signs of compassion. This is met by the presence of officials at the scene of the disaster and regular press conferences. After major shocking events the risk that people look for culprits or turn to conspiracy theories for explanation, will be prevented as much as possible by building up trust. An important point is that nowadays a greater appeal is made on the resilience of a community. A more flexible and cautious approach is needed, and sometimes the tragedy of life must be accepted. Yet, the idea of resilience also leads to discussions among experts. The questions are: Would well-intentioned citizens not interfere with issues they have little knowledge of? Would people not rely too much on resilience, whereas people are mainly unsettled? Would this way of thinking not fit a retreating government that relies too much on informal care? Would people not be drawn into the mobilization of a community too much, whereas they would prefer to live their own lives at a proper distance from this community? Propagating firmness and strength, when people are severely traumatized, may cause much more suffering. The strong bond that can manifest itself when relying on the resilience of a community has to be reduced to normal proportions later. That may be painful for people who have put in a lot of effort and derive status from that effort. Resentment about lack of appreciation may be the result.

8 The limits of the trauma regime

8.1. Complex traumas

People in modern societies are very attached to their own privacy. Infringements in this atmosphere by mistreatment, abuse or sudden death or mutilation of a loved partner, child, brother or sister hit people hard. Nuclear families are small, the distance with the extended family has grown and the expectation of a long and healthy life is high. The infringements are especially traumatic if mistreatment or abuse occurs by someone within the family. It leads to a breakdown in trust and if someone cannot escape the situation it causes serious problems. Especially if the situation persists, if one is forced to secrecy and if small children are concerned, the traumas are complex. These complex traumas with symptoms of dissociation as an attempt to escape from the oppressive reality, partial amnesia and psychotic symptoms are very persistent. Here the regime meets its limits.

Stopping domestic violence or violence in closed institutions is hampered by privacy rules. One cannot just suspect a family and go inside without solid evidence. Finding evidence is hampered by secrecy. Legal authorities may decide only after careful investigation. This is not easy due to this secrecy and a lack of witnesses. The removal of children from parental power leads to new problems in foster homes or institutions. Children are not always better off in an institution where there are other damaged children. The strong bond with the perpetrator and the dependency on him prevents the victim from ending the relation. After the break one often enters into relationships that have the same characteristics

The unimaginable horrors that may take place close by or around the corner evoke resistance in other people. One feels disgust or wants to deny the events. It is difficult to keep the public interested in this issue permanently. Experts in this field often work in the margins of the trauma regime. Their approaches are less clear and more difficult to investigate as to effectiveness because of the long duration. Talk therapies are often ineffective, because the victims have lost segments of time and stress has been stored on a deeper level in the body. The health and insurance industry benefits from short and fast solutions, but those are not very effective in this area. However, dealing with this problem requires a huge investment in mental health care, which could certainly bring returns, but that is something society has not yet ventured to do. Only when the burden of suffering becomes too great, the readiness to help groups of victims in this area will grow.

In the mid 1990s there was a heated debate about the veracity of memories that had long been forgotten and were later recovered. These were often memories of incest which had been recovered with the help of a therapist. Therapists reported memories that had been lost for many years. However, only a few cases were known in which serious offenses had previously been recorded and not been remembered years later.[371] The seriousness of the facts made amnesia implausible. In several countries working groups gathered incest memories that had been recovered during psychotherapy sessions and in which the patient's parents were accused of sexual abuse. The debate drew attention to the reliability of recall. Some insights that resulted from this debate will be presented here.

Remembering is a process of reconstruction. What is remembered and what is forgotten depends on the importance that someone attaches to certain events and its details. In the memory details are sometimes sharp, whereas the context is vague. Physical symptoms may arise that are hard to understand, even for the victims involved. The accusation of simulation lurks when the pain is diffuse and its origin is located in a distant past. This also happens when only certain forms of expression are socially accepted or the memories are too painful to acknowledge. This had already been indicated with the ancient notion of hysteria. And hysteria often manifests itself in new guises. Remembering as an individual process is constantly influenced by social norms, which are formed and changed in the collective process of remembering.

In a depth analysis of trauma in modern culture the sociologist and psychoanalyst Jeffrey Prager pointed out that traumas do not manifest themselves as pure re-experiences. The memory of an extreme event is incomplete and is therefore difficult to reproduce in a coherent whole. It is a reference to the event, a way to try to free oneself from blocked emotions associated with the memory but the attending pain is too severe. The victims try to maintain their self-image within the available schemes of the culture. So remembering is not the same as thinking back of a photo or film, but a process in which references to events change and obtain new meaning all the time. Statements that are common in a culture, such as sexual abuse, can even be used to hide deeper traumas.[372] Freud had focused on the distorted process of remembering. This incomplete process is reflected in affective components such as repetitions. They only refer to the event, which refuses to be seen so to speak. The stories continuously change, due to cultural changes. Their status grows when they become stories of a respected survivor. Redefining the past in terms of traumatic events has even become a global business, in which states play an active role with memorials, museums and monuments.

An example is the memory of the Second World War, which has strongly been influenced by the Nuremberg tribunal and is seen from a dominant Anglo-Saxon perspective. The perspective of the Jewish victims remained underexposed because of this. Only with the trial of the war criminal Adolf Eichmann, 15 years later, was there a beginning of recognition. Another example is the trial of Lieutenant Calley, responsible for the massacre at My Lai during the Vietnam War in 1968. During this trial there were no Vietnamese witnesses present and the perspective of the Vietnamese victims was ignored. Lieutenant Calley was released three years after the trial. Therefore, in the United States the veterans and not the Vietnamese people are considered victims of the war.[373] Other analyses during this debate highlighted the role of the media. According to them, media institutions play a major role in public perception and they can contribute to a distorted picture. Especially film images have come to play a crucial role in the public memory.[374]

According to Pierre Nora, the explosion of interest for memories can be explained by a profound change in the traditional relationship with the past in countries and social or ethnic groups. This was reflected in the rediscovery of areas that had been hidden or suppressed, more interest in social roots, new museums and the opening of archives. The uncertainty about the future stimulates people to look for their roots. "What have we lost?" has become the central question. This search is not an official activity, but it is fragmented, with numerous groups who seek recognition and compete for empowerment. Identity is derived from what has been done to the group in the past, and what traces it has left in the present: slavery among blacks, sexual violence among women, the Holocaust among the Jews or the great famine among the Irish.

The debate was not completed, but the sting had gone out of it when the pressure of victims to recognize incest had decreased and the feminist movement, which had placed the issue on the agenda, had arrived in calmer waters. However, the wider public debate on the recognition of severe damage in youth continues and there is only a beginning of recognition. At least for the time being, here are the limits of the trauma regime.

8.2. Medicalization

In 1995 the anthropologist Allan Young sharply criticized the concept of trauma.[375] According to him, radical suffering had been conceived as suffering from a memory for the first time at the end of the nineteenth century. One spoke of a "pathogen secret" with the effect of a "mental parasite". Previously, the notions of despair or confusion had been used. At the end of the nineteenth century suffering caused by memory was even extended to collectively suffering caused by a memory, when victims search for recognition by the community. According to Young, this way of thinking was based on a social construction: neurologists had medicalized the experiences of victims and had transformed them into a form of pathology. It was an attempt to provide responses which differ from culture to culture, with an objective description. This was the reason that the figures on the extent of the problems varied significantly in different societies.

Young's critique fitted a broader debate on medicalization. Critics indicated that if the rediscovery of a meaningful existence after shocking events did not run smoothly, the victim was placed in the role of patient. This was problematic because doctors often treated disorders with medication and did not examine the cause. The DSM classification system, that was used a century later, paid no attention to the causes and with every new version included more disorders, which were increasingly treated with medication.[376]

Further criticism entailed that by describing problems in terms of a disorder, valuable support from the immediate vicinity of the victim and the wider community was absent, because of the excuse that medical help was available. This was certainly the case when the stories were too difficult to listen to, because they evoked too much fear and grief. In addition, recognition of the "disease" resulted in loss of social function.[377] Life in the patient role was usually dominated by medical rules of conduct which would often result in isolation. If the effectiveness of treatment was uncertain, the price could be high. However, victims struggled with the question why something like this could happen and how it could be prevented. According to the critics, an answer to this question was only possible if factual event and responsibility were discussed in public. If the victims were sent to experts these questions would not be answered and they would be silenced.[378]

For an answer to the victim's questions a shared story in which the answer can be found, must be available in the wider society. However, sometimes the truth is too horrible to be discussed in public, for instance when a society has to admit that it was fearful or cowardly. One prefers to be proud of the past. By using the term trauma, there is no difference between a victim of a serious accident and a victim of a mass murder. However, the latter case is not trauma in the sense of a severe form of stress, but a serious crime that affects the core of civilization. The concept of stress conceals this special meaning.

In other words, shocking events cause more than a pathological response. According to Arthur Kleinman, they are a threat to the meaning of life and to the connection with others.[379] He claims that severe suffering after a shocking event, or suffering in the face of death, is a direct confrontation with "what matters in life." It is a confrontation with the limitations of life and what is really important. This creates the need to participate in a world in which humanity counts and life matters. The problem will not be solved by removing the pathology, changing the behavior and cognitions or suppress them by medication. It is the search for meaning in a life that is finite.[380] The Dutch psychiatrist Van Dantzig considered it the task of psychotherapy to help patients to regain pleasure in life. But the power of psychotherapy is limited. It can free people from too strict demands of the conscience and free them from repressed feelings, so they can handle life in a more realistic way. However, this release does not remove the task of finding meaning in life. This becomes complicated if there is no collective meaning in a chaotic world.

Especially in the face of severe suffering the question of the value of life is urgent. When suffering remains trapped within the subject and has no resonation in collective rituals of acknowledgment and commemoration and is not explored in art and literature, people may search for extreme forms of expression. This may result in an even more extreme confinement within themselves with self-torture and self-mutilation or in attempts to artificially experience reunification with others. These attempts can take the form of mass experiences, intoxication and distraction, extreme violence, closed religious communities or worship of heroes and idols. It is therefore essential that people search for meaning in their own life story and in the place they occupy in the chain of generations, in which one picks up the tradition, edits it and passes it on to future generations. The way a society deals with this value determines the extent to which subjective suffering is bearable and withdrawing oneself is counteracted. When everything is focused on the removal of a pathology, there is no opportunity to learn how to come to terms with the pain.

8.3. Effectiveness

As long as there has been psychotherapy, the reliability of the diagnosis and the effectiveness of the treatment are subject of discussion. Due to cuts in the welfare state and the increasing importance of evidence based therapy, the discussion gained momentum in the nineties.

Various definitions of effectiveness have been proposed. A basic definition focused on the disappearance of the signs and symptoms or part of them. A broader definition emphasized the increase in resistance and resilience, the strengthening of self-esteem or obtaining a life perspective in which the trauma is less central or contributes to new meaning. Examining the effects was mostly based on the basic definition. Part of the criticism focused on that. It stated that in that case many effects were excluded. Indeed, symptoms could persist, whereas the resilience and self-esteem of a person had increased.

Measuring the effectiveness of psychotherapy through controlled studies also evoked much criticism about the composition of the research group and the control group. Finding people for a stable control group was not easy. There were many drop outs in a group on a waiting list. Keeping other factors constant besides the interventions, was not easy. Meta-analyses were unreliable due to the use of different study designs, different definitions of what was meant by symptoms and effects, and different measuring instruments.[381] Most controlled studies have been done on brief interventions, such as cognitive behavioural therapy, in which exposure turned out to be the most effective element. According to the critics, isolating success factors showed unspectacular things: a good working relationship and a clear working model.[382]

Based on research and experience with disasters and other shocking events that concern many people, there was consensus about the fact that debriefing aimed at evoking emotions immediately after the event was harmful; that initially focusing on practical support, understanding and attention to the social network and later selection with a view to increased risk of PTSD was effective; that to talk or not to talk should be left to the person concerned initially; and unsolicited delving into emotions or speaking about personal experiences was counterproductive.

In case of very severe events, such as mass persecution, the effectiveness of treatments was even more difficult to measure. The need to find the words and to talk about the atrocities or the indifference of bystanders was intense, as appeared from the recognition of the atrocities in the camps in World War II. According to experts, the therapy that worked best, was to restore trust, build a new system of meaning, and to set the memory free by writing and talking. The sense of desolation, being at the mercy of the executioners and the indifference of bystanders, was the worst feeling that had to be overcome.[383] The controversy continued. Short-term forms of psychotherapy could be researched best with the current experimental method. Therapies focused on complex traumas remained very much at a disadvantage.

8.4. Safety

The trauma regime calls for vigilance. This may extend to protecting the state against malicious dictators who threaten democracy, or criminals and their organizations that undermine safety. And even far beyond that, such as protection against disasters, calamities, risk of infection, food poisoning, environmental degradation, traffic fatalities or accidents in the home. Not all measures are directly related to psychological trauma, but lack of safety can be so severe that they eventually lead to traumas. Yet, a society is never completely safe, because in that case all social traffic would be shut down. Every action carries risks and many risks arise unintentionally and unexpectedly. Security will always be limited.

Modern societies are barely able to accept limits to safety. Some sociologists speak about a safety utopia in which all setbacks must be eradicated. In a safe and prosperous society t is hard to accept that people can be affected by fate and have to face the tragedy of life. Dangerous behavior is tempting, especially for young people looking for challenges. In a dynamic society the quest for excitement and danger is widespread. Defying fate in dangerous sports, use of intoxicants or risky behavior is even encouraged. Modern societies thus always navigate between the need for security and the need for excitement and danger.

If an entire society is threatened, or if a threat is magnified, mass violence may be provoked. The threshold is high, but when communism fell in the nineties, Europe was faced with situations, such as in Yugoslavia and more recently in Ukraine, in which people resorted to mass violence. When political leaders incite people to hatred against certain groups of populations or make people think that compatriots are threatened in neighboring countries, then violence is imminent. Serbs and Croats did this in Bosnia, the Russians in Georgia and Ukraine. Ethnic violence is a form of violence people will turn to, despite lessons from the past. Even an international legal system is often powerless, when certain interests of superpowers collide and a deadlock occurs in the UN Security Council. Peace Forces, if being deployed at all, usually have a limited mandate.

Terrorist attacks show most clearly what the pursuit of security and the fear of trauma may lead to and in which respect it is limited. Especially after the attacks on the Twin Towers in 2001, an unimaginable safety system has been installed to protect people and buildings, from border control to espionage, from large-scale data collection to deployment of police and army at political meetings and tours of politicians, above all the protection of the top, such as the President of the United States. Citizens are encouraged to be wary of suspicious people and packages at airports, on public transport or in squares and shops. Camera surveillance has been extended and warning systems via the Internet and mobile phone continue to be refined. Border controls of intercontinental travels are intensified. When the danger decreases, alertness and security measures are reduced, such as large scale espionage, but it does not require much to activate these systems again.

Despite extensive measures, the danger persists. An unobtrusive loner or a small network of people may cause huge damage. There is always the risk of an attack with major consequences. The prevention of the proliferation of dangerous nuclear material is always limited. But even with simpler means much damage can be done to a vulnerable infrastructure that connects many people. Sabotage of the Internet, adding substances to the food, spreading hazardous biological material, cannot be ruled out. And there are always people who are capable of anything for ideological reasons or simply out of revenge or for the thrill of it. Saving the world by destroying it, is an attractive idea for some people and it is hard to prevent.

8.5. Victim culture

The thesis of the victim culture is that people in developed societies increasingly adopt the role of victim to acquire attention and sympathy. In this role they are able to absolve themselves from guilt, exempt themselves from labor, claim compensation and sue perpetrators. Victimization may take many forms. One of the most far-reaching is when one feels permanently wronged as a victim of history. A symbolic story, a myth, that makes somebody inviolable may arise. In less drastic forms emotions, such as sadness and anger, are presented as dramatically as possible. This creates competition with other victims or alleged victims for attention, apologies and reparation. Draconian penalties are claimed. Critical and relativistic opinions are not allowed in this wave of emotions. The shame about emotions turns into an assertive culture of claims for satisfaction.

A victim culture may occur in particular in a commercial media culture which is looking for drama and emotions, fueled by an impatient public that has a short attention span. Media are captivated by the event. They look for similar incidents which can confirm the news and supply news again. Every detail is widely reported and all becomes a one-sided picture with half-truths, magnification or exaggeration. In this regard, journalists are powerful catalysts. Media can mobilize many people, select information and enhance the emotional effect. More intense and sharper images in close-up help to create a greater psychological confrontation.

The English psychiatrist Dalrymple uses children being looked upon as victims as an example of abuse of victimhood and exaggerated sentimentality. Discipline is out of the question here. They get what they want. Their violence is condoned and they should never ever incur any frustrations. According to him, this undermines children's learning process. Steven Pinker's critique is in line with this.[384] Adults try to banish every expression of violence from children's culture. Sometimes they are only allowed to wear positive costumes at parties. Their health must be protected by a ban on playing in the grass (ticks) or in the sun (skin cancer), on eating cake (salmonella) or buying lemonade at a stall (bacteria). They are only allowed to cycle or climb with helmets on and are not allowed to accept cookies from strangers or be alone in the street. They must always be accessible by cell phone. Though in the United States, only one in one million children is murdered, there is extreme attention for missing children who have usually been taken by a family member temporarily.

Dalrymple states that victims must not be contradicted, the blame always lies with the authorities. People present their suffering as dramatically as possible: "I am devastated", "My career is in ruins", "I dare not leave my house anymore." As a result, the suffering seems insurmountable. For the audience, there is only sorrow when grief is displayed. Someone who is in pain without tears is insensitive. Refusing to take part in public expressions of mourning is considered inappropriate and even as a sign that one might be the perpetrator. According to Dalrymple, victims who show they have been seriously affected, can also claim higher penalties. Compassion is sometimes ostentation, such as a pop star who earns a lot of money, evades taxes, but gives a benefit concert to fight hunger in the world. Especially abuse stories receive much attention in the media, evoke much sympathy and ensure extreme pressure on the perpetrators and their lawyers, who are often threatened. That victims can also be perpetrators, is ignored.

In these analyses it seems that the trauma regime encounters its limits in a commercial media culture in which victimhood is sacrosanct. However, there are objections to this analysis. The first is that there is much reluctance in a media culture, too. Often there is a careful independent investigation into the facts. In many developed societies there is certainly no claim culture. Victims of disasters often receive only small amounts. Research among experts shows that most victims of PTSD suffer in silence and are ashamed of their symptoms. Veterans wait a very long time before seeking help, refugees keep their suffering often hidden out of fear for rejection. Considerations of privacy and fear of reprisals often refrain people from reporting domestic violence.

A second objection is that victims struggle against disbelief and doubts, when the suffering points to the failure of others or when offenders deny. Experts usually need a long time to find out what has really happened. This may be due to lack of information or lack of witnesses, but in case of larger events to the vast amount of information to be collected or browsed through.

A third objection is that victims may unintentionally be faced with a dynamic of increasing rivalry which cannot be considered a victim culture. The dynamic is as follows. Revelations of victims evoke a claim for recognition. When the suffering is recognized, this may provoke more new revelations with new claims for recognition. Recognition may provoke new revelations. In this spiral of revelation and recognition victims do play an active role, but they are also inadvertently dragged into it. A similar dynamic occurs with respect to satisfaction. In order to obtain satisfaction liability should be recognized. This is often accompanied by a claim for compensation, causing perpetrators or the authorities responsible to avoid liability. The victim feels wronged and may harden in his position. This is also the case if the compensation is covered by insurance or a fund: the perpetrator does not have to make sacrifices himself and insurance and funds seldom cover all the damages. In such cases, one can focus on retribution. Limiting the need for retribution is difficult. One possibility is to give the victim an active role in the judicial process.

Another objection is that people in modern societies derive their morality more and more from aversion to cruelty, humiliation and suffering. Showing that you are a victim has become a way to indicate moral boundaries.[385] Usually, it is not the victim who claims draconian punishments and threatens lawyers, but this is done by extreme right-wing groups and anonymous "lone wolves". Finally, there is the objection that there are simply very many victims of shocking events, who suffer severely and worry so much about the event that this hampers their daily functioning. People have high demands and invent or exaggerate their stories, especially when big compensations are within reach. This is not a modern phenomenon, but it was already the case with railroad accidents in the nineteenth century. It may increase when cuts that affect the welfare state continue. It may also increase when changes in the structure of the media make it more difficult to access objective information.

8.6. Global humanity
Some philosophers have raised the question whether humanity can control itself enough to build a peaceful society on a global scale. According to them, the desire

for thrills, violence and the intoxication of destruction and living recklessly is too strong. They claim that human beings have a strong tendency to warfare, aimless luxury, hero worship or perversity and are fascinated by death and violence. In that vision the human ability to feel solidarity is limited. Too much self-control leads to equalization, so that there is no goal in life that appeals anymore and special occasions, such as holidays and commemorations, do not evoke a sense of depth. Crusades for the good may kindle violence. That violence may escalate without ritual containment in religions. The detached attitude of the intellectual who sympathizes, but in moderation and within feasible limits, does not provide a way out. This also applies to the overloaded news consumer who believes that suffering cannot be remedied.

This argument has also been criticized. Critics argue that it is possible to build a more peaceful world when people realize that they need each other. On a much smaller scale, but still encompassing millions of people, this indeed succeeded when building the welfare state. In that case, large groups of people exchanged their bonds with family and village clan for solidarity for all people within a country. This was the case, even if the residents remained strangers to each other: to live in the same country was sufficient. For the time being it will still not work on a global scale, but when people become more interdependent in order to be able to counter major world problems, such as the deterioration of the global environment and the spread of nuclear weapons, more solidarity may be possible. At the moment the self-control needed for this solidarity is still limited, however.

According to Ian Morris some threats become bigger and bigger. Many areas in the world are unstable. Some people speak of the arc of instability, which runs from Somalia to the north, deflecting to the Middle East and South Asia, and then south to Indonesia. The spread of nuclear weapons and the ability to buy them, provides malicious individuals with more power to make countless victims, but the biggest problem is the degradation of the biosphere. By 2050, the earth will be inhabited by nine billion people, by 2100 probably 11 billion. The energy consumption will have doubled in 2050 compared to 2010 and even more, if more and more people gain access to electricity and live in energy-intensive cities.[386]

The question is when the world will run out of fossil fuels and whether it will be able to use the large amount of energy from the sun in time. Biodiversity decreases at great speed, and scarcity of resources provokes new conflicts. Global warming makes many areas uninhabitable and promotes major migration flows. These threats can be seen as the harbingers of a crisis in the biosphere, which directly threatens the lives of people on earth. The survival of humans as a species is at stake. This is the biggest crisis since the appearance of man on earth and can only be solved by global crisis management and involvement of all mankind.

However, technological development progresses by leaps and bounds, the capability of computers to store and process information greatly expands and awareness of the global threat to the survival of mankind increases. The question is whether this development can reduce the threats sufficiently. According to Ian Morris, the next fifty years will be crucial. It is the period that must be bridged in order to find new energy sources, and the infinite possibilities of artificial intelligence. During this period, humanity will have to muster the self-control to preserve human life for the planet and to avoid conflicts that lead to millions of deaths.

The threat that shocking events have become for the functioning of modern societies is the reason that the trauma regime led by trauma experts will acquire a crucial function. Crisis management has become a key task of modern governments and trauma experts play a key role in that. Conflicts in the legal sphere are increasingly dominated by what has been done to the victims. Retribution for victims is more and more often the motive when resolving conflicts and providing legal certainty. The quality of health care is increasingly determined by the quality of life. As to losing quality of life, psychological problems with a traumatic background take up a growing share. It is for this reason that solving problems in these three areas increasingly requires the expertise of trauma experts.

According to the German philosopher Peter Sloterdijk, the global crisis in which mankind finds itself is authoritative, because it relies on the unimaginable: the global catastrophe.[387] It consists of a global environmental crisis, the deployment of nuclear weapons by unstable regimes, a global pandemic or large-scale migrations due to a shortage of raw materials, food and energy. The global catastrophe is a prospect that is the only authority that can say now: "You must change your life" and "Behave in such a way that the consequences of your actions will be in line with the survival of human life on earth." This transcends religions, cultures and local interests. Sloterdijk describes the warning as follows:

> "Because it has the aura of the awesome, it gets the fundamental features that were hitherto attributed to transcendent powers: it keeps itself hidden but reveals itself already in signs; (...) In its name its delegates turn to fellow human beings, but they are banned by most as troublemakers (...) Overall, the crisis hardly differs from

the experiences of the God of monotheism when he came on stage barely three thousand years ago. His message was too big for the world and only few were willing to lead another life for his sake."

When we take the warning seriously, then all attempts from the past to actually lead a better life are no more than exercises in self-discipline to cope with the challenge that arises now. The great ideologies and religions have made all sorts of attempts to encourage people to withdraw from the world or to unite under the banner of nationalism, communism or fascism. The latter with disastrous consequences. The present challenge now transcends all these attempts. The "imperative" assumes a global catastrophe if we continue on this path. The "imperative" is embodied in the system of rules and practices to prevent events or to protect itself from the pain caused by these events. The trauma regime is the protection shield, the immune system that defends people from the damage caused by shocking events, but its power is limited. To understand what is happening in modern societies, requires more insight into the lessons in life that the regime offers.

Traditionally, people have tried to free themselves from the world and to arm themselves against its injuries and distractions by withdrawing or leading ascetic lives. The task was to distinguish themselves from those who did not. This required intensive and continuous exercise and the avoidance of self-pity and envy. Their basic attitude was to live life more intensely and with more spiritual content by exercising. It was a form of imaginary anticipation and mental reinforcement against mortality and injuries caused by fate. People often made excessive efforts during that process. However, exercise by withdrawal is not the appropriate means in modern times, because this day and age asks for the provision of security not outside, but in the world. To build resilience now, a new combination of knowledge, technology and organization is needed in which mental capital, mental support and mental resilience play a crucial role.

Conclusion: civilization and empathy

In thinking about shocking events two distinct processes can be distinguished: rationalization and psychologizing. During these processes, people became more sensitive to the effects of events in the long term, could analyze the events with more aloofness and became more open to feelings of being overwhelmed, of humiliation and disregard due to the events. The limitation that people had imposed on themselves was aimed at preventing traumas by avoiding harmful and reckless behavior and curbing revenge. They kept more aloof from their own thoughts and feelings that were evoked by the intense thoughts and feelings of the affected individuals. All this requires much self-control and can be considered as a process of civilization.

Despite the fact that major controversies in the professional world have decreased, it remains difficult to keep on investing in the care for severe traumas. The challenge is twofold. Firstly, the urgency of global control of the effects of environmental and technological disasters and large-scale violent conflicts is increasingly felt. There is a growing awareness that the psychological consequences may now far surpass the material damage. Secondly, the discovery and recognition of the many consequences of breaches of privacy, especially when young children are concerned, are still only at an early stage. It requires a much larger effort of mental health services to promote the health and quality of life of the population. These two constitute the greatest challenge facing humanity in the coming decades.

The complex dynamics evoked by shocking events require a professional approach in order to manage them. The emotional impact of shocking events may be an important driving force for the search for solutions at a higher level of integration and self-control and thereby to further civilization.

Acknowledgements

This book is the result of an investigation that has taken more than ten years. I am indebted to many experts. In the first place the sociologists who offered me the theoretical framework, especially Nico Wilterdink, my supervisor during a part of my research and Johan Goudsblom, founder of the historical school of sociology in the Netherlands, both professors Emeritus at the University of Amsterdam. I am very grateful to them. Furthermore, I thank the many experts in the field of professional trauma in the Netherlands, particularly those with knowledge of the international context: Eric Vermetten, professor in medical-biological and psychiatric aspects of psychotrauma at the University of Leiden, who offered me a lot of insight into this field. Thanks also to Onno van der Hart and Berthold Gersons, professors Emeritus at the University of Utrecht, respectively Amsterdam and former president of the International Society of Traumatic Stress Studies, respectively the European Society. I received a host of information during a series of interviews with the most influential trauma experts in the Netherlands, particularly Jos Weerts, Hans Hovens, Anton Hafkenscheid, Rolf Kleber, Peter van de Velden, Iris Engelhardt and Evert Bloemen.

Most of the historical material has been gathered during my earlier research into the history of the international trauma field in the past 150 years, accompanied by an intensive literature review. I am grateful to the staff of the library of the Radboud University in Nijmegen for their help in collecting the material. I discussed the early history with my son Erik who, being a classical scholar at the Institute of Ancient Studies in New York, made many resources on early and late antiquity available (he has specialized in the latter). He offered me also much insight in Byzantium, the realm of the Abbasids in Baghdad and the Carolingian Empire. Thanks also to my very dear friend Paul Wessing, a lawyer and an expert on the history of culture, with whom I had many long discussions. Thanks also to Willy Schaap who supported me with my translation into English.

Finally, thanks to my wife and my adult children Irene and Erik. In particular, the support of my wife, who combines empathy with Amsterdam level-headedness common sense, has made it possible to bring this work to fruition.

Endnotes

1. Sociologists use the concept regime in various fields, such as a medical or a pedagogical regime.
2. See: Book 6, Revelation of the New Testament.
3. The sociologist Johan Goudsblom speaks about an extending antroposphere (2003).
4. Sloterdijk (2013).
5. For example: Summerfield (2001).
6. Elias (2000, orig. 1939), part II: Design of a theory of civilization. See also Dunning & Mennell (eds.) (2003).
7. De Waal (2010).
8. About compartments of violence: De Swaan (2003, 2015); about humanitarian sensitivity: Haskell (1985); about the motive to help other people and the widening of circles of identification: De Swaan (1988, 1995).
9. Diamond (2011, orig. 2005) Introduction and chapter 14.
10. Elias (2000), vol. II, Design of a Theory of Civilization, part V.
11. Nussbaum (2004), Taylor (2007), Collins (1998).
12. There are historical and sociological studies on the worldwide web or world system and the rise of the West; about civilization processes, state formation and the development of welfare states, the emergence of the global system of language, the impact of epidemics in the history of mankind, the formation of networks and heydays of intellectual creativity. See for example: McNeill (1977); McNeill and McNeill (2003); De Swaan (1988, 2001); Abu Lughod (1989); Goudsblom (1992); Collins (1998); Wickham (2009); Rifkin (2009); Morris (2010); Ferguson (2011); Pinker (2012).
13. The term culture experts has been derived from the dissertation of Goudsblom Nihilism and Culture (1980), in which he explored the social origins of humanistic ideals.
14. The dynamics of professional networks: Heilbron (1995) about sociologists, Bourdieu (1984, 1988) about scientists and Collins (1998) about Philosophers.

15 Within the "sociology of disasters" one speaks of "social amplification of crises and disasters" (SACD). Quarantelli, Lagadec, Boin (2006), 33. Boin and 't Hart (2006), 42-55. In the transition to a service economy the emotional investment in the work increases, and hence vulnerability to stressful emotional confrontations. Weehuizen (2008).

16 See note 15.

17 About the vulnerable society: Beck (1992); De Vries (2002); Hermans (2010). About complex systems and interaction effects: OECD (2003), 34; Boin and 't Hart (2006), 42-55. About disasters: Barton (1969); Dynes (1988); Kreps (1989); Rodriguez, Quarantelli, Dynes (eds) (2006). Sociological classics on health care and psychiatry: Goffman (1961 and 1963); Scheff (1966); Freidson (1970); Zola, (1972). More generally: Szasz (1961); Starr (1982); Grob (1991); Healy (1997); Showalter (1998); Healy (2004); Horwitz, Wakefield (2007). A "sociology of suffering": Wilkinson (2005) and Sznaider (1996, 2001). In the transition to a service economy the emotional investment in the work increases, and hence vulnerability to stressful emotional confrontations: Weehuizen (2008). On indebtedness: Bernstein (2008), about the possibilities of artificial intelligence: Morris (2010).

18 See Richard Sennett: The Corrosion of Character (2000) and The Craftsman (2008).

19 About the emancipation of emotions which he calls in line of Norbert Elias a process of Informalization: Wouters (2008), especially the introduction.

20 These two paragraphs are based on Wil Roebroeks' Dies lecture (2004) at the University of Leiden. Large groups, he said, were much more efficient in hunting, but always have to spend much time on communication about each other's reputation. For a comparison of the two energy sources: Goudsblom (2012).

21 Goudsblom (1992), Fire and civilization. This section is largely based on that description. See also McNeill & McNeill (2003), Chapter 1. As in this book, they constantly focus on the expansion of human networks, the human web, as they call it.

22 Morris (2010).

23 Diamond (2013), 317-365.

24 Ó'Grada (2009), 108-128 about the demographic impact of famines.

25 Goudsblom (203), 34-42.

26 Taylor (2010), 861-870.
27 De Swaan (1988), Introduction.
28 Goudsblom (1992) chapter 2, (2003), 40.
29 Pinker (2011), 88-91.
30 Gosch en Stearns (2008), 21.
31 McNeill & McNeill (2003), 52 en 53.
32 Translated from a Dutch text: Veenhof (1974), 4-6.
33 Horden en Purcell (2000), 306.
34 Horden en Purcell (2000), hoofdstuk IX.
35 Horden en Purcell (2000), 447.
36 Pinker (2012), 944; McNeill & McNeill, (2003), 11 en 12.
37 Miles (2012), 51-56.
38 Miles (2012), 43-49, 73-79. In the fifth century BC Sierra Leone and Brittania were seized by Hanno and Himilco respectively. See: Gosch and Stearns in their fascinating Premodern Travel in World History (2008), 31. There are historians who claim that migration to the West was not caused by the Assyrians, but by better trade opportunities for the Phoenicians. See also: Morris (2010), 239-240.
39 Wickham (2009), 24.
40 Grosch en Stearns (2008), 48.
41 Wikipedia, crisis of the third century, (cons. 6/28, 2013).
42 Morris (2010), 289.
43 Rifkin (2009), chapter 6.
44 Chua (2007), 66-79, 83.
45 Pinker (2011), 457.
46 Pinker (2011), 38; Wickham (2009), 21/22.
47 De la Vassière, E. (2012) Central Asia and the Silk Road, in: Oxford Handbooks online.
48 Pulleyblank (1989, 2011), "An Hsi, in Iranian Encyclopaedia Iranica. See also Chinese-Iranian relations in pre-islamic times in the same encyclopedia, and Beckwith (2009).
49 Morris (2010), 273.
50 Abu Lughod (1989), 265.
51 Bernstein (2008), 135 and 136 on the spread by rats. He mentions the descriptions of Hippocrates, Thucydides and Procopius who do not disclose the nature of the disease.
52 Morris (2010), 296-297.
53 Morris (2010), 323, 326-329.
54 Niederer (1952), 285-293.

55 Morris (2010), 315-317, 347 en 352
56 Green (1992), 23. Gibbon, E. (1787), chapter 71, final conclusion. http://www.ccel.org/g/gibbon/decline/volume2/chap71.htm (cons. 6/14, 2014)
57 Thomas (2012, orig. 1971).
58 Paton (2009), chapter 1 and 2.
59 Taylor (2007), gives a detailed description of this worldview.
60 Ellenberger (1970) introduction.
61 Blok (2013), 118.
62 http://classics.mit.edu/Thucydides/pelopwar.html (cons, 6/17, 2014).
63 Nussbaum (2004), 350-351.
64 Morris (2010), 333, 334 and 337.
65 McNeill and McNeill (2003), 95; Chua (2007), 100-103 and 115; Chen da-Sheng (1991, 2011).
66 Tyrwhitt (1968), 30, 33, 37.
67 Collins (1998), 288-290, see also Cook (1972), especially 404-407 and Internet Encyclopaedia of Philosophy, Fa Tsang, (cons. 8/23, 2012) and Libbrecht (2003), 395-396.
68 Libbrecht (2003), 33-34.
69 De la Vassière (2012), 4.
70 De la Vaissière (2012), 5.
71 Shown by images in a house of a Sogdian nobleman, de la Vassière (2012), 5. Sogdians in the west traded with the Byzantines and opened a route for them out of the range of their enemies, the Persians.
72 According to the medical compendium of Ali ibn Raban al-Tabari, the plague came from Sudan. Following a comment by Ibn al-Nafis Ibn Sina Ethiopia was a major source (as with the plague in Athens according to Thucydides). Ibn Abi Hajalah made a report which with some modifications is included in the epilogue of a well-known compendium of Ibn Hajar al-Asqualami. Axis Suyuti made a short summary which is usually used by later writers in the West. See Dols (1979), 372.
73 Procopius, History of the Wars, parts of Chapters 22 and 23.
74 Morris (2010), 309.
75 Wickham (2009), 290-302.
76 Herrin (2007), 104 en 161-163; Roland (1992), Conclusion.
77 Browning (1964), 8-14 gives an older article a detailed overview of the quality of education and science in the Byzantine Empire;

Miller (1984) on the nature of the hospitals in the Byzantine Empire.
78 Kennedy (2008), 50, 65; Morris (2010), 412.
79 Alexander (2001), 46-50. The "frontier" for the slave trade was in the eighth century in East Africa, extending to the mouth of the Zambesi River; Bernstein (2008), 112-115; Obert Voll (1994, 218) speaks of a world system that was primarily held together by a common way of looking and thinking.
80 Bernstein (2008), 59, 60.
81 This was already described by the Roman Pliny. It took the Roman Empire a lot of silver. For a more detailed description: Bernstein (2008), Chapter 3: Camels, Perfumes, and Prophets.
82 Hoyland (2011); http://www.iranicaonline.org/articles/sogdiana-iii-history-and-archeology (cons. 8/8, 2013).
83 http://www.nlm.nih.gov/exhibition/islamic_medical/islamic_03.html, (cons. 8/22, 2012).
84 Gutas (1998) provides a thorough analysis of these motives in the first part of his wonderful work; Green (1988), 457 provides an overview of the development of libraries in the Arab world.
85 Wolfson (1976) gives a very thorough description of the philosophy of the Kalam in his great life's work. Collins (1998) describes the flow as a major breakthrough, not by imitation of the Greeks, but on their own.
86 See the detailed description of Michael Dols (1984). See the doubts regarding Gundashapur in a fascinating article by Peregrine Horden on the first hospitals in Byzantium, Western Europe and Islam. Hurdles (2005). See also: Imaduddin (1978), 48; Wael (2008).
87 Hamarneh (1974), 168. The degree of innovation is the subject of intense debate. See Wael (2008). The city of Cordoba became a haven for Jews when in 711 an Islamic regime was established there. In the tenth century, the court physician Albucasis (Abu al-Qasim) would write about surgery and hygiene. In Toledo, the vizier al-Lakhmi was an authority in the field of diet and medication, as well as elsewhere in Spain Edrisi and Ahmad al-Ghafiqi. In the twelfth century, Ibn Zur (Avenzoar) from Seville discovered that parasites were the cause of scabies. In the thirteenth century, Ibn al-Baytar wrote about 3,000 plants, many of which were not known in ancient times and all Nafis on circulation three centuries before the circulatory system was discovered in the West. His work was only discovered in the twentieth century. Hamarneh (1974), 173,

174, 182 and Encyclopaedia Britannica Ibn Al Nafis, (cons. 8/21, 2012).
88 Encyclopedia Britannica: Avicenna, Averroës en Moses Maimonides (cons. 9/2, 2013).
89 Wickham (2009), 378 a.n.
90 Bachrach (2002), 328 a.n., 348.
91 Wickham (2009), 384; On the content of the course: Rompf (1973), 24.
92 Bachrach (2002), 356.
93 McNeill and McNeill (2003), chapter 4.
94 Beaujard and Fee (2005), 412, 413, 421.
95 Abu Lughod (1989) wrote one of the classics about this period. The connections: 353.
96 Bernstein (2008), 78.
97 Mainly derived from Abu Lughod (1989), 176-178. About the size of the Islamic Empire:. Houben (2003), 153. See also: McNeill and McNeill (2003), 141-145.
98 Chua (2007), 127-129 and Iranian Encyclopaedia, Cengiz Kahn.
99 Chua (2007), 138. Nisapur 1.7 million, Herat 2 million see Iranian Encyclopaedia, Cengiz Kahn.
100 Abu Lughod (1989), 316. According to Landes (1998, chapter 4) and Morris (2010, 449), 125,000 ton of iron had been produced between 1050 and 1100.
101 Morris (2010), 453-463.
102 Ferguson (2011), 53-55.
103 Morris (2010), 486 en 503 e.v.
104 Abu Lughod (1989), 102-105.
105 Bernstein (2008), 111.
106 Day (1978), 6, 10 and 36.
107 Lucas (1930), 351 in an older overview article: Bailey (1998), 246; Clark (1987), 422, see also Kershaw (1973), 6-16 and Jordan (1996), 20, 23, 36/37.
108 Bernstein (2008), 139; Tuchman (1980), 119; Goudsblom (1987), 192.
109 Abu Lughod (1989), 125, 215, 238; Bernstein (2008), 147-149.
110 Thomas (1989, orig. 1971), 35-40.
111 Thomas (1989, orig. 1971), 49.
112 Taylor (2010), 116-119.
113 Taylor (2010), 120-130, 156/157.
114 De Swaan (1989), 31- 60.

115 McNeill (2004), 6.
116 Blaffer Hrdy (1999), 329.
117 Morris (2010), 370.
118 Collins (1998), 457.
119 Landes (1998), chapter 4.
120 Collins (1998), 461-462.
121 Collins (1998), 454
122 Rifkin (2009), 260.
123 McNeil and McNeill (2003), 166, 174-191.
124 Bernstein (2008), 164-167.
125 McNeil and McNeill (2003), 185.
126 McNeill and McNeill (2003), 221. Bernstein (2008): 11 million between 1519 and 1860.
127 Bernstein (2008), 167, 169-170, 184-187, 193. According to him, 25,000 European soldiers died of these diseases in the Royal Hospital in Goa in the seventeenth century.
128 Acemoglu, Johnson and Robinson (2005, 547) claim that here the foundation was laid for the future of Europe.
129 Morris (2010), 454.
130 According to Geoffrey Parker, in a review article on the crisis, Parker (2008), 2.
131 Parker (2008), 6; Morris (2010), 513-515.
132 Morris (2010), 451.
133 McNeill and McNeill (2003), 187.
134 Morris (2010), 539.
135 Atwell (1988), 321.
136 Atwell (2005) about the debate about the silver supply.
137 Lynn Struve gives a wonderful analysis of the document using the PTSD concept, tempered by D. Pillemer, in a special issue of the journal History and Memory on the use of psychological concepts in historical research. Struve (2004) and Pillemer (2004).
138 Struve (2004), 21.
139 De Vries, van der Woude (1995), 203 en 749.
140 De Vries, van der Woude (1995), 88.
141 De Vries, van der Woude (1995), 227, 320-356, 427-437, 470-473 and 831-832.
142 De Vries, van der Woude (1995), 500. The "mother trade": Goudsblom (1988), 53.

143 In 1625 7700 people worked in the Dutch East India Company, of which in Asia 4500 to 22,000 in 1688, of which 16,000 in Asia. De Vries, van der Woude (1995), 99, 503.
144 Goudsblom (1988), 37.
145 With 25 students in every thousand men: De Vries, van der Woude (1995), 212.
146 Wijsenbeek-Olthuis (1997), 71-86.
147 Osterhammel (2014), 122.
148 Thomas (1989, orig. 1971), ch. 1; Encyclopædia Britannica, 2005; Pinker (2011), 104.
149 Thomas (1989, orig. 1971), 15-20 en 20-29.
150 Thomas (1989, orig. 1971), 80-82.
151 Wikipedia Glorious Revolution, 2 juin, 2012.
152 Bernstein (2008), 248. The English shipping tonnage increased between 1675 and 1688 from 200,000 to 340,000 tons. Also: De Vries, van der Woude (1995), 479. About the benefits of maritime trade:. Acemoglu, Johnson and Robinson (2005), 563-566.
153 Bernstein (2008), 275.
154 Fletcher (1995), 286.
155 Elias (1982, 1), 240, 257-260, 269, 280.
156 Simissen (2003), 822-837.
157 Elias (1982, orig. 1939) part II, 280-302. An overview: Pinker (2011); Sznaider (1996).
158 Pinker (2011), 225.
159 Taylor (2010), 190-205.
160 McNeill and McNeill (2003), 193.
161 Collins (1998), 642- 644.
162 Morris (2010), and Osterhammel (2014, 643) point to other factors, such as a large area without barriers to rates, good supply lines, raw materials from the colonies, a well-functioning monetary system, a practical attitude of scientists with extensive knowledge about making tools, a productive agriculture so that labor was released for industry and cheap energy from coal.
163 Bernstein (2008), 263.
164 Osterhammel (2014), 122; Morris (2010), 5050-513.
165 Osterhammel (2010), part I and chapter 14.
166 Bernstein (2008), 329.
167 Brands (2010), 22 en 23; Wikipedia: Gilded Age, 16 july 2012.
168 Brands (2010), 22-30.
169 Osterhammel (2014), 334.

170 Osterhammel (2014), 135-156. Not included are the people who returned, sometimes a significant percentage.
171 Osterhammel (2014), 134-135.
172 Osterhammel (2014), 212.
173 Osterhammel (2014), 121.
174 Osterhammel (2014), 203.
175 Osterhammel (2014), 190-191.
176 Bernstein (2008), 359-360.
177 Osterhammel (2014), 197.
178 Franke (1990), 767.
179 Franke (1990), 124, 775, 778.
180 Pinker (2010), 580-623.
181 Costin, Karger, Stoesz (1996), 46. The organization consisted of prominent members of the New York community and was the initiative of the lawyer Gerry, the son of a vice president of the United States who had signed the Declaration of Independence yet.
182 Pinker (2010), 610.
183 Reil (1803), 473-478; Vijselaar (2001), 176, 177, 208; Ellenberger (1970), 211.
184 In 1910, there were 659 organizations in the United States, 247 of which were concerned also with child protection. Sznaider (1996), 340-342.
185 Elias (1982).
186 Rifkin (2009), 371.
187 Reiss, B. (2004) The Springfield somnambulist: or the end of the enlightment in America, www.common-place.org. (cons.: 11 januari 2007).
188 Dickens knew, and had demonstrated, that the giving up of secrets could be freeing. At the age of 32, he had met one Madame de la Rue, an English woman married to a Frenchman, who was beset by what we would recognize as obsessive-compulsive fears and anxieties. During the winter of 1844-45, Dickens repeatedly hypnotized the woman and encouraged her to relate her secrets. This amateur "treatment" was a success – not only did she begin to sleep more peacefully; the improvement lasted for years, and Dickens became obsessed by the efficacy of it. (http://books.rpmdp.com/archives/v01.n1928, cons. 2 jan. 2007).
189 About anesthesia: Gauld (1992), 223, 257. The statement Ellenberger (1970), 112.

190 Porter (2002), 39, 40-42.
191 Lutz (2000), 51-74.
192 Figes (2011), 34-37 en 43.
193 Figes (2011), 64-69. A Greek uprising in 1821 was brutally beaten by the Turks. On the island of Chios 20,000 Greeks were hanged and 70,000 people deported as slaves (painted by Delacroix).
194 Figes (2011), 18, 19, 334, 335 en 455.
195 Anderson (2010); Clarke (2007).
196 http://en.wikipedia.org/wiki/United_States_military_casualties_of_war, (cons. 4/10, 2012).
197 Encyclopedia Britannica: American Civil War en Battle of Gettysburg.
198 Mc Pherson (2008), 42-44.
199 Da Costa (1871).
200 Anderson (2010). Derived from Medical and Surgical History of the War of the Rebellion 1861-65 published by the Surgeon General's Office of the War Department.
201 Jones (2006), 536-539; Anderson (2010); Clarke (2007).
202 Osterhammel (2014) 199 The disasters in Japan in 1891 with 73,000 deaths and at Sumbawa in 1815 with 117,000 dead were larger but had less global impact.
203 Simmons, Biddle (eds.) (1997), 493.
204 Kostal (1994), 258, 259, 281. In the period 1843-1871 there were 1036 victims in train disasters, but 1389 in mining disasters. Among railway employees there were a lot of deaths and injuries in this period: 6200 deaths and between 20,000 and 60,000 wounded. See also Wilson (1909); Rolls (1982 orig. 1955). See also: Harrington (2001), 33, note 11.
205 George Hudson of the York and North Midland Railway Company spent several years in prison. Miller (2003), 55. Spencer (1868, 256) says: "(...) that the corruptions here glanced at are not merely exceptional evils, but result from some deep-seated vice ramifying throughout our system of railway-government (...)."
206 Simmons, Biddle (eds.) (1997), 300.
207 Kostal (1994), 282.
208 Erichsen described symptoms such as bursting into tears, getting excited, bad sleep. pallor, bad dreams and tinnitus, Schivelbusch (1986, orig. 1977), 140.
209 Fischer-Homberger (1975, 20) says: "Nevertheless, they clearly indicated how the new technological-industrial reality, so palpably

demonstrated in the railroad accident, gradually and in the face of much resistance infiltrated and ultimately transformed traditional medical thought."

210 Harrington (1999), 7; Caplan (1995), 396.
211 It fitted in with thinking about nervous irritation, a term which was just as popular in the nineteenth century as the term stress nowadays. See Ferrari, Shorter (2003).
212 For him, hypnosis was not a form of therapy, but a way to indicate hysteria, a degenerative disease. Hulspas (1999). According to Hulspas, Charcot went to work in the Salpêtrière in 1862 to prove his theory, because there were so many patients with "hystero-epileptic" symptoms, who stayed in one department.
213 Ellenberger (1970), 97 and 99. According to Ellenberger, also Westphal, the famous German neurologist, Bernheim in Nancy and Beard in New York criticized him.
214 Goetz, Bonduelle, Gelfant (1995), 245-252.
215 Lerner (2003), 27-28. The German psychiatrist Hermann Oppenheim and Max Nonne became interested in male hysteria through the agency of Charcot. Nonne visited Charcot in 1889 for six weeks, considered him too arrogant.
216 Ellenberger (1970), 93.
217 Herman (1993), 29.
218 Koehler (1995), 2177, 2178.
219 Koehler (1995), 2179. Micale (2001), 116, 117.
220 Oppenheim (1889) gives a detailed description of a large number of cases.
221 Lerner (2003), 37 and 38, see Lerner (2003) on the fall of Oppenheim.
222 Brinkgreve (2008), 103.
223 Panhuysen (1990), 112; Brinkgreve (2008), 102.
224 Schaffner (2001), 86; Gabbard (1997), 3-6.
225 De Swaan (1982, orig. 1977), 302-313.
226 De Swaan (1982, orig. 1977), 302, 308 and 313; Gabbard (1997).
227 Gomperts (2000), 348, 350, 353-358.
228 Van der Kolk, Weisaeth, McFarlane (1996), 52 and 53.
229 Young (1995); Ellenberger (1970).
230 Young (1995); Ellenberger (1970); Van der Kolk, Van der Hart (1991), 1.
231 Van der Kolk, Weisaeth, McFarlane (1996), 52; Van der Hart, Friedman (1989), 3. Ellenberger (1970, 407, 409) says: "Pierre

Janet is a remarkable example of the way in which fame and oblivion are unequally distributed among scientists (...) it is as if he slowly slipped aside from the general current (...) Thus Janet's work can be compared to a vast city buried beneath ashes, like Pompeii (...)."

232 The French had eight million people in the army on a population of forty million. They suffered half a million deaths and two million disabled people. In Germany 35% of the boys between 19 and 22 died in the war. Van Bergen (2001), 98, 99, 330.

233 Binnenveld & Binnenveld (1997), 34-42; Leed (1979) 181, cited in Van der Hart (2000); Van Bergen (2001), 222; Babington (1997) 10.

234 Van Bergen (2001), 33-35, 46-48, ch. 2; 117-129, 278, 398; Binnenveld & Binnenveld (1997), 27, 46; Rouzeau, Becker (2004), 33-35 en 46-48; Van Eecke (2007), 423-432.

235 Binnenveld (1995), 9, 21 and 29 in the Second World War desertion was easier, because soldiers were not trapped in trenches, but the maximum was 63 per 1,000 in the Vietnam War, desertion was a lot more difficult and it fluctuated between 29.1 per 1000 in 1968 and a peak of 73.4 in 1971. Shay (1994), 213.

236 Babington (1997) 54, 109 See also Shephard (2000), 89, 158. Between April 1915 and April 1916 1300 officers and 10,000 soldiers were sent to England. Babington (1997), 81; van Bergen (2001), 218, 219.

237 Babington (1997), Chapter 1 and 92-94. According to Babington, it was a total of 346 executions.

238 Binnenveld & Binnenveld (1997), 49.

239 Winter (2000) speaks of: "a kind of English genius of linguistic compression, in which a host of allusions are fused in two simple vertical syllables".

240 Young (1995), 60, Showalter (1985), 168; Babington (1997), 81; Shephard (2000), 47.

241 Van der Hart (2000), 41.

242 Pat Barker wrote a trilogy about the fate of British officers with "shell shock": Regeneration (1990), The Eye in the Door (1993) and The Ghost Road (1995).

243 Marlowe (2000), hoofdstuk 5.

244 Merridale (2000), 39-55.

245 Hale (1995), 16; Artiss (1963).

246 Salmon (1917); Ozarin (2002).

247 Babington (1997), 91-92 en Hale (1995), 17.
248 The historian Bodnar (2000), 959 points this out in a "review" of a contribution from Nora, Combs and Giddens.
249 Bodnar (2000), 959-960.
250 Eyerman (2004), 160.
251 Véray (2010), 417, 421.
252 Simissen (2006), 891.
253 Geurst (2010), 13, 14, 41 describes the many sides of the design process, accompanied with beautiful pictures.
254 About "punctum": Palmer, Minogue (2010), 168, referring to Roland Barthes.
255 Bogacz (1986, 645) provides a good overview of the literature of World War I.
256 This designation of Norris is mentioned in a review of Heather Lusty (2008, 149) about the book by Norris, Writing War in the Twentieth Century.
257 Lusty (2006, 201-204) points to this in a review on some of the reviews about this literature. About the poems of amateurs, see Bogacz (1986), 647. The pomposity is explained by the function poetry had in English education with an emphasis on Romanticism, the classics and religion.
258 Palmer, Minogue (2010), 164.
259 Lunn (2005), 722-725 makes a detailed comparison between the two writers.
260 Lunn (2005), 726.
261 Roudebush (2001).
262 Winter describes this insistent in his masterpiece: Sites of Memory, Sites of Mourning (1995).
263 Cox (2001), 281-284, 291.
264 Arthur Schlesinger Jr. spoke of a land of "joiners": "one of the strongest taproots of the nation's well-being." Schlesinger (1944), 1-25.
265 The material on the Legion and GAR is mainly taken from Pencak (1989), 26-30 and 43. The figures for the losses vary considerably. The Encyclopedia Britannica provides this figure, others speak of 114,000 deaths.
266 The organization also helped veterans who were not members (Pencak, 1989). It was successful in its fight for compensation – the so-called bonus – for veterans in 1924. During the Depression in the thirties, violent protests against proposals to abolish the

bonus ended in riots. It would only strengthen the organization in its mission. Ross (1969), 7-18. About shell shock: Pencak (1989), 170-208, on the number of beds, 187.
267 Pencak (1989), 176; Ross (1969), 24, 25.
268 They would settle in centers such as the Menninger Clinic in Topeka, Kansas, Chestnut Lodge in Rockville, Maryland, Sheppard-Pratt in Baltimore, Maryland and Saint Elizabeth's in Washington DC. Friedman (1990), 110-111.
269 About the numbers Crocq, Crocq (2000), 54; see also: Shephard (2000), 150; Young (1995), 89.
270 Kardiner (1941). His anthropological work was The Individual and His Society: the psychodynamics of primitive social organization (1939).
271 Hale (1995), chapter 7; about psychology: Capshew (1999), 30.
272 Yerkes brought his experience of the First World War and his contacts with the National Resource Council in Washington, where he had continued to work for several years after the war, before returning to the academic world. Blocher (2000), 93, 94.
273 Grob (1991, 3 and 4) provides a thorough overview of this development.
274 Schwartz (1996).
275 Schwartz (1996), 909-923. The description of three approaches of collective remembering is taken from his article. The first author to point to the construction of the past and to use the term collective memory, was Maurice Halbwachs in an article titled Social Frameworks of Memory from 1925, see Olick & Robbins (1998). Both authors point to several sociologists, anthropologists and psychologists in the twenties, thirties and forties who paid attention to the social context of remembering. The big boom came with the fall of communism, the rise of multiculturalism and the politics of victimization and mourning in the eighties. Other factors were the focus of the political elites on recalling their purposes to deploy and marginalizing the memories of other groups, the focus of Bourdieu and others on cultural practices and the emergence of theories of social construction.
276 Schwartz (1996), 921-923.
277 For the explanation of the persecution by the Nazi regime Norbert Elias (2003) has highlighted the special position of Germany – sandwiched between other nations and vulnerable to raids – the exceptional progress of the German process of state formation and

the position of the bourgeoisie with little access to the elite with a strong military tradition and unrealistic beliefs about the founding of a large empire in Europe.

278 In the American Civil War 620,000 people were killed in a much smaller population. McPherson (2008), 44. and: Wikipedia, casualties in World War II, consulted, November 2, 2008.

279 O'Grada (2009), 236-241. Further refinement: Ellman (2007).

280 The Medical Department of the United States Army in the World War, (1929) ch. 10 about neuropsychiatry in the "American Expeditionary Forces"; Menninger (1948), 267.

281 Herman (1995) speaks of 2.5 million, Friedman (1990, 168) of 1.1 to 1.8 million. Logistical problems frustrated Sullivan, who resigned in 1942. Of a group of 2054 rejected soldiers who were still deployed later, 18% was sent away in the end and the rest continued to function properly. A group of 316 soldiers who were previously treated for mental health problems at the front and then returned and monitored, functioned properly afterwards. Jones, Wessely (2005), 107-114.

282 For example: Psychology for the fighting man (400.000 copies edited) and "twelve rules on meeting battle fear". Herman (1995), 102.

283 Perkins (1955), 175.

284 Among them: Paul Lazarsfeld, John Dollard, Carl Howland, Hadley Cantril, Frank Stanton and Nathan Maccoby: Herman (1995), 67.

285 Stouffer c.s. (1949) is the most cited study about the American Army and the behavior and motivation of the soldiers. See also: Herman (1995), 67-70.

286 Shephard (2000), 235, 237, 243.

287 Hale (1995), 278; Binnenveld & Binnenveld (1997), 181.

288 Menninger (1948), 12-13, 26-27, 32, 38, 40.

289 Grinker, Spiegel (1945, 1), vii. Better known is Men under stress from the same year, which contains almost the same data. Grinker, Spiegel (1945, 2). About the traumatic consequences: "The holocaust of battle exposes the primitive forces within every man's personality and permits detailed studies to be made of his ego reactions in various stages of dissolution and repair (...) Therefore such observations are not limited in value to wartime psychiatry alone, but furnish experimental data for understanding of anxieties from the stresses of civilian life." Grinker, Spiegel (1945, 1), vii, viii.

290 Developed by the company Eli Lilly in Indianapolis in 1929. Amobarbital is mainly used now as a sleep aid. William Sargant used it at the crisis center for civilians during the bombing of England, more for the soothing than for the psychedelic effect. By 1942 he had treated 3,000 patients in England. Shephard (2000), 207, 209; Binnenveld & Binnenveld (1997), 121.
291 Snelders (1999), 21-23.
292 They made a further distinction between extreme anxiety, depression, somatic regression, psychosomatic reactions, conversion symptoms, exhaustion and psychotic states. Grinker, Spiegel (1945, 1), 115.
293 Grinker, Spiegel (1945, 1), 69. In 1969 Richard Lazarus said about the work of Grinker and Spiegel: "The title of their book helped establish the term "stress", although their proposed specific mechanisms for battle fatigue emphasized the terminology of anxiety, threat, and defense (Lazarus, 1966). Van der Kolk also indicates the important influence of Grinker and Spiegel on postwar thinking: Van der Kolk, McFarlane, Weisaeth (1996), 59.
294 Elias (2003), 408. See also: Durst (2000); Solomon (1995).
295 Withuis (2010), 288-302.
296 Cohen (1952), chapter 1 and 3. A theoretical perspective: Goffman (1961).
297 Cohen (1952), 22 en 67-83.
298 Kaas (1946), 409-422; Kaas (1968), 138 and chapter 1.
299 Vogelaar (2006), 44, 45, 50-53 and 61. According to Jacq Vogelaar, the question is if the experiences described can be explained psychologically or that they are physiological sketches or ethnographic reports: a report of man at his wits' end. Perhaps these experiences can be made visible only by using literary means, not by naming them, but by showing them. See also Vogelaar (2006, 2).
300 Saito (2006), 353-376.
301 Based on the first publication of his research: Lifton (1963).
302 Herman (1995), 248. 242-244, 248; Shephard (2000), 330.
303 Hale (1995), Chapters 14 and 212; Plant (2005), 2: www.historyweb.ucsd.edu, 1-22. (cons. 10/12, 2007).
304 Friedman (1990), 119-120. Will had a conflicted relationship with his older brother. Will died in 1966 at the age of 67, Karl died in 1990 at the age of 96. Friedman (1990) Chapter 6, 7 and 9 and www.menninger.edu, (cons. 1/20, 2008).

305 Lindemann (1944), 141-148. Trauma and stress: Binnenveld & Binnenveld (1997), 98; Selye (1950). See also www.nlm.nih.gov/hmd/emotions/stress.html Slater (cons. 10/3, 2006), Slater (1965), 1399 and Shephard (2000), 332-337.
306 Bauer (1996), 15.
307 Novick (1999).
308 Felman (2000), 103-150.
309 Robbins (1987), 249.
310 Robbins (1987), 251.
311 Davoliute (2005), 1.; Boym (2008), 342-363.
312 Davoliute (2005), 7.
313 Vogelaar (2006), 31-33.
314 Vogelaar (2006), 36.
315 Vogelaar (2006), 39.
316 Bourguignon (2005), 66-69.
317 De Swaan (2007, orig. 2003), 104, 107.
318 De Swaan (2007, orig. 2003), 112.
319 De Swaan (1999), 297; de Swaan (2000).
320 Gomperts (2000), 349-363.
321 Zwaan (2001).
322 Zwaan (2001), 347-349.
323 De Laender (1996), 46 e.v.
324 Lifton (2001), 30.
325 The sociologist Cas Wouters (1990, 227) speaks about an emancipation of emotions.
326 De Swaan, A. (1989), 228-236.
327 Goffman (1961), 23-33.
328 Blok (2004), 139.
329 Pfohl (1977).
330 Dijkstra (2000), 269. The prevalence of severe physical abuse of girls is estimated at 10%. Retrospective prevalence estimates of sexual abuse range from 12 to 33% among adult women and from 10 to 55% among inpatients. Draijer (1999), 153.
331 Komen (1999), 89 en 100-102.
332 Krystal (1968); Krystal en Niederland (1968). About the congress: Bohleber (2002).
333 Herman (1993).
334 Vasterman (2004).
335 Van den Bogaard (1992), 101, 123, 127.
336 Bourguignon (2005), 66-69.

337 Keilson (1979).
338 Trimble (1984, orig. 1981); Beall (1997).
339 Andreasen, who with Spitzer ensured that the concept was included in the DSM III, wrote in a memoir that PTSD is a complex concept. "The DSM-III formulation emphasized that the stressor should be significant – outside the range of normal human experience. It assumed, but did not explicitly state, that there would be a temporally close juxtaposition between the stressor and the development of symptoms" (...) In fact, that stringent requirement was dropped in DSM-III-R and DSM-IV, providing a much broader concept than was originally intended. (In my view, this broadening should be reconsidered. Giving the same diagnosis to death camp survivors and someone who has been in a motor vehicle accident diminishes the magnitude of the stressor and the significance of PTSD)." Andreasen (2004), 1322.
340 Binnenveld (1995), 226, 227.
341 Binnenveld (1995), 230.
342 See the fascinating description of Lifton in his Home from the War (1973).
343 Shephard (2000), 356-357; Scott (1990), 300, 301.
344 Binnenveld (1995), 229.
345 To justify a separate diagnosis more proof was needed, which Shatan gathered in a working group, which also consisted of experts who had experience with other shocking events. For the model, see Horowitz (1976).
346 Young (1995), 140.
347 Binnenveld (1995), 233; Young (1995), 109-114.
348 Brett (1996), 117-128.
349 Allan (2002), 108. Overviews: Trimble (1984, orig. 1981); Herman (1993); Healy (1993); Van der Kolk, Mc Farlane, Weisaeth (1996); Binnenveld & Binnenveld (1997); More critical: Young (1995); Dean (1997); Shephard (2000).
350 Brewin (2001), 9; Van der Kolk (1996), 419.
351 Smith (2004), 629. Citaat: Smith (2004), 619. Also see Herman (1993), chapter 2 and de Swaan (1982, 1), 140-150. "Therapy is just another way of creating synaptic potentiation in brain pathways that control the amygdale." Le Doux, cited in Smith (2004), 620.
352 Rorty (1992), 223; Janoff-Bulman (1992).
353 Gomperts (2007).
354 Herman (1993), 129-152.

355 Healy (1997), 108.
356 Shay (1994).
357 Collins (1989), 366, 372-375
358 Healy (1997).
359 See for the term regime the introduction to this book. The examples in this section are taken from previous chapters of this book.
360 Goffman (1961) and (1963).
361 Rifkin (2009) gives a detailed description in chapter 14.
362 The National Comorbidity Study was the first large-scale survey in the USA of the mental health of the population as a whole, based on criteria of the DSM III-R. See Kessler, Sonnega, Bromet (1995) and Kessler, Chiu, Demler, Walters (2005). The National Vietnam Readjustment Study was held with the aim of getting an accurate picture of the prevalence of PTSD and other psychological problems in Vietnam veterans. Use was made of several methods, including clinical interviews and self-reports. Kulka, Schlenger, Fairbank (1990).
363 Norris and Slone (2013), 2, 3. Also: Davidson, Stein, Shalev, Yehuda (2004), 137, 138.
364 Site of the NIMH, accessed, January 4, 2008.
365 Verheule, C., study WSNS 3504, 2013.
366 Weehuizen (2008).
367 Bessel van der Kolk (2014).
368 Lifton (1973), 77: Young (1995), 142. Scott (1990), 294-310.
369 In his last book The body keeps the score (2014) Bessel van der Kolk pays special attention to this aspect in his epilogue.
370 The American trauma expert Sandra Bloom speaks of the establishment of a culture of trauma "Within all which it is understood that must behavioral pathology is related to overwhelming experiences or exposure to abusive power, disabling losses and disrupted attachment." Bloom (1997), Chapter 1.
371 In a well-known study of Bagley and McDonald (1984), in which twenty women were surveyed who had been placed in care for sexual abuse, three of them could not remember this abuse. Williams (1994) detected 66% of the girls in the period 1973-1975 who were examined for sexual abuse in a hospital. 38% did not report the original incident (because they did not want to tell or could not remember). Van der Kolk and Kadish (1987) describe the case history of a 55-year-old woman and her treatment. She was a survivor of a major fire, without remembering it.

372 Prager (1998), chapter 1.
373 Oliver (2002).
374 Lembcke (1998), 188.
375 Young (1995), chapter 4.
376 Healy (1993, 1997).
377 De Swaan (1982, 2 en 3).
378 De Swaan (1982, 1), 140-150.
379 Kleinman (1997) "Everything that really matters", Social Suffering, Subjectivity, and the Remaking of Human Experience in a Disordering World.
380 Taylor (2010), 875.
381 Schagen (1994), ch. 2. Drop out: Schottenbauer, Glass, Arnkoff, Tendick, Gray (2008).
382 Schagen (1994), chapter 3 and 5.
383 Herman (1993).
384 Pinker (2010), 618-623.
385 Boutellier (1993).
386 Morris (2008).
387 Sloterdijk (2010).

Literature

Acemoglu, D., Johnson, S. & Robinson, J. (2005) The Rise of Europe: Atlantic Trade, Institutional Change and Economic Growth, in: *American Economic Review*, 95, 3, pp. 546-579.

Alexander, J. (2001) Islam, Archaeology and Slavery in Africa, in: *World Archaeology*, vol. 3, no. 1, pp. 44-60.

Allen, J.G. (2001) *Traumatic relationships and serious mental disorders*, Chichester: John Wiley & Sons.

Anderson, D. (2010) Dying of Nostalgia: homesickness in the Civil War, in: *Civil War History*, vol. LXVI, 3, pp. 247-282.

Andreasen, N.C. (2004) Acute and Delayed Posttraumatic Stress Disorders, in: *American Journal of Psychiatry*, 161, 8, pp. 1321-1323.

Artiss, K. (1963) Human behavior under stress: from combat to social psychiatry, in: *Mil. Med.*, 128, pp. 1011-15.

Atwell, W.S. (1988) Ming Observers of Ming Decline: Some Chinese views of the "Seventeenth-Century Crisis" in Comparative Perspective, in: *The Journal of the Royal Asiatic Society of Great Britain and Ireland*, no. 2, pp. 316-348.

Atwell, W.S. (2005) Another look at the silver imports into China, in: *Journal of World History*, vol. 16, no. 4, pp. 467-489.

Audoine-Rouzeau, S. en Becker, A. (2003) *14-18, Understanding the Great War,* New York: Hill & Wang.

Babington, A. (1997) *Shell shock. A history of the changing attitudes to war neurosis*, London: Leo Cooper.

Bachrach, B. (2002) Charlemagne and the Carolingian General Staff, in: *Journal of Military History*, vol. 66, no. 2, pp. 313-357.

Bailey, M. (1998) Peasant Welfare in England 1290-1348, in: *Economic History Review*, vol. 51, no. 2, pp. 223-251.

Barnouw, D. (2001), The Certainties of Evil: Memory Discourse of the Holocaust. Review of The Holocaust in American Life by Peter Novick, in: *Monatshefte*, vol. 93, no. 1, pp. 98-111.

Barton, A.H. (1969) *Communities in disaster. A sociological analysis of collective stress situations,* New York: Doubleday.

Bauer, Y. (1996) The Impact of the Holocaust, in: *Annals of the Academy of Political and Social Science*, vol. 548, pp. 14-22.

Beall, L. (1997) "Post-Traumatic Stress Disorder", in: *Choice*, 34, pp. 917-930.

Beaujard, P., Fee, S. (2005), The Indian Ocean in Eurasian and African World Systems before the Sixteenth Century, in: *Journal of World History*, vol. 16, no. 4, p. 411-465.

Beck, U. (1992) Risk Society: Towards a new modernity, London: Sage.

Beckwith, C.L. (2009), *Empires of the Silk Road: A History of Central Eurasia from the Bronze Age to the Present*. Princeton: Princeton University Press.

Bentall, R.P. (2006), The environment and psychosis: Rethinking the evidence, in: Larkin, W. and Morrison, A. (red.), *Trauma and psychosis*, London/New York, Routledge, pp. 8-22.

Van Bergen, L. (2009), *Before my helpless sight. Suffering, dying and military medicine on the western front 1914-1918*, Ashgate: Franham: Surrey and Burlington.

Bernstein, W.J. (2008) *A splendid exchange, How trade shaped the World*, New York: Grove.

Binnenveld, J. en Binnenveld, H. (1997) *From Shell Shock to Combat Stress,* Amsterdam: Amsterdam University Press.

Blaffer Hrdy, S. (2000) *Mother nature. Maternal instincts and how they shape the human species*, New York: Ballantine Books.

Blazer (2005) *The age of melancholy. Major depression and its social origins*, New York: Routledge.

Blocher, D.H. (2000) *The evolution of clinical psychology*, New York: Springer.

Blok, A. (2013), De vernieuwers. De zegeningen van tegenslag in wetenschap en kunst 1500-2000, Amsterdam, Prometheus-Bert Bakker. (The innovators. The blessings of adversity in science and the arts 1500-2000, Amsterdam, Prometheus-Bert Bakker).

Bloom, S.L. (1997*) Creating sanctuary, Toward the evolution of sane societies*, New York: Routledge.

Bodkin, J.A., Pope, H.G., Detke, M. en Hudson, J.I. (2007) Is PTSD caused by traumatic stress?, in: *Journal of anxiety disorders*, 21, pp. 176-182.

Bodnar, J. (2000), Pierre Nora, National Memory and Democracy: A Review, in: *Journal of Contemporary History*, vol. 87, nr. 3, pp. 951-963.

Bogacz, T. (1986), "A Tyranny of words": Language, Poetry and Antimodernism in the First World War, in: *The Journal of Modern History*, vol. 58, no. 3, pp. 643-668.

Bohleber, W. (2002) The development of trauma in psychoanalysis, in: Varvin, S. en Popovic, T. (2002) *Upheaval: Psychoanalytical perspectives on Trauma*, Belgrado, International Aid Network, pp. 207-235.

Boin, A en 't Hart, P. (2006) The crisis approach, in: Rodriguez, R. Quarantelli, E. en Dynes, R. (eds) *Handbook of disaster research*, New York, Springer, pp. 42-55.

Bourdieu, P. (1988) *Homo Academicus*, Cambridge: Polity Press.

Bourdieu, P. (1984) *Distinction. A social criticism of the judgement of taste*, Cambridge: Harvard University Press.

Bourguignon, E. (2005) Bringing the Past into the Present: Family Narratives of Holocaust, Exile and Diaspora: Memory in an Amnestic World: Holocaust, Diaspora and Exile, and the Return of the Suppressed., in: *Antropological Quarterly*, vol. 78, no. 1, pp. 63-88.

Boutellier, J. and Boutellier, H. (2000) *Crime and Morality: The significance of criminal justice in Post Modern Culture*, New York: Springer.

Boutellier, H. (2002) *The Safety Utopia: Contemporary discontent and desire as to crime and punishment*, Deventer: Kluwer Academic Publishers.

Bowlby, J. (1969) *Attachment and Loss, volume 1: Attachment*, New York: Basic Books.

Bowlby, J. (1973) *Attachment and Loss, volume 2: Separation: Anxiety and anger*, New York: Basic Books.

Bowlby (1980) *Attachment and Loss, volume 3: Loss: sadness and depression*, New York: Basic Books.

Boym, S. (2008), Mimicry and the Soviet Subject: Varlam Shalamov and Hannah Ahrendt, in: *Slavic Review*, vol. 67, no. 2, pp. 342-363.

Branch, T. (2007) Justice for Warriors, in: *New York Review of Books*, 12 april, pp. 40-43.

Brands, H.W. (2010) *American Colossus. The Triumph of Capitalism, 1865-1900*, New York: Anchor Books.

Brett, E. (1996) "The classification of Posttraumatic Stress Disorder", in: Van der Kolk, B.A., McFarlane, A.C., Weisaeth, L. (eds.)., *Traumatic stress. The effects of overwhelming experience on mind, body and society*, New York/London: The Guilford Press, pp. 117-128.

Brewin, C. R. (2001) Cognitive and emotional reactions to traumatic events: implications for short-term intervention. In: *Advances in Mind-Body Medicine*, 17, pp. 163-168.

Brinkgreve, C., Onland, J.H., de Swaan, A. (1979) *Sociologie van de psychotherapie 1. De opkomst van het psychotherapeutisch bedrijf*, Utrecht/Antwerpen, het Spectrum.

Brinkgreve, C. (2008) Cultuur en hysterie. Sociologische beschouwingen, in: Dirkx, J. en Heuves, W. (red.), *Hysterie. Psycho-analytische beschouwingen*, Amsterdam, Boom, 103.

Browning, R. (1964), Byzantine Scholarship, in: *Past and Present*, no. 28, juli, 3-20.

Cannon, W.B. (1914) The interrelations of emotions as suggested by recent physiological research, in: *American Journal of Psychiatry*, 25, pp. 256-281.

Cannon, W.B. (1915) *Bodily Changes in Pain, Hunger, Fear and Rage: An Account of Recent Researches into the Function of Emotional Excitement*, New York: Appleton.

Caplan, E. (1995) Trains, Brains and Sprains: Railway Spine and the origins of psychoneuroses, in: *Bulletin History of Medicine*, 69, pp. 387-419.

Capshew, J. (1999) *Psychologists on the march*, Cambridge: Cambridge University press.

Chen da-Sheng (1991, 2011) Persian Settlements in Southeastern China during the T'ang, Sung, and Yuan Dynasties, in: *Encyclopaedia Iranica*.

Chua, A. (2007) *Day of Empire: How Hyperpowers rise to global dominance – and why they fall*, New York: Knopf Doubleday Publishing Group.

Clark, G. (1987) Productivity Growth without Technical Change in European Agriculture before 1850, in: *The Journal of Economic History*, vol. 47, no. 2, pp. 419-432.

Clarke, F. (2007), So lonesome I could die. Nostalgia and debates over emotional control in the Civil War, in: *Journal of Social History*, 41, pp. 253-282.

Collins, R. (1989) Sociological theory, Disaster Research, and War, in: Kreps, G. (eds) *Social Structure and Disaster*, Cranbury, Associated University Press, pp. 365-386.

Collins, R. (1998) *The Sociology of Philosophies. A global theory of intellectual change*, Cambridge and London: The Belknap Press of Harvard University Press.

Cook, F.H. (1972) The meaning of Vairocana in Hua-Yen Buddhism, in: *Philosophy East and West*, vol. 22, no. 4, pp. 403-415.

da Costa, J. M. (1871) On irritable heart, a clinical study of a form of functional cardiac disorder and its consequences, in: *The American Journal of the Medical Sciences*, 61, pp. 18-52.

Costin, L., Karger, H. J. en Stoesz, D. (1996) *The politics of child abuse in America*, New York/Oxford: Oxford University Press.

Cox, C. (2001) Invisible Wounds: The American Legion, Shell-Shocked Veterans, and American Society, 1919-1924 in: Micale, M.S., Lerner, P. (eds.) *Traumatic Pasts. History, Psychiatry, and Trauma in the Modern Age, 1870-1930*, New York: Cambridge University Press, chapter 13.

Crews, F.C. (2007) Talking back to prozac, in: *New York Review of Books*, 54, 19, p. 6.

Christian, D. (2000) Silk roads or steppe roads? The silk roads in World History: in *Journal of World History*, vol. 11, no. 1, pp. 1-26.

Crocq, M.A. en Crocq, L. (2000) From shell shock and war neurosis to posttraumatic stress disorder: a history of psychotraumatology, in: *Dialogues in clinical neuroscience*, 2, 1, pp. 47-57.

Davidson, R., Stein, D., Shalev, A., Yehuda, R., (2004) Posttraumatic Stress Disorder: Acquisition, Recognition, Course and Treatment, in: *Journal of Neuropsychiatry and Clinical Neurosciences*, 66, 135-147.

Davoliute, V. (2005), Shalomov's Memory, in: *Canadian Slavonic Papers, Revue Canadienne des Slavistes*, vol. 47, no. 1 en 2, pp. 1-21.

Day, J. (1978) The great Bullion Famine of the Fifteenth Century, in: *Past and Present*, no. 79, 3-54.

Dean, E.T. Jr. (1997) *Shook over Hell*, Cambridge, Harvard University Press.

Dennis, G.T (2001) Death in Byzantium, in: *Dumbarton Oak Papers*, vol. 55, pp. 1-7.

Diamond, J. (2011, orig. 2005) *Collapse: How societies choose to fail or succeed*, London: Penguin.

Diamond, J. (2012) *The World until yesterday: What can we learn from traditional societies*, New York: Viking Adult.

Dols M. (1974), Plague in Early Islamic History, in: *Journal of Oriental Society*, vol. 94, no. 3, pp. 371-383.

Dols, M. (1984) Insanity in Byzantine and Islamic Medicine, in: *Dumbarton Oaks Papers, Symposium on Byzantine Medicine*, vol. 38, pp. 135-148.

Dunning, E. and Mennell, S.(eds.) (2003) *Norbert Elias* (Four Volumes), London: Sage.

Drinka, G.F. (1984) *The birth of neurosis, myth, malady, and the Victorians*, New York: Simon and Schuster.

Dunning, E. & Mennell, S.(eds.) (2003) *Norbert Elias*, 4 volumes, London: Sage.

Van Dijk, J.J.M. (1997) Het victimologisch perspectief in verleden, heden en toekomst, in: *Tijdschrift voor Criminologie*, 4, 292-310.

Van Dijk, J.J.M. (2006) *Het abelsteken; over de sociale etikettering van slachtoffers van misdrijven*, oratie 24 november.

Dynes, R.R. (1988) Cross cultural international research: sociology and disaster, in: *International Journal of Mass Emergencies and Disasters*, 6, 2, pp. 101-129.

Elias, N. (1984) *What is sociology*, New York: Columbia University Press.

Elias, N. (2000) *The Process of Civilization: Sociogenic and Psychogenetic investigations*, Oxford: Blackwell.

Elias, N. (1996) *The Germans, Power Struggles and the Development of Habitus in the Nineteenth and Twentieth Centuries*, Cambridge: Polity Press.

Ellenberger, H. (1970) *The Discovery of the Unconsciousness. The history and evolution of dynamic psychiatry*, Allen Lane: The Penguin Press.

Ellman, M. (2007) Discussion article. Stalin and the Soviet Famine of 1932-1933 Revisited, in: *Europe-Asia Studies*, vol. 59, no. 4, pp. 663-693.

Van Emmerik, A.A.P. (2005) *Prevention and treatment of chronic posttraumatic stress disorder*, Amsterdam, dissertation University of Amsterdam.

Eyerman, R. (2004), The past and the present: culture and the transmission of memory, in: *Acta Sociologica*, vol. 47, no. 2, pp. 159-169.

Felman, S. (2000) In an Era of Testimony: Claude Lanzmann's Shoah, in: *Yale French Studies*, no. 97, pp. 103-150.

Ferguson, N. (2011) *Civilization: the West and the Rest*, London: Penguin.

Ferrari, R. en Shorter, E. (2003) From railway spine to whiplash – the recycling of nervous irritation, in: *Medical Science Monitor*, 9, 11, pp. 27-37.

Figes, O. (2011) *The Crimean War, a History*, New York: Henry Holt and Company.

Finkelstein, N. (2003) *The Holocaust Industry: Reflections on the Exploitation of Jewish Suffering*, New York: Verso.

Fitzgerald (1985), *China: a short cultural history*, Boulder: Westview Press.

Fletcher, J. (1995) Toward a theory of decivilizing processes, in: *Amsterdams Sociologisch Tijdschrift*, 22, 2, pp. 283-296.

Franke, H. (1995) *The emancipation of prisoners, a social-historical analysis of the Dutch prison experience*, Edinburgh: Edinburgh University Press.

Freedman, A.H., Kaplan, H.I., Sadock, B.J. (1976) *Comprehensive textbook of psychiatry*, Baltimore: Williams&Wilkins.

Freidson, E. (1970) *Professions of medicine. A study of the sociology of applied knowledge*, New York: Harper&Row.

Freud, S. (1896). The aetiology of hysteria, *Standard Edition*, vol. 3, pp. 191-221.

Friedman, L. (1990) *Menninger. The Family & the Clinic*, New York: Knopf.

Furedi, F. (2002) Culture of fear, London: Continuum International Publishing Group.

Gabbard, G.O. (1997) Challenges in the analysis of adult persons with histories of child sexual abuse, in: *Canadian Journal of Psychoanalysis*, 5, pp. 1-25.

Gauld, A. (1992) *A History of Hypnotism*, Cambridge: Cambridge University Press.

Goetz, C.G., Bonduelle, M. en Gelfand, T. (1995) *Charcot: constructing neurology*, Oxford: Oxford University Press.

Goffman, E. (1961) *Asylums. Essays on the Mental Patients and Other Inmates*, New York: Doubleday.

Goffman, E. (1963) *Stigma. Notes on the management of spoiled identity*, Englewood Cliffs: Prentice Hall Inc.

Gosch, S. en Stearns P. (2008) *Premodern Travel in World History*, New York en Londen: Routledge.

Goudsblom, J. (1967) *Dutch Society*, New York: Random House.

Goudsblom (1992) *Fire and Civilization*, London: Penguin.

Goudsblom, J., Jones, E.L. and Mennell, S. (1996) *The Course of Human History: Economic Growth, Social Processes and Civilization*, Armonk, New York: M.E. Sharpe.

Goudsblom, J. (1980, orig. Dutch 1960) *Nihilism and Culture*, Washington DC: Rowman and Littlefield.

Goudsblom, J. (2003) Introductory Overview: the Expanding Anthroposphere, in: de Vries, B. & Goudsblom, J. *Mappae Mundi*, Amsterdam: Amsterdam University Press, 21-46.

Goudsblom, J. (2012) Energy and Civilization, in: *Human Figurations*, vol. 1, no. 1, (Norbert Elias Foundation website).

Gray, P., Oliver, K. (eds.) (2004) *Memory of Catastrophe*, Manchester: ManchesterUniversity Press.

Green, W. (1992) Periodization in European and World History. In: *Journal of World History*, vol. 3, 1, pp. 13-53.

Green, A. (1988) The History of Libraries in the Arab World: a Diffusionist model, in: *Libraries and Culture*, vol. 23, no. 4, pp. 454-473.

Grinker, R. and Spiegel, J.P. (1945,1) *War Neuroses*, Philadelphia/Toronto: The Blakiston company.

Grinker, R. and Spiegel, J.P. (1945, 2) *Men under stress*, Philadelphia/Toronto: The Blakiston company.

Grob, G.N. (1991) *From asylum to community. Mental health policy in modern America*, Princeton: Princeton University Press.

Gutas, D. (1998), *Greek thought, Arabic culture. The Graeco-Arabic translation movement in Baghdad and early Abbasid society (2nd-4th/8th-10th centuries)*, New York: Routledge.

Hale, N. (1995) *The rise and crisis of Psychoanalysis: Freud and the Americans, 1917-1985*, New York: Oxford University Press.

Hamarneh, S. (1974) Ecology and Therapeutics in Medieval Arabic Medicine, in: *Suddhoffs Archiv*, 58, 2, pp. 165-185.

Harrington, R. (1999) *The railway accident: trains, trauma and technological crisis in nineteenth-century Britain*, Institute of railway studies, York, University of York, pp. 1-22. www.york.ac.uk/inst/irs/irshome/papers/rlyacc.htm

Harrington, R. (2001) Travel and Trauma in the Victorian Era. The railway accident – trains, trauma and technological crisis in nineteenth-century Britain, in: Micale, M., Lerner, P. (eds.) (2001) *Traumatic Pasts. History, Psychiatry, and Trauma in the Modern Age, 1870-1930*, New York: Cambridge University Press, chapter 2.

Harrington, R. (2003) On the Tracks of Trauma: Railway Spine Reconsidered, in: *The Journal of the Society for the History of Medicine*, 16, 2, pp. 209-223.

Van der Hart, O. en Friedman, B. (1989) A Readers' Guide to Pierre Janet: a neglected intellectual heritage, in: *Dissociation*, 2, 1, pp. 3-16.

Van der Hart, O., van Dijke, A., van Son, M. en Steele, K. (2000) Somatoform Dissociation in Traumatized World War I Combat Soldiers:

A Neglected Heritage, in: *Journal of Trauma and Dissociation*, 1, 4, pp. 33-66.

Haskell, T.L. (1985) Capitalism and the Origins of the Humanitarian Sensibility, in: *American Historical Review*, 90, 2, 339-361 and 90, 3, pp. 547-566.

The Health Council of the Netherlands (2004), *Disputed Memories*, Government Printing Office: The Hague.

Healy, D. (1997) *The Antidepressant Era*, Cambridge: Harvard University Press.

Healy, D. (2004) *Let them eat Prozac. The unhealthy relationship between the pharmaceutical industry and depression*, New York: New York University Press.

Heemskerk, M.T. (2000) *Suffering in the Mu'tazilite Theology. Abd al-Jabbar's teaching on pain and divine justice*, Leiden: Brill.

Heilbron, J. (1995) *The Rise of Social Theory*, Minneapolis: University of Minnesota Press.

Hekster, O. (2010) *Romeinse keizers. De macht van de magie*, Amsterdam: Bert Bakker.

Herman, E. (1995) *The romance of American Psychology. Political culture in an age of experts*, Berkeley and Los Angeles: University of California Press.

Herman, J.(1992) *Trauma and Recovery, the Aftermath of Violence, from domestic abuse to political terror*, New York: Basic Books.

Hermans, F. (2010) Trauma and Civilization: a Historical-Sociological Study of the rise and expansion of the care of victims of traumatic events, In: Hermans, F. (2010) Trauma en Beschaving, Summary, Amsterdam, Arq/Boom, pp. 269-273.

Herrin, J. (2007) *Byzantium: The surprising life of a medieval empire*, London: Allan Lane.

Horden, P. en Purcell, N. (2000), *The Corrupting Sea. A study of the Mediterranean history*, Oxford: Blackwell.

Horden, P. (2005), The earliest Hospitals in Byzantium, Western Europe and Islam, in: *Journal of Interdisciplinary History*, vol. 35, no. 3, pp. 361-389.

Horstmanshof, H.F.J. (1989) *De pijlen van de pest. Pestilenties in de Griekse wereld, 800-400 v. C.*, dissertation, University of Leyden.

Horowitz, M. (1976) *Stress response syndrome*, New York: Jason Aronson.

Horwitz, A. en Wakefield, J. (2007) *The loss of sadness. How psychiatry transformed normal sorrow into depressive disorder*, New York: Oxford University Press.

Houben, V. (2003) Southeast Asia and Islam, in: *Annals of the American Academy of Political and Social Science*, vol. 588, july, pp. 149-170.

Hoyland, R. (2011) Book review: de la Vaissière, E. (2007) Samarcande et Samarra: Élites d'Asie Centrale dans l'Empire Abbasside, in: *Cahiers de Studia Iranica*, 35, Leuven: Peeters Publishers, in: JESHO (51), 559-561.

Hughes, R. (1994) *Culture of Complaint: the Fraying of America*, Clayton: Warner Books.

Imamudin, S.M. (1978), Maristan (Hospitals) in Medieval Spain, in: *Islamic Studies*, vol. 17, no. 1, pp. 45-55.

Israel, J. (2010), *A Revolution of the Mind. Radical Enlightenment and the Intellectual Origins of Modern Democracy*, Princeton: Princeton University Press.

Janoff-Bullman, R. (1992) *Shattered Assumptions. Towards a new psychology of trauma*, New York: Simon & Schuster.

Jenkins, E. (1999) *The Muslim diaspora: a comprehensive reference to the spread of Islam in Asia, Africa, Europe and the Americas*, Jefferson: McFarland.

Jones, E.L. (2010) *Locating the Industrial Revolution: Inducement and Response*, Singapore/ London: Hackensack.

Jones, E. and Wessely, S. (2005) *Shell Shock to PTSD. Military Psychiatry from 1900 to the Gulf War,* Hove and New York: Psychology Press.

Jones, E. (2006) Historical approaches to post-combat disorders, in: *Philosophical transactions of the Royal Society B Biological Science*, 361(1468), pp. 533-542.

Jordan, C.W. (1996), *The great famine. Northern Europe in the early fourteenth century*, Princeton: Princeton University Press.

Kardiner, A. (1941) *The traumatic neuroses of war*, New York: Hoeber.

Keilson, H. (1979) *Sequentielle Traumatisierung bei Kindern*, Stuttgart: Ferdinand Enke Verlag.

Kempers, B. (1992) *Painting, Power and Patronage: The Rise of the Professional Artist in Renaissance Italy*, London: Allan Lane.

Kennedy, H. (2008), *The great Arabian Conquests: How The Spread Of Islam Changed The World We Live In*, New York: Da Capo Press.

Kershaw, I. (1973), The great Famine and Agrarian Crisis in England 1315-1322, in: *The Past and Present Society*, no. 59, pp. 3-50.

Kessler, R.C., Sonnega, A., Bromet, E. et al. (1995) Posttraumatic stress disorder in the National Comorbidity Survey, in: *Archives of General Psychiatry*, 52, pp. 1048-1060.

Kessler RC, Chiu WT, Demler O, Walters E.E. (2005) Prevalence, severity, and comorbidity of twelve-month DSM-IV disorders in the National Comorbidity Survey Replication (NCS-R), in: *Archives of General Psychiatry*, 62, pp. 617-627.

Kleinman, A. (1997) "Everything That Really Matters": Social Suffering, Subjectivity, and the Remaking of Human Experience in a Disordering World, in: *the Harvard Theological Review*, vol. 90, no. 3: pp. 315-335.

Kloocke, R., Schmiedebach, H.P. en Priebe, S. (2005) Psychological injury in the two World Wars: changing concepts in German psychiatry, in: *History of Psychiatry*, 16, p. 44.

Koehler, P.J. (1995) Freud, Charcot en de neurologische visie op hysterie, in: *Nederlands Tijdschrift voor Geneeskunde*, 193 (43), pp. 2177-2183.

Van der Kolk, B. and van der Hart, O. (1989), Pierre Janet and the breakdown of adaption psychological trauma, in: *American Journal of Psychiatry*, 146 (12), 1530-1540.

Van der Kolk, B.A., Weisaeth, L., en van der Hart, O. (1996) History of Trauma in Psychiatry, in: Van der Kolk, B.A., McFarlane, A.C. en Weisaeth, L. (eds.), *Traumatic stress. The effects of overwhelming experience on mind, body and society*, New York/London: The Guilford Press, pp. 47-76.

Van der Kolk, B.A., McFarlane, A.C. en Weisaeth, L. (eds.) (1996) *Traumatic stress. The effects of overwhelming experience on mind, body and society*, New York/London: The Guilford Press.

Van der Kolk, B. (2014) *The Body keeps the score. Brain, Mind and Body in the healing of trauma*, New York, Viking.

Kostal, R.W. (1994) *Law and English Railway Capitalism 1825-1875*, Oxford: Clarendon Press.

Kreps, G. (eds) (1989) *Social structure and Disaster*, Cranbury: Associated University Press.

Krystal, H. (1968), *Massive psychic trauma*, New York: International Universities Press.

Krystal, H. and Niederland, W. (eds) (1971) *Psychic traumatization: aftereffects in individuals and communities*, Boston: Little brown.

Kulka, R., Schlenger, W., Fairbank J. et al. (1990), *Trauma and the Vietnam War Generation*, New York: Brunner/Mazel.

De Laender, J. (1996) *Het hart van de duisternis. Psychologie van de menselijke wreedheid*, Leuven: Davidsfonds.

Landes, D. (1998) The Wealth and Poverty of Nations. Why some are so rich and some so poor, New York/London: W.W. Norton & Co.

Lazarus, R.S. (1966) *Psychological Stress and the Coping Process*, New York: MCGraw-Hill.

Lembcke, J. (1998) *The spitting image. Myth, Memory and the Legacy of Vietnam*, New York: New York University Press.

Lerner, P. (2001) From Traumatic Neurosis to Male Hysteria. The Decline and Fall of Hermann Oppenheim, 1889-1919, In: Micale, M.S., Lerner, P. (eds.) *Traumatic Pasts. History, Psychiatry, and Trauma in the Modern Age, 1870-1930*, New York, Cambridge University Press, chapter 7.

Lerner, P. (2003) *Hysterical men. War psychiatry and the politics of trauma in Germany 1890-1930*, Ithaca: Cornell University.

Lifton, R.J. (1963) Psychological Effects of the Atomic Bomb in Hiroshima: The Theme of Death, in: *Daedalus*, vol. 92, no. 3, pp. 462-497.

Lifton, R.J. (1973) *Home from the war*, Cambridge University Press: Cambridge.

Lifton, R.J. (2001) Illusions of the Second Nucleair Age, in: *World Policy Journal*, vol. 18, no. 1, pp. 25-30.

Lindemann, E. (1944) The symptomatology and management of acute grief, in: *American Journal of Psychiatry*, 101, pp. 141-148.

Lucas, H.S. (1930) The great European Famine of 1315, 1316 and 1317, in: *Speculum. A Journal of Medieval Studies*, vol. 5, no. 4, pp. 343-377.

Lunn, J. (2005) Male Identity and Martial Codes of Honour: A Comparison of the War Memoirs of Robert Graves, Ernst Jünger and Kande Kamara, in: *The Journal of Military History*, vol. 69, no. 3, pp. 713-735.

Lusty, H. (2006), Shaping the National Voice: Poetry of WWI, in: *Journal of Modern Literature*, vol. 30. no. 1, pp. 199-209.

Lusty, H. (2008), Looking Back: New Studies in the Literature of the Twentieth-Century War, in: *Journal of Modern Literature*, vol. 31, no. 4, pp. 145-151.

Lutz, T. Varieties of Medical Experience: Doctors and Patients, Psyche and Soma in America, in: Gijswijt-Hofstra, M. (2000) *Introduction: Cultures of Neurasthenia from Beard to the First World War*, Amsterdam: Rodopi, pp. 51-74.

Marlowe, D. (2000) *Psychological and Psychosocial consequences of combat and deployment with special emphasis on the Gulf War*, Rand Corporation.

Mazlish, B. (2013) The Advancement of Humanity, in: *Human Figurations*, vol. 2, 1.

McNeill, W. (1977) *Plagues and People*, Garden City, NY, Anchor Press/ Doubleday.

McNeill, J.R. en McNeill, W. (2003) *The Human Web: A Bird's-Eye of World History*, New York: W.W. Norton &Company.

McNeill, Weapons of Mass Destruction, in: *The New York Review of Books*, 2004, april, 6.

McPherson, J. (2008) Was it more restrained than you think, in: *New York Review of Books*, 14 feb., 42-44.

Mennell, S. (2007) *The American Civilizing Process*, Cambridge, Polity Press.

Menninger, W. (1948) *Psychiatry in a troubled world. Yesterday's war and today's challenge*, New York, The MacMillan Company.

Merridale, C. (2000), The Collective Mind: Trauma and Shell Shock in Twentieth Century Russia, in: *Journal of Contemporary History*, vol. 35, no. 1, 39-55.

Micale, M.S. (2001) Jean-Martin Charcot and *les névroses traumatiques*: From Medicine to Culture in French Trauma Theory of the Late Nineteenth Century, In: Micale, M., Lerner, P. (eds.) (2001)*Traumatic Pasts. History, Psychiatry, and Trauma in the Modern Age, 1870-1930*, New York, Cambridge University Press, chapter 6.

Miles, R. (2012) *Carthago must be destroyed: The rise and fall of an Ancient Civilization*, London, Penguin.

Miller, R. (2003) *Parallels between the early British Railways and the ICT Revolution*, London, Institute of Economic Affairs.

Miller, T. (1984), Byzantine Hospitals, in: *Dumbarton Oaks Papers, Symposium on Byzantine Medicine*, vol. 38, 53-63.

Morris I. (2010) *Why the West Rules – For Now: The Patterns of History, and what They Reveal about the Future*, Farrar Straus and Giroux.

De Mul, J. (2013) *Destiny Domesticated. The Rebirth of Tragedy Out of the Spirit of Technology*, Albany: State University of New York Press.

Nicolaï, N.J. (2003) Nieuwe ontwikkelingen in psychodynamische psychotherapie, in: Nicolaï, N.J., *Handboek psychotherapie na seksueel misbruik*, Utrecht, de Tijdstroom, hoofdstuk 12.

Niederer, F.J. (1952) Early Medieval Charity, in: *Church History*, vol. 21, no. 4, 285-295.

Norris F.H en Slone, L.B (2013), Understanding Research on the Epidemiology of Trauma and PTSD. *Special Double Issue of the PTSD Research Qarterly*, 24, 2-3.

Novick, P. (1999) *The Holocaust in American Life*, New York, Houghton Mifflin.

Nussbaum, M. (2004), *Upheavels of Thought: The Intelligence of Emotions*, Cambridge: Cambridge University Press.

Obert Voll, J. (1994) Islam as a special World System, in: *Journal of World History*, vol. 5, no. 2, 213-226.

Ó'Grada, C. (2009) *Famine. A short history,* Princeton and Oxford: Princeton University Press.

OECD (2003) *Emerging Risks in the 21st Century, an Agenda for Action*, OECD Publications Service.

Olick, J.K en Robbins, J. (1998) Social Memory Studies: From Collective Memory to the Historical Sociology of Mnemonic Practices, in: *Annual Review of Sociology*, vol. 24, 105-140.

Oliver, K. (2004*)* "Not much of a place anymore": The reception and memory of the massacre at My Lai, in: Gray, P. and Oliver, K. (eds.) (2004) *Memory of Catastrophe*, Manchester, Manchester University Press, 171-189.

Osterhammel, J. (2014, orig. 2009) *The transformation of the world: a global history of the nineteenth century*, Princeton, Princeton University Press.

Ozarin, L. (2002) Thomas William Salmon. Psychiatry in time of war, in *Psychiatric News*, 37, 13, 38.

Palmer, A. & Minogue, S. (2010) Memorial Poems and the Poetics of Memorializing, in: *Journal of Modern Literature*, vol. 34, no. 1, 162-181.

Parker, G. (2008) Crisis and Catastrophe, the Global Crisis of the Seventeenth Century Reconsidered in: *American Historical Review*, vol. 113, no. 4, (no numbers).

Paton, L.W. (2009) *Spiritism and the cult of the dead in antiquity*, New York, Mac Millan Company.

Pemberton, A., Winkel, F.W. & Groenhuijsen, M.S. (2007). Taking victims seriously in restorative justice, *International Perspectives in Victimology*, 3 (1), 4-14.

Pencak, W. (1989) *For God & Country. The American Legion, 1919-1941*, Boston, Northeastern University Press.

Perkins, M. (1955) Preventive psychiatry during World War II in: *Preventive medicine in World war II, Vol. III*, chapter 6, Office of the Surgeon General Department of the Army, Washington DC.

Pfohl, S.J. (1977) The "Discovery" of Child Abuse', in: *Social Problems*, 24, 310-323.

Pillemer, D. (2004) Can the Psychology of Memory enrich Historical Analyses of Trauma?, in: *History and Memory*, vol. 16, no. 2, Special Issue: Traumatic Memory in Chinese History, 140-154.

Pinker, S. (2012) *The better Angels of Our Nature: Why Violence has declined*, London, Penguin.

Plant, R. (2005) Menninger and psychoanalysis, 1946-1948, in: *History of psychiatry*, 16, 2, (copyright 2005, www.historyweb.ucsd.edu, London, Sage, 1-22).

Porter, R. (2002) *Madness: a Brief History*, Oxford: Oxford University Press.

Prager, J. (1998) *Presenting the Past. Psychoanalysis and the Sociology of Misremembering*, Cambridge, Harvard University Press.

Pulleyblank (1968) An Lushan Rebellion, in: *Encyclopedia Britannica*.

Pulleyblank (1989, 2011), "An Hsi", in: *Iranian Encyclopaedia Iranica*.

Pulleyblank (1991, 2011), Chinese-Iranian relations in Pre-Islamic Times, in: *Encyclopaedia Iranica*.

Quarantelli, E.L., Lagadec, P., Boin, A. (2006) A heuristic approach to future disasters and crises: new, old and in-between types, in: Rodriguez, R. Quarantelli, E. en Dynes, R. (eds) *Handbook of disaster research*, New York, Springer, 16-42.

Rayner Wilson, H. (1909) *The Safety of British Railways*, IRSE.

Read, J. (2006) Breaking the silence; learning why, when and how to ask about trauma, and how to respond to disclosures, in: Larkin, W. and Morrison, A. (red.), *Trauma and psychosis*, London/New York, Routledge, 196-221.

Read, J., Rudegeair, T. and Farrelly, S. (2006) The relationship between child abuse and psychosis: Public opinion, evidence, pathways and implications, in: Larkin, W. and Morrison, A. (red.), *Trauma and psychosis*, London/New York, Routledge, 23-57.

Reil, J. (1803), *Rhapsodieen über die Anwendung der psychischen Curmethode auf Geisteszerruettungen*, Halle, Curtsche Buchhandlung, 473-478: www.sgipt.org/gesch/reil1.htm.

Reilly, K. (2012) *The Human Journey: A Concise Introduction to World History*, Volume I, Prehistory to 1450, Rowman & Littlefield.

Rifkin, J. (2009) *The empathic civilization. The race to global consciousness in a world in crisis*, Cambridge: Polity Press.

Robbins J. (1987) The Writing of the Holocaust: Claude Lanzmann's Shoah, in: *Prooftexts*, vol. 7, no. 3, pp. 249-258.

Rodriguez, R. Quarantelli, E.L. en Dynes, R. (eds.) (2006) *Handbook of disaster research*, New York: Springer.

Roebroeks, W. (2004) *Voedsel en de menselijke niche: la Grande Bouffe*, Leiden, Universiteit van Leiden, diësrede.

Roland, A. (1992), Secrecy technology and war: Greek fire and the defense of Byzantium, 678-1204, in: *Technology and Culture*, vol. 33, no. 4, pp. 655-679.

Rolt, L.T.C. (1982, oorspr.1955) *Red for Danger: a History of Railway Accidents and Railway Safety*, London: The Bodley Head.

Rorty, R. (1989) *Contingency, Irony and Solidarity,* Cambridge: Cambridge University Press.

Rosenwein, B. (2002) Worrying about emotions in History, in: *American Historical Review*, vol. 107, no. 3, 821-845.

Ross, D.R.B. (1969) *Preparing for Ulysses. Politics and veterans during World War II*, New York and London: Columbia University Press.

Roudebush, M.O. (2001) A Battle of Nerves, Hysteria and Its Treatments in France During World War I, In: Micale, M., Lerner, P. (eds.) *Traumatic Pasts, History, Psychiatry, and Trauma in the Modern Age, 1870-1930*, New York: Cambridge University Press, chapter 11.

Ruiz, T.F. (2011) *The Terror of History. On the Uncertainties of Life in Western Civilization*, Princeton: Princeton University Press.

Saito, H. (2006) Reiterated Commemoration: Hiroshima as National Trauma, in: *Sociological Theory*, vol. 24, no. 4, pp. 353-376.

Salmon, T.W. (1917) *The care and treatment of mental diseases and war neuroses ("shell shock") in the British Army*, in: *Mental Hygiene* 1 (4), pp. 509-547.

Schaffner, W. (2001) Event, Series, Trauma. The Probalistic Revolution of the Mind in the Late Nineteenth and Early Twentieth Centuries, In: Micale, M.S., Lerner, P. (eds.) *Traumatic Pasts, History, Psychiatry, and Trauma in the Modern Age, 1870-1930*, New York: Cambridge University Press, chapter 4.

Scheff, T.J. (1966) *Being mentally ill*, Chicago: Aldine.

Schivelbusch, W. (1986, orig. 1977) *The Railway Journey. The industrialization of Time and Space in the 19th Century*, New York: Berg.

Schlesinger, A.M. (1944) Biography of a Nation of Joiners, in *American Historical Review*, 50, pp. 1-25.

Schottenbauer, M., Glass, C., Arnkoff, D., Tendick, V. and Gray, S. (2008) Nonresponse and drop out rates in outcome studies on PTSD: review and methodological considerations, in: *Psychiatry*, 71, 2, pp. 134-168.

Schwartz, B. (1996), Memory as a Cultural System: Abraham Lincoln in World War II, in: *American Sociological Review*, vol. 61, no. 5, pp. 908-927.

Scott, W.J. (1990) PTSD in DSM.III: a case in the politics of diagnosis and disease, in: *Social Problems* 37, 3, 294-310.

Selye, H. (1950) *The Physiology and pathology of exposure to stress*, Montreal: Art.

Shay, J. (1994) *Achilles in Vietnam. Combat Trauma and the Undoing of Character*, New York: Touchstone book, Simon&Schuster.

Sennett, R. (2000) *The Corrosion of Character: the Personal Consequences of Work in the New Capitalism*, New York: W.W. Norton & Company.

Sennett, R. (2008) *The Craftsman*, New Haven: Yale University Press.

Shephard, B. (2000) *A War Of Nerves*, London: Jonathan Cape.

Showalter, E. (1998) *Hystories. Hysterical epidemics and modern media*, New York: Columbia University Press.

Simissen, H.G.J.M. (2003) Een aardschok in de filosofie. De aardbeving van Lissabon (1755) in het denken van de Verlichting, in: *Streven*, oktober, pp. 822-837.

Simmons, J. en Biddle, G. (eds.) (1997) *The Oxford Companion to British Railway History*, Oxford: Oxford University Press.

Hanigan, W., Sloffer, C. (2004) Nelson's wound: treatment of spinal cord injury in 19th and early 20th century military conflicts, in: *Neurosurgical Focus* 16 (1), pp. 3, 4.

Sloterdijk, P. (2013) *You must change your life*, Cambridge: Polity.

Smith, J. (2004) Examining psychotherapeutic action through the lense of trauma, in: *Journal of the American Academy of Psychoanalysis and Dynamic Psychiatry*, 32 (4), pp. 613-631.

Snelders, S. and Kaplan, A. A.M. (2002) LSD Therapy in Dutch Psychiatry: Changing Socio-Political Settings, in: *Medical History*, 26, pp. 221-240.

Solomon, Z. (1995) From denial to recognition: attitudes toward holocaust survivors from World war II to the present, in: *Journal of Traumatic Stress*, 8, 2, pp. 215-228.

Spencer, H. (1868) *Essays: Moral, Political and Aesthetic*, New York: Appleton and Company.

Spiegel, D. and Vermetten, E. (2007) Post-traumatic stress disorder: medicine or politics (not both), in: *the Lancet*, 369 (9566): p. 992.

Starr, P. (1982) *The social transformation of American medicine*, New York, Basic.

Stoicea, G. (2006) The Difficulties of Verbalizing Trauma: Translation of the Economic Loss in Claude Lanzmann's "Shoah", in: *The Journal of the Midwest Modern Language Association*, vol. 39, no. 2, pp. 43-53.

Stouffer, S. e.a. (1949) *The American Soldier. Combat and its Aftermath*, Princeton New York: Princeton University Press.

Struve, L.A. (2004) Confucian PTSD. Reading Trauma in a Chinese Youngster's Memoir of 1653, in: *History and Memory*, vol. 16, no. 2, Special Issue: Traumatic Memory in Chinese History, pp. 14-31.

Summerfield, D. (2001) The invention of post-traumatic stress disorder and the social usefulness of a psychiatric category, in: *British Medical journal*, 322, pp. 95-98.

De Swaan, A. (1988) *In Care of the State: Health Care, Education and Welfare in Europe and the USA in the Modern Era*, Oxford: Oxford University Press.

De Swaan, A. (1995) Widening circles of identification: Emotional concerns in sociogenetic perspective, in: *Theory, Culture and Society*, vol. 12.1, pp. 25-39.

De Swaan, A. (2001), *Words of the World*, Cambridge, Polity Press.

De Swaan, A. (2003) On the Sociogenesis of the Psychoanalytic Setting. In: *Norbert Elias,* Eds. Dunning E. & Mennell, S., London: Sage, vol. 4, pp. 171-202.

De Swaan, A. (2003) Dyscivilisation, mass extermination and the state, in: Dunning E. & Mennell, S. *(Eds.) Norbert Elias, London, Sage*, vol. 2, pp. 137-148.

De Swaan, A. (2015) *The Killing Compartments: The mentality of mass murderers,* New Haven: Yale Univerity Press.

Szasz, T.S. (1961)*The myth of mental illness*, New York: Harper & Row.

Szasz, T.S. (2003). The cure of souls in the therapeutic state, in: *The Psychoanalytic Review*, 90: pp. 45-62.

Sznaider, N. (1996), Pain and Cruelty in Socio-Historical Perspective, in: *International Journal of Politics, Culture and Society*, vol. 10, no. 2, pp. 331-354.

Sznaider, N. (2001) *The compassionate temperament. Care and cruelty in modern society*, Lanham: Rowman & Littlefield.

Taylor, C. (2007) *A Secular Age*, Cambridge: The Belknap Press of Harvard University Press.

Terr, L. (1991) Childhood trauma, an outline and overview, in: *American Journal of Psychiatry*, 148, pp. 10-20.

Thucydides (2001) *The history of the Peloponnesian War* http://classics.mit.edu/Thucydides/pelopwar.html

De Tocqueville, A. (1945, orig. 1850) *Democracy in America*, Cambridge, Severe and Francis.

Thomas, K. (2012, orig. 1971), *Religion and the Decline of Magic*, London Penguin.

Trimble, M.R. (1984, orig. 1981) *Post-Traumatic Neurosis, From Railway Spine to the Whiplash*, Chichester: John Wiley & Sons.

Trompf, G.W. (1973) The concept of the Carolingian Renaissance, in: *Journal of the History of Ideas*, vol. 34, no. 1, pp. 3-26.

Tuchman, B. (1987) A Distant Mirror: *The Calamitous 14th Century*, New York: Random House.

Tyrwhitt, J. (1968) The city of Ch'ang-an: capital of the Tang dynasty of China, in: *Town Planning Review*, vol. 39, 1, 1968, pp. 21-37.

De la Vassière, E. (2012) Central Asia and the Silk Road, in: *Oxford Handbooks online*.

Vasterman, P. (2005) Media-Hype: Self-Reinforcing News Waves, Journalistic Standards and the Construction of Social Problems *In: European Journal of Communication 2005*; 20; p. 508.

Veenhof, K., (1974) *Mesopotamië, het land en het water*, Amsterdam, VU.

Véray, L. (2010) 1914-1918, the first media war of the twentieth century: The example of French newsreels, in: *Film History*, vol. 22, no. 4, Cinema during the Great War, pp. 408-425.

Vermetten E, Dorahy M, Spiegel D (eds) (2007) *Traumatic Dissociation: Phenomenology, Neurobiology and Treatments*, Arlington: American Psychiatric Press.

De Vries, G.C. (2002) *Transformations in vulnerability*, Paper presented at the ISA World Congress of Sociology, Brisbane, Australia.

De Vries, J. en van de Woude, A. (1997) *The first modern economy: success, failure, and perseverance of the Dutch economy, 1500-1815*, Cambridge: Cambridge University Press.

Vijselaar, J. (2010) *Psyche and Electricity*, http://www.dwc.knaw.nl/wp-content/uploads/2010/08/psyche_and_electricity_woud-2.pdf

De Waal, F. (2009) *The Age of Empathy: Nature's Lessons for a Kinder Society*, New York: Broadway Books.

Wael, M. (2008) *History of Neuroscience: Arab and Muslim contributions to modern neuroscience*, http://www.ibro.info/Pub/Pub_Main_Display.asp?LC_Docs_ID=3433], Weehuizen, R. (2008*) Mental Capital: The economic significance of mental health.*

Dissertation University of Maastricht file:///C:/Users/Frank/Downloads/Thesis_Weehuizen_final.pdf

Wickham, C. (2009) *The inheritance of Rom. A History of Europe from 400 to 1000*, London: Allen Lane.

Wilkinson, I. (2005) *Suffering, a sociological introduction*, Cambridge: Polity Press.

Wilson, R. (1925) *Railway Legislation and Statistics 1825 to 1925*, London: Raynar Wilson.

Wilterdink, N. (2009), Civilizing Processes in an Evolutionary Perspective, Introduction, congress 10-13 november, Recife, Brasilia.

Wilterdink, N. (1995) Increasing Income Inequality and Wealth Concentration in the Prosperous Societies of the West, in: *Studies in Comparative International Development*, Volume 30, 3, pp. 3-23.

Winter, J. (1995) *Sites of Memory, Sites of Mourning. The Great War in European Cultural History*, Cambridge: Cambridge University Press.

Winter, J. (2000) Shell-Shock and the Cultural History of the Great War, in: *Journal of Contemporary History*, 35, 1, pp. 7-11.

Withuis, J. & Mooij, A. (eds.) (2010) *The Politics of War Trauma. The aftermath of World War II in eleven European countries*, Amsterdam: Aksant.

Wolfson, H.A. (1976), *The Philosophy of the Kalam*, Cambridge: Harvard University Press.

Wood, M. (1998) *Op zoek naar de bronnen van onze beschaving*, Utrecht, Stichting Teleac.

Wouters, C. (2004) *Sex and Manners: Female Emancipation in the West 1890-2000*. London: Sage.

Wouters, C. (2008) *Informalization: Manners and Emotions since 1890*, London, Sage.

Wouters, C., Mennell, S. (2013). Discussing Civilisation and Informalisation: Criteriology, in: *Política y Sociedad*, vol. 50, 2: pp. 553-579.

Young, A. (1995) *The Harmony of Illusions*, Princeton: Princeton University Press.

Zola, K. (1972) Medicine as an institution of social control, in: *Sociological Review*, 20, 4, pp. 487-504.

Zwaan, T. (2001) On Civilizing and Decivilizing Processes: A Theoretical Discussion, in: Dunning, E. and Mennell, S. eds. *Norbert Elias*, Volume 4, pp. 167-175.

Zwaan, T. (2008) *On Genocide. An Introduction*, NIOD Institute for War, Holocaust and Genocide Studies, http://www.niod.nl/sites/niod.nl/files/Introduction%20on%20Genocide.pdf

Zwaan, T. (2003) *On the Aetiology and Genesis of Genocides and other Mass Crimes Targeting Specific Groups*, Centre for Holocaust and Geno-cide Studies University of Amsterdam/ Royal Netherlands Academy of Arts and Sciences.
http://www.srebrenica-mappinggenocide.com/files/SMG-en-doc-mapping-genocide-ton-zwaan.pdf